THE FEAR OF BEGGARS

The Eerdmans Ekklesia Series

Editors

Michael L. Budde
Stephen E. Fowl

The Eerdmans Ekklesia Series explores matters of Christianity and discipleship across a wide expanse of disciplines, church traditions, and issues of current and historical concern.

The Series is published in cooperation with the Ekklesia Project, a network of persons for whom "being a Christian" is seen to be the primary identity and allegiance for believers — superseding and ordering the claims on offer by the modern state, market, racial and ethnic groups, and other social forces. The Ekklesia Project emphasizes the importance of the church as a distinctive community in the world, called to carry into contemporary society the priorities and practices of Jesus Christ as conveyed in the Gospels.

The Ekklesia Series will draw from the broad spectrum of the Christian world — Protestantism of many traditions, Roman Catholicism, Anabaptism, Orthodoxy — in exploring critical issues in theology, history, social and political theory, biblical studies, and world affairs. The Series editors are Stephen E. Fowl, Professor and Chair, Department of Theology at Loyola College in Baltimore; and Michael L. Budde, Professor of Political Science and Catholic Studies and Chair, Department of Political Science, at DePaul University in Chicago.

Additional information about the Ekklesia Project, including submission guidelines for the Eerdmans Ekklesia book series, may be found at www.ekklesiaproject.org.

THE FEAR OF BEGGARS

Stewardship and Poverty in Christian Ethics

Kelly S. Johnson

WILLIAM B. EERDMANS PUBLISHING COMPANY

GRAND RAPIDS, MICHIGAN / CAMBRIDGE, U.K.

Published 2007 by
Wm. B. Eerdmans Publishing Co.
2140 Oak Industrial Drive N.E., Grand Rapids, Michigan 49505 /
P.O. Box 163, Cambridge CB3 9PU U.K.

Printed in the United States of America

12 11 10 09 08 07   7 6 5 4 3 2 1

Library of Congress Cataloging-in-Publication Data

Johnson, Kelly S., 1964-
The fear of beggars: stewardship and poverty in Christian ethics /
Kelly S. Johnson.
p.   cm. — (Ekklesia project)
Includes bibliographical references and index.
ISBN 978-0-8028-0378-8 (pbk.: alk. paper)
1. Stewardship, Christian. 2. Poverty — Religious aspects —
Christianity. 3. Christian ethics. I. Title.

BV772.J576 2007
241'.68 — dc22

2006039056

www.eerdmans.com

In memory of my father,
who asked me whether to invite a beggar home with us
and waited for my answer

Contents

Acknowledgments

Adam Smith noted that before the advent of the printing press, scholars sometimes were beggars. In my own pre-publication era, I have received generous support from many people. The Delores Zohrab Liebmann Foundation funded me during a year in which I began the research for this project, and the Center for the Study of Philanthropy and Voluntarism at Duke University provided support during work on Chapter Four. I have been fortunate for extended periods during the writing of this work to be the houseguest and dependent of Bill Cavanaugh and Tracy Rowan; Casa Guadalupana Catholic Worker; Ed and Ghislaine Miller; Iredell House; the Derthick family and the Vine Street community; and Anna and Tuck Satterfield. In New York, the Peter Maurin Farm welcomed me for working holidays, and I found there some of my most perceptive conversation partners. My mother has offered more support, emotionally, materially, and even physically through these years of travel and writing than I could ever hope for from anyone but a mother, and even at that she surprises me.

I received helpful comments on this project from the History of Economic Thought Reading Group at Duke; the Ekklesia Project; the Kenan Ethics Colloquium at Duke; and the New Wineskins circle of Catholic moral theologians. Many people have read and commented on some or all of this project through its various stages, including Una Cadegan, Mary McClintock Fulkerson, John Inglis, Greg Jones, Brad Kallenberg, Sandra Yocum Mize, Bill Portier, and Terry Tilley. David Aers and Craufurd Goodwin were indispensable guides in my early transgressions of disciplinary boundaries. Therese Lysaught read several full-length drafts, offered timely and detailed comments on organization and content, and kept me from giving up on more than one occasion. Many friends from Iredell Street and colleagues from Duke, particularly David Cloutier, Laura Yordy, and Kristen Bargeron Grant, hammered out the original outlines of this work with good humor and patience, and Ethan Smith showed the same qualities when compiling the index. Stanley Hauerwas has taught me to take intellectual risks, cheerfully, and I am deeply grateful for his guidance. If I have managed to articulate these ideas intelligibly, it is principally thanks to these and many other friendships. Errors and misjudgments remain my own property.

Waking Up Lost

Even in the relief of common beggars we shall find that we are more frequently influenced by the desire of getting rid of the importunities of a disgusting object than by the pleasure of relieving it. We wish that it had not fallen in our way, rather than rejoice in the opportunity given us of assisting a fellow-creature. We feel a painful emotion at the sight of so much apparent misery; but the pittance we give does not relieve it. We know that it is totally inadequate to produce any essential effect. We know, besides, that we shall be addressed in the same manner at the corner of the next street; and we know that we are liable to the grossest impositions. We hurry therefore sometimes by them, and shut our ears to their importunate demands.[1]

Beggars do a reasonable thing: needing something and seeing someone who might have it, they ask for it. Put that way, the act is simple enough. Yet Malthus's description of the encounter remains a distressingly accurate account of how many people react when faced with beggars. Beggars alarm and disturb us. Like Malthus, the clergyman and economist, we find ourselves unable to act well, and can only try to remove ourselves from the offensive situation as quickly as possible.

A case in point: what happens when, walking through Grand Central Station, I see a man holding a sign that reads, "I am at your mercy"? My

---

1. Thomas Robert Malthus, *An Essay on the Principle of Population*, ed. Donald Winch (Cambridge: Cambridge University Press, 1992), 283.

normal perception of myself as reasonably just and kind is thrown into Protean contortions. If he is "at my mercy," then what am I? Am I the ruthless victor in a war of all against all? Am I nobility strolling through a world of misery, barely aware of the suffering that makes my life possible? Am I a sucker, the target of a scam that is working only too well, or an enabler, funding a soul's self-destruction? Am I, in fact, in some kind of danger? Or are the beggar and I both flotsam in an economic system which throws some of us on a sunny shore and drowns others, and against which resistance only increases the danger for all of us? I would gladly spot a friend some cash, perhaps a great deal of cash, but what will I do with the intimacy of this request from a stranger? Anyway, who says he is at *my* mercy, and not at *our* mercy? What about all the other people passing by without responding?

The cumulative effect of all this uncertainty about self and society is anxiety, confusion, and avoidance. Shopping malls provide merchants and shoppers a sphere free of this moral complexity, and laws controlling the location and behavior of beggars have been championed and denounced across the U.S., from California to Vermont and Florida, over the past eighteen years.[2] In 1988, Mayor Koch set off a storm of debate when he urged New Yorkers not to give to beggars on the grounds that giving only encouraged beggars and attracted more to the same behavior. Refusing to give would force the beggars to seek more acceptable ways to get their living. Koch added that those who were troubled in conscience by refusing a beggar should see their priest (presumably to be absolved without having

2. The ACLU and the Center for the Community Interest have both been involved in legal arguments over panhandling laws in several states in recent years, the ACLU opposing laws that threaten free speech and CCI working to set limits on aggressive panhandling and to keep beggars from approaching people in certain locations, such as near ATMs or on public transportation. See http://www.communityinterest.org/backgrounders/panhandling .htm. The National Coalition for the Homeless offers a survey of case law on panhandling with examples back to 1990, which indicates that laws forbidding begging must respect free speech, but may limit the circumstances of such speech for various reasons, such as concerns about safety, the flow of traffic, and implications for the tourist industry. The law in Orlando, Florida, was covered in *Harper's Magazine* 296:1775 (April 1998): 58-59. How to enforce the laws is as much a topic of conversation as how to word them. See, for example, the discussion around San Francisco's anti-panhandling laws: Kevin Fagan, "New panhandling law — S.F. to take it easy: City says it will use persuasion, not jail," *San Francisco Chronicle*, May 25, 2004; and comparisons with enforcement in Philadelphia: Kevin Fagan, "Success in the City of Brotherly Love," *San Francisco Chronicle*, June 13, 2004.

to change the pattern of not giving to beggars which sent them to the confessional).[3]

People have a visceral reaction to beggars, and not merely to stench or disfigurement, but to begging itself. Although abstractly most people recognize that all of us are in some respects dependent upon each other, the sight of a stranger asking for help outside the public order of rights and the private affection of the family shakes us. Uncertainty about the beggar's honesty and civility, concern that giving alms to one somehow makes things worse for others or may lead to endless demands, and knowledge that the "pittance" given is ineffective and may be only a sop to appease the giver's conscience have together undermined, without destroying, the traditional image of almsgiving as virtuous. The anxiety remains. Ethicists, as often as anyone else, get trapped at traffic lights where beggars hold up signs, yet whether to give to beggars does not figure as a significant problem in contemporary works on economic ethics. Why the silence?[4]

If the gap in ethics generally were not remarkable enough, the fact that *Christian* ethicists have not addressed the problem recently is even more noteworthy. Almsgiving traditionally has played a conspicuous role in Christian sanctity.[5] Whether and when to give has been a topic of serious discussion among Christian moralists of other ages. Christians have even recognized as saints some people who begged not because of any catastrophe in their finances but as a component of their spiritual discipline. St. Francis is the most famous, but not the only, virtuous beggar of Christian lore. In fact, although popular imagination now sees Jesus as a self-employed carpenter, other societies have assumed Jesus to have been a beggar.

Beggars implicitly raise questions about the nature and limits of property rights; the efficacy and virtue of almsgiving; the uses of social control

3. "New Yorkers Growing Angry over Aggressive Panhandlers," *New York Times,* July 29, 1988.

4. I know of one fine exception to this silence: Tony Skillen, "Questions of Begging," *Philosophy and Public Affairs,* Royal Philosophy Supplements 45, ed. John Haldane (Cambridge: Cambridge University Press, 2000). On almsgiving more generally, see Luis Carlos Susin's excellent "Alms, Fasting, and Prayer: The Work or Circle of Mercy and Adoration," in *Concilium 2005/2: Hunger, Bread, and Eucharist,* ed. Christophe Boureux, Janet Martin Soskice, and Luis Carlos Susin (London: SCM, 2005).

5. The importance of almsgiving is not peculiar to Christianity. Notably among Muslims, Hindus, and Buddhists, as well as in ancient Greek thought, gifts to beggars are encouraged. Commentary on those traditions — their histories and the influence of modern sociology and economics on them — is beyond the reach of this project.

and surveillance to differentiate needy from greedy beggars; the possibility
of genuine altruism; the material meaning of 'dignity'; the moral importance of productivity; the distinction between public and private behaviors;
the working of justice among strangers; and the relationships of system and
person or intention and effect. Beggars stand in an untidy corner of ethics.
The presence of beggars, particularly those who beg as a theological act,
raises questions that those societies would sometimes prefer not to address.
According to a western-trained Indian sociologist lecturing in Bombay in
1945, due to the continuing presence of religious mendicants there,

> the solution of the beggar problem becomes well-nigh impossible. The
> beggar question will never be finally and thoroughly solved till the re-
> ligious heads of these two great communities [Hindu and Muslim] co-
> operate whole-heartedly with the Government, the Municipality and
> the social work agencies.[6]

Regardless of whether one desires a "final solution" to the problem
of beggars, the role of religious beggars in challenging the invisibility of
poverty, disregard for the poor, and the nature of property rights is real.

The phrase "the fear of beggars" indicates these anxieties from two
directions. One the one hand, beggars have fears: not only of cold, hunger,
and sickness, but also of being alone, of being beaten, of losing those last
few precious belongings, of being stripped of any possibility of self-
determination. But in conversations over the years while I have worked on
this project, I've heard many fears from the other side, from those who
meet beggars on our streets: fears that the beggar might turn violent; that
neither giving nor refusing will be morally satisfactory; that behind one
beggar stand a thousand others, whose needs will overwhelm any generosity; that the beggar sees an alarming truth about humanity, about *me:* that
had things gone differently, that beggar could have been any one of us.
These concerns deeply shape economic and political forms of life. Philosopher Annette Baier has argued that

> The conditions of the form of human justice that recognizes universal
> human rights include not just moderate scarcity, vulnerability to the
> resentment of one's fellows, and limited generosity, all of which Hume

6. J. M. Kumarappa, ed., *Our Beggar Problem: How to Tackle It* (Bombay: Padma Publications Ltd., 1945), 12.

4

recognized, but also a limited willingness to beg, a considerable un-willingness to ask, even when, if we did ask the powerful for a handout, it would perhaps be given us. What we regard as ours by right is what we are unwilling to beg for and only limitedly willing to say thank you for. We seem to be getting less and less willing both to beg and to give to beggars. The increasing tendency to talk of universal rights and the extension of their content correlates with this decreasing ability to beg or to respond generously to beggars.[7]

The ways Christians have acted and argued in order to overcome or repress or reroute those fears is the topic of this work. Facing beggars, we fear poverty, we fear conflict, we fear drowning in the demands that may arise if we open ourselves to the needs of others, we fear the entanglements of gratitude. We fear to be family to the poor because we fear becoming poor. And yet, many of us also fear that refusing to be family to the poor is refusing membership in the body of Christ, which is the greatest danger of all. What, then, will we do?

What This Book Is Not

Rather than raise false hopes from the beginning, let me say clearly that I make no promise to resolve the reader's anxiety about whether to give to beggars. In fact, I begin from the presumption that not being able to pro-vide a satisfactory response to this question, Christian ethics needs to back up and work out *why* we have so much trouble answering it. What role do beggars play in Christology, ecclesiology, ethics? How are our ideas on wealth and poverty, rights and economic systems, humility and work con-tributing to this confusion, or at least failing to help us through it? Like Dante's pilgrim, we wake up to discover ourselves "in dark woods, the right road lost." How did we get here, and how do we get out?

This work, then, is less about the ideal situation we ought to establish than it is about the pilgrimage we are making. It seems like an innocuous claim: the Christian life is a pilgrimage. That is, the Christian community is known by its movement toward and participation in the mutual love of

7. Annette Baier, *Moral Prejudices: Essays on Ethics* (Cambridge, Mass.: Harvard University Press, 1994), 225-26.

the Trinity. *Movement toward* matters because as yet the community has not come to the vision of God and is continually trying better to understand and to cultivate its calling. *Participation in* matters because in Word and sacrament, through the work of the Spirit, this community has already received this gift. The one who is the Way walks with us, instead of only waiting patiently at the end of the road. This quality in Christian life leads Thomas Aquinas to use the term *viator* (wayfarer) to describe the Christian, made by God, called and graced by God, and en route to the beatific vision and friendship with God. Being a wayfarer or pilgrim does not mean that life is merely a journey to an end, in which getting there is all that matters. In a pilgrimage, the path itself matters and is already sanctified, because of what it aims at.

For Christians concerned with economic justice, this means that we should not look for a static solution, one perfect system in which to rest.[8] We have here no lasting city. Fostering justice requires local and ongoing negotiation, as does the work of meeting human needs. But that is not to say that Christian ethics must resign itself to endless process, nor that Christians can hide behind abstract principles and leave the work of application to others. It means that ethical questions must be situated within their specific narratives of human life moving toward its fulfillment.

In that sense, approaching the moral life as a journey is no evasion. Christian ethics, I contend, cannot be a matter of acts or virtues apart from a form of life and the unfolding of histories as pilgrimage, and that means it must be grounded in specific realities. As human life is inevitably social and historical, attempting to understand the good life through abstract categories is likely to lead to distorted conclusions. Convictions about "the good"

8. Although through the twentieth century, Catholic encyclicals criticized both capitalist and socialist systems, and although those encyclicals offered on occasion specific proposals for addressing the abuses of those systems and specific teachings on matters such as private property and the just wage, John Paul II is quite right in refusing to make of Catholic social teaching an alternate system, a "third way." He claims in *Centesimus annus* that the Church advocates neither economic system, but rather "a society of free work, of enterprise and of participation" (#35). At the center of the Church's social teaching is anthropology as a chapter of theology, so that the Church's concern is not for humanity as an abstraction (the necessary center of economic systems) but for historical persons. "This man is the primary route the church must travel in fulfilling her mission . . . the way traced out by Christ himself, the way that leads invariably through the mystery of the incarnation and redemption" (#53).

are woven out of a warp and woof of evolving social forms and theological wisdom, and any attempt to treat pursuit of the good abstracted from social forms is likely to end up, at best, purely formal.[9] For Christian ethics, in particular, histories and social forms offer insight into the Christian plot line, moving, more or less, toward a comic end in beatitude.

These stories of voluntary beggars and their impact on the emergence of stewardship and classical economics tell us something about who we are and how we got here, not about who everyone must be for all times. Attending to the habits of property-holding at work in those stories aims to make us better pilgrims, not to establish a new home.

If this book cannot provide an answer to what one ought to do about beggars, neither is it a study of begging, per se. The beggars studied here are the odd breed called voluntary beggars, those who as an act of Christian devotion have embraced a life of mendicancy, usually following renunciation of means to live otherwise.[10] These — Alexis, Francis, Benoît-Joseph Labre, and so on — are related to other beggars in something like the same way

9. One study on the virtue of humility, for example, states simply that humility is the virtue of seeing one's own strengths and weaknesses in the proper perspective, as neither less nor more important than they really are. This reasonable suggestion nevertheless leaves the most important questions unanswered: What is this right perspective and how do I get it? On whom do I rely to assist me in finding it and what might indicate that I have gotten my perspective wrong? The author himself acknowledges that if one accepts Christian doctrines of creation and fall, then it is only through the work of grace that a person achieves any good, and therefore humility will involve the recognition that I myself am incapable of actual good, apart from God's work in me. Those who do not accept these doctrines, of course, will have an entirely different perspective on their own contributions and therefore will practice humility in a quite different way. Thus this study of the virtue indicates that those seeking the good life, with humility as a piece of it, will have their notions shaped by forces far outside the reach of a proper formal definition of humility. Norvin Richards, *Humility* (Philadelphia: Temple University Press, 1992).

10. "Voluntary" is the traditional descriptor to designate someone who has taken up begging as part of a religious vocation. It does not imply, necessarily, that the person was previously wealthy, although that is often the case. It only signifies that as the person begs, he or she intends it as an act of Christian devotion and does not aspire to escape from it. These beggars cannot be called "Christian" beggars, as many beggars who do not consider begging a vocation or gift may be Christian. "Vocational" might be better than "voluntary," but in current usage might seem only to suggest that begging is a career and neglect the sense in which it is embraced for the love of God. If I could recreate the terminology, I might prefer "joyful" beggars, but as the theological meaning of joy is not transparent at present, I have judged that all things considered, the traditional term will have to do.

martyrs are related to murder victims. Observers may or may not be able to distinguish them. Holiness may be present or absent in either groups, as some who die professing their faith may nevertheless be guilty of pride or hatred, while some murder victims may die in the odor of sanctity. Voluntary beggars have been seen both as allies of other beggars and as competition or a convenient replacement for them. Both types are liable to criticism of their work ethic and honesty. But the two types are distinct in that one begs principally because of the violence of poverty and as a symptom of some disease within the social body, whether famine, unemployment, or alienation; the other begs as love's discipline, to cultivate charity in themselves and their community. In the heavenly city, no one will be forced to beg, but it is just possible to imagine voluntary beggars there, playing love's game of asking and receiving and giving it all away again with delight.

Voluntary beggars serve two purposes in this work. First, in them we can see the question of begging specifically intersecting Christian devotion and thought on property. They act as a focus for larger questions about property. Second, these histories of voluntary beggars are a valuable foil to changes in the life of the church regarding ownership, particularly the deveolpment of the term "stewardship" and the emergence of classical economics.

This book is, then, a historically-informed theological study of Christians' responses to the fear of beggars. The argument is, admittedly, anecdotal and dauntingly interdisciplinary. The histories engaged in this work are subject to ongoing debates, and the breadth and complexity of the material involved ensure that the author will not be able to engage, for good or ill, in neat proof-making. But it will be worth the risk if we can begin to understand how it is that something as simple as someone asking for some change can reduce so many of us to anxious silence.

Overview

To begin investigating the fear of beggars in Christian thought, the first two chapters will consider the practice of voluntary begging. Such begging, sometimes considered virtuous, sometimes sacrilegious, functioned as rich theological critique of new economic relations within an emerging market economy. It is no insult to Francis's sanctity, though, to recognize that this practice was not merely open to abuse, but held within itself points of fundamental instability, such as in the role of rights and duties in property relations. One of the most revered Christian saints became the founder of its most contentious order.

The third chapter will suggest how Christians disciplined the disorderly holiness of begging and rehabilitated the virtue of humility under the language of stewardship. Existing histories associate stewardship with Protestant missionary ventures in the nineteenth century, but in fact stewardship gains wide use first in the English Reformation, with a set of associations and rhetorical purposes proper to that context. The ideal of poverty is fractured. Its material practice was pressed on the church for the sake of humility, and the ideal of spiritual poverty was linked to lay holders of wealth, who demonstrated their humility and obedience by exercising the power of their wealth.

The fourth chapter treats begging as a focal point in the emergence of classical economic thought. Adam Smith, a Christian philosopher, and T. R. Malthus, a clergyman, constructed systems that make all economic life into exchange among competing strangers, so that beggars, who in the past had been suspected of dishonesty, laziness, and disturbing the social order, now appear unnatural, a kind of irrational margin to real life. Their near-contemporary, Benoît-Joseph Labre, begged his way across western Europe during a particularly well-organized attempt to enclose and reform beggars in France. The same era that produced these rational accounts of Christian political economy excluded, in every sense, beggars, even as many French and Italian Christians were hailing Labre as a saint.

The fifth chapter will take up twentieth-century proposals concerning poverty and just ownership, including the U.S. Catholic bishops' letter on stewardship, the work of Douglas John Hall, and post-liberal philosophers of gift. These contributions indicate that the concerns raised by earlier chapters remain unresolved, and in some cases, unacknowledged, so that the shape of present-day Christian ethics remains ill equipped to face beggars.

Finally we turn to Peter Maurin, who gave the beggar a decisive role in his account of a good Christian society. His synthesis argues that virtuous dependence and voluntary poverty are essential to a vibrant and practical Christian social order. In Maurin we find grounds for a fertile conversation on charity and poverty as serious categories for economic ethics.

Christian teaching on wealth has never been a simple matter, and the problem is not merely the perennial vice of greed. Or rather, the many guises in which greed as well as gluttony, anger, envy, and pride meet up with such virtues as prudence, courage, hope, justice, and humility with respect to the goods of providing for health, worship, and pleasure mean that a continual discernment about the particulars of economic life is inevitable, and inevitably complex. We can draw lessons and insight from the past, but our present awkwardness has its own shape. Catholic leadership continues to offer teaching on economic matters, but the status of this teaching remains uncertain, for the papacy itself acknowledges that encyclicals teach on moral issues and not on matters of "technical" economics.[11] Economics, while marching on toward mathematical certainty, is at least on its periphery concerned that gift and charity may be necessary, irreducible categories.[12] In congregations, leaders find themselves unsure how to advise their people, whatever their economic status. Pastors turn to guides on running small businesses for help organizing their parish finances.[13] Believers look to the facile answers of prosperity theology or face their finances presuming a separation of fact and value. Nations of poor Christians work for nations of rich Christians (sometimes in the same city) in a decentralized and hidden system of wage-slavery. Calls for good stewardship ring out on all sides, but with little agreement on what, exactly, that would look like. A wayfarer from another age tells what we fear will be our story as well.

> Midway on our life's journey, I found myself
> In dark woods, the right road lost. To tell
> About those woods is hard — so tangled and rough

---

11. See *Quadragesimo anno*, #41. Note, however, that it is "the Church," not only the papal office, that lacks this competence. The significance of the terminology is critical: does the whole Church have no comment to make on "technical economics"? Is the core of modern economics slipping through that loophole? The rousing call to battle in the end of this letter urges the clergy to gather the laity about them in order to concentrate their good works and make them more effective, indicating awareness of the many attempts among the laity to address economic concerns on the ground. This terminology, however, leaves the impression that the body of the Church has no economic competence or power.

12. This periphery, which I will consider primarily with reference to Smith and Malthus, lives on in Kenneth Boulding's work and more recently in Oded Stark, *Altruism and Beyond: An Economic Analysis of Exchanges within Families and Groups* (Cambridge: Cambridge University Press, 1995). In sociology, the classic work is Richard Titmuss, *The Gift Relationship: From Human Blood to Social Policy* (New York: Vintage Books, 1971).

13. See, for example, Lyle Schaller, *44 Ways to Increase Your Church's Financial Base* (Nashville: Abingdon Press, 1989).

And savage that thinking of it now, I feel
The old fear stirring: death is hardly more bitter.
And yet, to treat the good I found there as well

I'll tell what I saw, though how I came to enter
I cannot well say, being so full of sleep
Whatever moment it was I began to blunder

Off the true path. . . .[14]

We have woken up lost, perplexed and afraid. But the Christian pilgrimage is, for all that, a comedy. We set out, then, in search of wisdom in the strange company of Christianity's joyful beggars.

---

14. Dante, *The Inferno,* trans. Robert Pinsky (New York: Farrar, Straus and Giroux, 1994), Canto I, 1-10.

CHAPTER ONE

Begging and Christian Economy

In the thirteenth-century novel *Blanquerna,* a pious couple argues because the husband wants to become a beggar as penance. The wife cries,

> Great merit has he that is in the world and possesses temporal things without sin, and devotes himself to the service of the poor of Jesus Christ; and great merit has he that is rich in the goods of this world yet poor in spirit; and if it be virtue to beg for the love of Jesus Christ, it cannot be a vice to give to the poor who beg for love of him.[1]

"If it be virtue to beg for the love of Jesus Christ": she does not question the virtue of her husband's intent. It *is* virtue to beg for the love of Jesus Christ, and therefore it cannot be vice to give to the poor. Confidence in the goodness of almsgiving is made dependent upon confidence in the goodness of begging "for the love of Jesus Christ."[2]

Before we can begin to sort out what voluntary beggars are up to, we

---

1. Ramón Llull, *Blanquerna,* trans. E. A. Peers (London: Dedalus/Hippocrene Books, 1987), 50-57.

2. With apologies to scholars of literature and history, I am drawing not only on accounts of historical people and movements, but also on legendary, fictional, and poetic material, insofar as each of these attests to the ways Christians have understood the renunciation of property and embrace of mendicancy. Recognizing the dangers of rifling through such an array of sources, I have tried to attend to the contexts in which texts were produced and to respect their foreignness as well as their internal coherence. But ultimately, as this is a theological work, they are grist for the mill as we try to understand present-day problems of humility and property.

have to know what we mean by "beggars." Beggars, properly speaking, are not simply poor. Indeed, reluctant almsgivers often ask whether the beggars they meet *are* genuinely poor. Begging remains a distinct subfield within the world of the poor, though its boundaries vary with the society. In some contexts, "beggars" refers to the lowest stratum of the poor, those who have no means of earning even a low wage. To be in such a position is in effect to be a beggar: such a person lives on alms, even if the impoverished body is not on public display. To have any other recourse is to be higher on the social ladder. Such mendicancy could result from injury, physical or mental illness, old age, or even childhood. These beggars of other eras are in the modern nation often enclosed in systems or buildings run by the government for their care, remaining dependent without making public appeals or relying on gifts or alms. Their dependence becomes instead a matter of law, policy, and right. It is in the public domain, but hidden, controlled, and rendered impersonal. These are not the beggars with whom this chapter is chiefly concerned, although movement from one form of dependence to another is simply a fact of life to the poor.

More precisely, a beggar is one who begs. Even here, some ambiguity remains, for one may beg by going door to door, by calling out to strangers walking by, by holding a sign, or even by waiting silently in a public place, exposing one's disability. This last case assumes that the passersby know how to read the appeal, perhaps because of the location (by the church door), the manner (leaving a hat or other container nearby for contributions), or simply because of the beggar's familiarity in the community.[3] One may beg by offering the pretense of a petty sale (a pencil) or service (windshield washing). Street entertainers rest uneasily on the border between wage labor and begging, and in them we see the persistence of a long association between troubadours and beggars. The boundary between the two may be drawn with reference to their talent, or lack thereof. But workers can also be beggars. Seasonal, occasional, or badly-paid workers may now, as in the past, resort to begging in off-periods, or during the journey to new work. Some churches in the U.S. are becoming more accustomed to appeals from migrant workers in need of shelter or food as they travel to new jobs.

3. Wordsworth's "Old Cumberland Beggar" names the import of such a well-known local beggar: "While from door to door,/This old Man creeps, the villagers in him/Behold a record which together binds/Past deeds and offices of charity,/Else unremembered . . ." (lines 87-91). In *The Complete Poetical Works of Wordsworth* (Boston: Houghton Mifflin, 1932), 93-96.

Regardless of the particular circumstances, a person who begs, suffering from no apparent disability or crisis, is frequently presumed to be morally diseased by laziness or misanthropy. In an era in which public bureaucracies are expected to provide alms systematically, many people associate beggars with addiction, mental illness, or crime. Beggars can be bearers of disorder. Accounts of famine tell of hoards of beggars descending on a town or farm, employing threats, arson, or violence to back up their pleas for food. The line between begging and robbery can be fragile, and survivors of famine offer horrifying illustrations of the war of all against all in a world of scarce goods.[4]

The beggars of this book, usually called voluntary beggars, are both at home and strange among other beggars. Like other beggars, they are a varied lot. The earliest Franciscans engaged in menial day labor, begging when that income was insufficient; Benoît-Joseph Labre lived on the road much of his life; *Piers Plowman* draws on images of slackers, people who fake their own or their children's disfigurement, and the desperate honest poor, as well as friars, a saintly pilgrim, jongleurs, and lunatics. What distinguishes voluntary beggars is that, however they came to it, they embraced public dependent poverty as part of their attempt to live the good life. Most of these beggars were not thrown unwillingly into poverty, but renounced whatever security and prestige their families and labor could

4. During a famine in Lyons, 1529, some 2,000 people rioted and looted the grain supplies of the city, the Franciscan monastery, and the homes of wealthy citizens. See Natalie Zemon Davis, *Society and Culture in Early Modern France* (Stanford: Stanford University Press, 1975), 27-29. The problem of theft in case of starvation was discussed at great length among canonists and theologians of the late twelfth and early thirteenth centuries. Although it served certain rhetorical purposes, evidence suggests that it was a practical issue which did not have merely theoretical significance for the scholars who wrote about it. Famine stalked the poor of northwestern Europe in the last two decades of the twelfth century. Around Paris, the years 1194-1198 saw five consecutive failed harvests. The abbey of Vicoigne regretted that it could no longer give alms in 1197, recording that the poor were dying by the thousands. Consensus emerged that the famished person was not guilty of theft. The decision left unresolved questions such as whether the wealthy person was then guilty of murder for not volunteering property in time of famine; what constituted sufficient desperation; and what could be done when a large group of people were all in danger of starvation. The ecclesial consensus did not change civil law. See Giles Couvreur, *Les pauvres ont-ils des droits? Recherches sur le vol in cas d'extrême nécessité depuis la Concordia de Gratien (1140) jusqu'à Guillaume d'Auxerre (+ 1231)* (Rome: Libreria Editrice dell'Università Gregoriana, 1961); and Michel Mollat, "Pauvres et pauvreté a la fin du XIIe siècle," *Revue d'ascetique et de mystique*, Tome XLI, 3:163 (1965): 310-11.

have gained them.[5] Why would anyone do such a thing, and why would a community support them, much less honor them for doing it?

A number of responses follow, raising in turn various functions of voluntary begging which, in practice, are often closely entwined. Considering each one separately offers us the chance to recognize a thread that runs through them all: voluntary begging is not merely about an individual's pursuit of holiness, but rather concerns the possibility of a Christian social order.

To Make a Living

Most obviously, begging is a way to get food and other necessities without earning wages. Insofar as being poor includes by definition occasional begging — as was the case when Francis embraced poverty — the voluntarily poor may beg as any poor person would, to obtain necessities. Pilgrims, who cannot engage in daily work, may take to begging as a means of completing the pilgrimage if they lack resources to finance an entire trip ahead of time. Similarly, the wandering hermit-preachers of the twelfth century, for example Robert of Arbrissel, were apparently dependent upon alms, since they were accused of being parasites, wandering in search of donations.[6] The anonymous nineteenth-century Russian work *The Way of a Pilgrim*[7] tells of a pilgrim walking through Russia, searching for wisdom and teaching others about prayer. Injured early in life, having lost his family and property, he turned to permanent pilgrimage. He takes up occasional jobs that leave him in the solitude he so desires for cultivating ceaseless prayer, but when the jobs run out or he takes again to the road, he depends upon charity. The pilgrim's begging is a matter of no more than passing interest to the characters, hardly more notable than the basket-weaving of a desert father. It is simply one of the miserable ways the poor

5. Evidence suggesting that voluntary beggars usually came from the ranks of the monied and not from among peasants or the "garden variety" poor has provided historian Kenneth Baxter Wolf grounds to claim that Franciscan-style poverty served, both materially and spiritually, the purposes of the moneyed, increasing the material and ecclesial marginalization of the poor. *The Poverty of Riches: St. Francis of Assisi Reconsidered* (Oxford: Oxford University Press, 2003).

6. Lester K. Little, *Religious Poverty and the Profit Economy in Medieval Europe* (Ithaca: Cornell University Press, 1978), 77, 82.

7. Trans. R. M. French (New York: Harper & Brothers, 1952).

survive, regardless of their virtue or vocation. If his economic dependence mirrors his spiritual dependence, or if it serves to engage him in a sort of missionary activity toward his benefactors, this is not a matter he or they discuss. Begging is just a way of getting food.

Or rather, begging is just a way of getting food as long as donors are willing to give. Accounts of voluntary beggars often include stories of individuals or towns hostile to the beggar, places where a beggar cannot survive, unless some dissenter provides a haven. Beggars beg to survive, but they depend upon the existence of social order that accepts begging as part of the social fabric (not as a crime or absurdity). The possibility of successful begging indicates a strong social bond so that sharing with a needy stranger is reasonable. It also indicates a culture that tolerates substantial variations in wealth so that almsgivers do not presuppose a need to change the beggar's status.

But begging as a way to survive need not imply desperation. Thomas Aquinas, a Dominican mendicant, argued that although begging to avoid work was unlawful, a religious could beg either because he has no other means of living or in order to finance some useful work. "Thus alms are besought for the building of a bridge, or church, or for any other work whatever that is conducive to the common good: thus scholars may seek alms that they may devote themselves to the study of wisdom." Begging for a living can be a diffuse sort of wage, paid on behalf of the whole community to one who works without wages for the common good. This arrangement presupposes, again, a kind of social bond in a community that possesses a sense of such a common good and has some trust that the beggars in question are actually contributing to it. Such begging may be "disgraceful" or "uncomely" according to Thomas, but it is not sinful.[8]

These rules governing begging are no different for religious than for other people. Thomas notes in particular that preachers who beg actually have a right to wages. They accept alms, instead, as an act of humility. Without rejecting the category of rights, those friars who willingly renounce just claims to put themselves at the mercy of others do so for virtuous reasons, in keeping with their state of life.[9]

---

8. Thomas Aquinas, *Summa Theologica: Complete English Edition in Five Volumes,* trans. Fathers of the English Dominican Province (Westminster, Md.: Christian Classics, 1948), II-II, Q.187, a.5. Hereafter ST.

9. ST II-II, Q.187, a.5

Recognizing that begging can be a manifestation of sloth or avarice, Thomas repeatedly makes it clear that those who accept alms for such purposes act sinfully. He assumes that religious who live on alms do so in recompense for their work on behalf of the whole church. Their begging is not freeloading, but transformation of a claim of justice into the practice of patient humility and an invitation to charity. They forgo the salary they earn, preferring to wait on gifts. Yet in this argument, these "gifts" remain strongly connected to work for the common good. Using them would become unlawful if the recipient were not doing the religious work in honor of which the gift was given. They "would be thwarting the intention of those who bestowed those gifts."[10]

Thomas is working on two levels: first, he is eager to demonstrate that reception of alms and even begging for them is in no way unjust, given the work that the friars do. They are, in fact, a financial bargain for the church since they could legitimately claim greater support as a right. But he wants to claim further not only that their begging is not wrong, but also that it is virtuous in a way that supersedes these issues of justice and right. They have made the greatest act of liberality possible in surrendering all of their goods at once, rather than parceling them out over time, and surrendering claims to their just wages continues their life of self-sacrifice. While Thomas takes a Dominican line on poverty (perfect poverty is poverty well-suited to the work of the order) rather than a Franciscan enthusiasm for absolute poverty, he does claim that Jesus was a beggar and that humble dependence upon others is a proper element of the imitation of Christ. Nevertheless, for readers of a pragmatic mind, he is also careful to justify begging as less expensive than the wages friars could legitimately charge for their services.

While remaining cautious about the uses of poverty, Thomas defends his order's begging as an exercise of humility toward support that could just as well be claimed as a right, and a right particularly due to them since they are living the highest possible Christian life. Without undermining the validity of wages for other workers, without raising questions about the necessity of paying just wages in ordinary circumstances, Thomas demonstrates the excellence of the friars' receiving alms in lieu of wages.

Begging for a living has, however, been problematic for women reli-

10. ST II-II, Q.187, a.4.

18

gious, whose begging is also subject to the approval of the donors. Francis's female followers were cloistered, as religious generally were at that time and as women's orders continued to be for some centuries. Since begging involves mobility, exposure to public view, and contact with all manner of people, respectful and disrespectful, virtuous and vicious, it was considered incompatible with cloistered life and therefore largely incompatible with women's virtue. The fictional nuns of *Blanquerna,* under the guidance of a new abbess, end the practice of sending a sister out to beg for the convent. The mendicant sister saw worldly sights not conducive to her virtue, and she sometimes bore tales back to the other sisters. Instead, the wise abbess endows the convent with funds for a certain fixed number of sisters. If others want to join, they may, provided they pay their own way. In Llull's world, their segregation and stability in the cloister trumps the importance of their precarious poverty.

Exceptions may be allowed: the wife quoted at the beginning of this chapter does become a beggar along with her husband, as the final stage of her commitment to the active life and to her marriage. But for celibate women, whose bodies bear the social role of perfecting modesty and purity, begging is too worldly an activity. The abbess acts to protect the purity of the women, for their own welfare, but the author's concern may indicate another concern altogether, that women should not take on such a public and controversial role.

To Conceal and Reveal

This question of a beggar's public exposure has a rich theological legacy. The Christian legend of Alexis, a fifth-century saint whose cult arrived in the West in the tenth century, served as the prototype of the voluntary beggar in its golden era. But in its early form, the legend of Alexis emphasizes less his begging than his discipline of obscurity.[11] In this version, Alexis grew up in great wealth, the long-awaited child of a well-known couple,

---

11. I am using the French translation of the Syriac version of the legend, *La legende Syriaque de S. Alexis, l'homme de Dieu,* by Arthur Amiand (Paris: Vieweg, 1889). The earliest versions of the legend actually concern an unnamed saint. Studies of the French poem of the life of Alexis can be found in T. D. Hemming, ed., *La Vie de Saint Alexis* (Exeter: University of Exeter Press, 1994) and Maurizio Perugi, ed., *La Vie de Saint Alexis: Edition Critique* (Genève: Librarie Droz S.A., 2000).

originally placed in Constantinople and later in Rome. On the eve of his wedding, however, he eloped with poverty, fleeing to Odessa where he could live in poverty and anonymity. He was unrecognized even by the slaves sent from his parents' house to try to find him. Only one man, a church porter, noticed that Alexis, among the many homeless sleeping out, often prayed during the night. Having sworn not to tell during Alexis's life, he was able to elicit the truth of his identity. When Alexis fell ill, the porter offered to care for him, but Alexis was only willing to receive what the porter would have done for any stranger. The porter took him to the hospital and visited him there regularly. One day, the porter was delayed. When he arrived, Alexis had died and his body had already been removed to a paupers' grave. Now released from his vow of secrecy, the porter begged the bishop to come and help him find the saintly poor man. The bishop and his retinue searched the paupers' grave, but all they could find there were the rags that Alexis had worn. His body had disappeared. Thereafter, the bishop pledged to be vigilant in caring for the poor, since he would never know when another such saint might be among them.

A second story of Alexis may be a conflation of that first story with the life of St. John the Calybite, who after abandoning his wealth to enter a monastery was told by a heavenly voice to return home. Unrecognized by his family, he lived as a beggar in a hut near them, only revealing his identity on his deathbed. This second version of Alexis's life has him deciding after some years that he was too well-known in Odessa. He boarded a ship to Tarsus, but in a storm the ship was forced off course and came to Rome. Certain that no one would recognize him, he returned to his home as a stranger, pleased no longer to be dependent on anyone outside his family. Invoking the story of Lazarus and Dives, Alexis begged from his own father, and the father consented to keep the poor man and care for him. Over seventeen years, no one in his father's house recognized Alexis. Shortly before he died, he wrote out an account of his life. He was discovered, dead, on Good Friday morning by a group of clerics and nobles miraculously directed to him. The account he had written was read, and his family — amazed that this pauper had been their long-lost son — mourned, while crowds rushed to the body to pray for healing. The distinguished company trying to take the body to St. Peter's were so mobbed that they threw money onto the ground to try to distract and disperse the crowds pressing on them. The people nevertheless ignored the money and continued to try to touch the corpse. The body was displayed for seven days at St. Peter's, and when it was placed in a reliquary, a sweet-smelling ointment appeared on the outside of it. All those who touched it were aided.

In this legend, the element of Alexis's mendicancy is given little attention per se, yet it contributes to his charism of hiddenness. The poverty he embraced is called "not ordinary poverty, but that complete poverty which is a shame and opprobrium."[12] In making himself an object of shame, Alexis deflects the view of the world. If beggars feel shame, they cannot allow it to move them to avoid being seen. To win a living, beggars must be seen. Beggars expose their failure to earn a living and in doing so reveal their disfigurement or imbecility or moral disease to the public eye. The working of shame, as the story of Alexis demonstrates, actually has more power over the almsgiver than the beggar, for whom it is an unaffordable luxury. In exposing himself thus, Alexis becomes completely hidden, for few are willing to look a beggar in the eye. Even his family pass by him every day, but fail to look at him.

Having ceased to be recognized, Alexis loses the security of family and social status. In an economy not fully monetized, recognition and social status are the primary sources of power and security, and so Alexis's anonymity is the deepest of poverties. Nevertheless, the story does not affirm anonymity entirely, or we would have no story. Alexis must be recognized. In the first version, it is the good porter (the doorkeeper, who had charge of keys, guarded the relics, and was responsible for ringing bells for the call to prayer, and who recalls Peter's office of holding the keys) who sees Alexis's devotion and attests to his holiness so that others can know him after his death. He cries to the bishop, "Recognize me, and take pity on me."[13] Even then, however, the bishop only hears the story. Alexis himself evades his sight. As in the empty tomb narrative, Alexis's story ends with an openness that asks the reader to continue looking for him in the flesh, and to be ready to find him anywhere. In the second version, God leads the church to find the saint they have not seen in their midst, and Alexis leaves a witness to himself. The letter he has written revealing his identity is clenched in his dead hand, and his father cannot remove it. The family has failed to recognize the beggar as their own.

When Alexis regains recognition, it is by a different family and in a

---

12. "Non pas de la pauvreté ordinaire, mais de cette pauvreté complète qui est une honte et un opprobe." Amiand, *La legende Syriaque*, 1.

13. "Reconnais-moi, et prends pitié de moi." Amiand, *La legende Syriaque*, 8.

new social hierarchy, as a saint of the church. Alexis's recognition is his service to the church, as well as his testimony against its late arrival. In seeing him at last, his family and the church see their own refusal to look at the beggar. Recognizing him and repenting of their blindness, they find his body a haven of grace and healing for, among other ailments, blindness. Who knows, the story teaches, but that many other such saints may be hidden around us, even in our own households? The bishop of the first story cries out, "May the Lord preserve me hereafter to do no other thing than to make my one care relieving strangers! For who knows if there are not many like this saint, seeking humility, great in the eyes of God and ignored by men on account of their humility?"[14]

Alexis's poverty is a shame to him in that it brings ridicule on him from passersby and servants. But this shame is a discipline for Alexis, stripping from him concern for any eyes on him except God. When he is seen rightly, as by the bishop who seeks him in Odessa, the vision is not of shame, but of humility. The question is, again, not merely the beggar's virtue, but the power of the community to see and respond rightly to his action. His life bears fruit in their new vision.

To Preach

Closely related to the importance of the beggar's being seen is the power of a beggar to admonish or inspire. The Dominican Order, mendicant preachers whose history is closely entwined with the Franciscans, emerged from a mission to the Cathars that adopted evangelical poverty in order to counter the argument that Catholic clergy were corrupted by wealth. Their imitation of Christ's poverty was a necessary credential for their preaching, and their begging, as we saw with Thomas, was a way to fund their

---

14. "Me préserve désormais le Seigneur de faire autre chose que de mettre mon unique soin à soulager les étrangers! Car qui sait s'il n'y en a pas beaucoup comme ce saint, recherchant l'humilité, grands par eux-mêmes aux yeux de Dieu, et ignorés des hommes à cause de leur humilité?" Amiand, *La legende Syriaque*, 9. The idea that hidden among beggars are people beloved of God and unseen by people reminds me of Lear's plan to be with Cordelia as "God's spies" (V:iii, 17). My analysis of the legend of Alexis is much indebted to Stanley Cavell's essay on Lear, "The Avoidance of Love," *Must We Mean What We Say? A Book of Essays* (New York: Charles Scribner's Sons, 1969), which Peter Dula pointed out to me.

work, rather than itself a central part of their work. The brothers led by Dominic did not originally beg. Rather, they received a portion of what the parishes in the area had set aside for the poor. Thus although they were poor and dependent on donations, they were secure in food and a place to live. They did not publicly beg. Only in 1220, four years after papal approval was given to Dominic's new group, did they cease accepting rents, revenues, and alms in cash. Their poverty was internally connected to their preaching, but their begging was one of several possible appropriate means.

But begging itself can be seen as a kind of preaching. We have already met Evast and Aloma, Blanquerna's parents, who round out their holy married life as beggars. At the wife's request (perhaps in authorial deference to her femininity), they preach only through their actions, but they are depicted as converting sinners from each of the seven deadly sins, including a friar suffering from vanity. Their success is related to their being recognized as voluntary beggars, in whom the observed poverty is an inspiring example of humility. Because their poverty is taken on for the love of God, the sight of this couple is edifying. Alexis's effect on those who saw (or failed to see) him refers us instead to the discomfort many experience passing by beggars presumed to have no other means. As Baudelaire put it, "I know nothing more disquieting than the mute eloquence of those supplicating eyes that contain at once, for the sensitive man who knows how to read them, so much humility and so much reproach."[15] Begging implicitly raises questions about the almsgiver, and perhaps about the whole social order.

Within Christian discourse, this kind of silent preaching touches a sore spot. We should pause here to review the tradition's uneasiness with wealth and property. While the Old Testament is not lacking in demands for justice and laws for the protection of the poor, the New Testament makes wealth itself problematic.[16] Cautions against wealth (e.g., Mt. 6:19, 31; 13:22; 19:23; 1 Tim. 6:17; 2 Tim. 3:2; James 1:10; Rev. 3:17), the examples of

15. Charles Pierre Baudelaire, "Counterfeit Money," reprinted in Jacques Derrida, *Given Time: 1. Counterfeit Money*, trans. Peggy Kamuf (Chicago: University of Chicago Press, 1992).

16. For a very brief survey of the pervasive scriptural anxiety concerning wealth peppered with a salutary consciousness of the rationalizations Christians attempt to use to justify the status quo of property, see Richard Hays, *The Moral Vision of the New Testament* (San Francisco: HarperSanFrancisco, 1996), 464-68.

renunciation of private property (partial or complete) as a component of becoming a follower of Jesus (e.g., Mt. 4:20; 10:9; 19:21, 29; Lk. 12:23; 19:8; Acts 2:44-45; 4:34) and commendation of or association with the poor (e.g., Mt. 25:40; Lk. 1:53; 6:20; 16:22; 2 Cor. 8:2; James 2:5-6; Rev. 2:9) appear frequently. While these passages do not amount to a prohibition of private property and while the just wealthy person is not unknown in the New Testament (e.g. 1 Tim. 6:18-19 and the oft-cited hospitality of Martha and Mary), poverty is preferred to wealth often enough that ownership has remained a troublesome topic for Christians.

In patristic literature, possession remained an issue.

> Tell me then, how did you come by your wealth? Did you receive it from someone? Where did he get it from? From his grandfather, you say, or from his father. Are you able to show, as you go back through the generations, that it was justly acquired? It cannot have been. No, the beginning and root of wealth must lie in injustice of some sort. And why? Because, in the beginning God did not create one person wealthy and another to go wanting; nor did he, at some point later in time, reveal great heaps of gold to one person and cheat another searcher. He gave one and the same earth to all alike. . . . Isn't the fact that you claim sole ownership of what belongs to the Lord, of what is common property, something evil? Or do you deny that the Lord's is the earth and its fullness? And so, if whatever we have belongs to our one common Lord, it belongs also to those who are his servants along with us.[17]

Chrysostom was not alone in raising this question to his congregation. Ambrose asked, "The earth was established in common for all, rich and poor. Why do you alone arrogate an exclusive right to the soil, O rich?"[18] Basil taught, "The bread that you keep belongs to the one who is hungry, and to him who is naked, the cloak that you keep in your chest; to him who has no shoes, the shoe that is rotting in your house; to the poor, the money that you keep hidden. Thus you commit as many injustices as there are persons to whom you could give."[19] According to sermons of both Leo the Great and Cesarius of Arles, the person who could but does

---

17. Chrysostom, Serm. 12.4 in *Ep. I ad Tim.*
18. *De Nabuthae*, 1.2.
19. Cited from Couvreur, *Les pauvres ont-ils des droits?* 95-96. P.G. 31, 1752.

not come to the aid of a starving person should be thought of as an assassin.[20] This set of teachings suggests, though not in a systematic way, that to claim goods as private property is implicitly an immoral act, at least as long as other people lack necessities. The right to hold and use goods as one's own is suspect in these preachers.

This is not to say that all Christians were required to dispossess themselves. On the contrary, those who taught that such renunciation was necessary for salvation, as the Pelagians did, were condemned as heretics, on the grounds that "nothing is impossible with God" (Mt. 19:26). Some patristic advice to the rich treats of the interdependence of the rich and poor, such that the gifts of the rich meet the needs of the poor now, and the prayers of the poor will meet the need of the rich for salvation later.[21] In such a view, a beggar who invites the rich to remember this mutuality and who prays for these benefactors provides a necessary service to the community, and the rich demonstrate their refusal to count their goods as entirely their own.

This irenic vision of mutual aid runs into trouble, however, under scrutiny. If riches are only innocent when they are not hoarded but are shared with the poor, then are the wealthy not in fact obligated over time to renounce all their superfluities, or as many as are needed by the poor? Who will define how much is to be shared, what counts as superfluous wealth, and what counts as a need that must be addressed? Furthermore, drawing on those patristic teachings which claim possession itself is rooted in sin, is it not restitution rather than alms that is needed? The claim that the wealthy depend upon the poor through whom they can win their salvation leads to the notion of poverty as a beneficial institution which neither the poor nor the rich should aim to dismantle, a notion of poverty the homilists cited above seem to oppose. What degree of poverty can be allowed to continue to exist among Christians? Even the phrasing of such a question is problematic: given the strong scriptural caution against riches, should it not be a matter of what degree of privately owned riches can continue to exist?

Nevertheless, the idea of a wealthy person's virtue resting in detachment and wise use does also appear in patristic writings. The most famous

20. Leo the Great, Sermons, App. 4,2. "Pasce fame morientem: quisquis enim pascendo servare hominem poteris si non paveris, occidisti" (P.L. 54, 491). Cesarius, Sermon 33 ". . . Et quanti paupers in locis, ubi ipse habitat, illo decimas non dante fame mortui fuerint, tantorum homicidiorum reus ante tribunal aeterni iudicis apparebit . . ." (ed. D. Morin, CCSL, 103, 2nd ed., 146). Both cited in Couvreur, *Les pauvres ont-ils des droits?* 81.

21. E.g., The Shepherd of Hermas.

early example is Clement's "Who Is the Rich Man Who Shall Be Saved?" in which 'spiritual poverty' is to be rich in virtue and therefore able to use wealth for good purposes. The rich need not despair, for their wealth, mastered and rightly used, will not keep them from heaven. Various wealthy characters of Scripture, such as Abraham, Job, Zaccheus, and Joseph of Arimathea, were used at times as examples of those who used wealth well rather than renouncing it altogether. These two strands of thought made peace with each other in the monastic compromise: poverty belongs with the contemplative life, and various forms of right possession of wealth to the active life. Poverty and contemplation are more perfect, as they more closely resemble the eternal goal of communion with each other and with God, but the active life remains morally serious, as a present necessity. Beggars, however, unsettle this compromise by raising the possibility of virtuous poverty in the very midst of the active life, in the streets of the city, among laity and clergy. Their appeal can be a disturbing critique or a confrontation.[22]

Llull turns that dangerous history to his own purposes when he includes an incident in which a canon appointed by Bishop Blanquerna to represent "Blessed are the poor in spirit" leads all the poor in the town not only in their begging, but even in a mass denunciation of a cleric who hoards grain. With the canon at their head, a mob of beggars gathers outside the cleric's residence and shouts, "Justice, justice!" until he is forced to distribute his grain. Llull authorizes the poor — at least in this fictional case and led by (controlled by) a delegate of the bishop — publicly and aggressively to denounce those who withhold what others need. Nor is such a move purely fictional: Raymond of Piacenza (d. 1200) is said to have led a group of beggars through the streets crying out in protest at the stinginess of the rich.[23]

Though the focus is a *cleric's* greed, Llull removes any taint of disrespect in his story by having a cleric lead the righteous denunciation. The

22. In the interest of maintaining any pretense of limitations to my topic, I will not here treat the evangelical movements of the twelfth and thirteenth century, with their various relations to wealth, work, begging, and Christian doctrine. Suffice it to say that the condemnations directed against some of them concerned their doctrinal orthodoxy, but often their unconventional forms of religious life, including itinerant poverty, were a crucial component of their suspect status, particularly when accompanied by a critique of the wealth of clergy. See Herbert Grundmann, *Religious Movements in the Middle Ages*, trans. Steven Rowan (Notre Dame: University of Notre Dame Press, 1995).

23. Wolf, *The Poverty of Riches*, 74. Raymond, Wolf writes, took the opportunity to upbraid the wealthy for giving to him, but not to the involuntarily poor.

image of a mob of beggars publicly condemning a hoarder in time of need could quite reasonably strike terror in the hearts of prosperous merchants in the thirteenth century, and putting an ecclesial authority at their head both tames their potential for violence and lends moral credibility to their condemnation. When Llull wants a powerful scene condemning economic injustice, he uses beggars paired with the authority of the church.

Still, ordinary boisterous beggars do not receive his approbation, nor do all owners of wealth merit condemnation. When Llull's Poverty canon criticizes a burgess for living in luxury, the burgess leads him to a hidden room in his house, poorly furnished, where he and his wife do penance. He maintains his rich goods, he explains, the more to increase his disregard for them. As a result, the Poverty canon sees no need for a mob to surround this house where hidden poverty is somehow lived secretly in the midst of wealth. But this approval comes from a voluntary beggar, who is taken to be the authority on such matters. Virtuous possession is possible, but for Llull it is authorized by approval from the church and the poor, two sources that conveniently coincide in his Poverty canon.

To Instigate Gift-Giving

It may seem only too obvious that begging is the instigation of gift-giving. Perhaps because it is so obvious, it receives little comment, or at any rate, little positive comment. In the story of Alexis, his return home layers irony into his begging — he is only asking for his own inheritance, that to which he has a legal right. Alexis, or his narrator, finds this a relief. The pilgrim of the Russian story admits to finding begging offensive, and Blanquerna, for all the virtuous begging of Evast and Aloma, never himself begs, though he seems to live a suspiciously long time on an all-too-allegorical seven loaves with which he leaves home. The actual appeal for the gift remains, even in these stories, a source of some narrative embarrassment. Self-contained voluntary poverty is admirable, but when a person pulls others into the circle of that poverty by asking for alms, suddenly poverty becomes more dubious. Still the most famous of all Christian voluntary beggars, Francis of Assisi, laid hold of precisely this part of begging with enthusiasm, relishing not only poverty but also the role of public dependent.

The end of the twelfth century saw a great outpouring of theological literature on poverty and almsgiving which was neither a romantic exalta-

tion of poverty nor an anti-materialist repudiation of wealth.[24] The writers concerned wrote of concrete issues: the rights of the poor to claim their
necessities in case of urgent need, the inability of monasteries to continue
giving alms in time of famine, the effect of usury on the poor, the purchase
of riches to adorn a church where the faithful were hungry and clad in
rags, the burden of tithes on the poor, whether to give alms to all or only to
the worthy. The authors did not think in terms of analyses of social mecha-
nisms, but of personal sin on the part of the wealthy and powerful in a period which saw across much of western Europe a long series of poor harvests and great misery among the poor.

This development in theology corresponds to a diffuse and complex
change in European society dating from the late eleventh century, often
called the rise of the money economy.[25] Though no unified event, the
transformation can be observed through a series of interconnected
changes. Agricultural techniques and expansion produced surplus which
aided and in turn was encouraged by the growth of towns and permanent
markets. Population increased approximately threefold. With the greater
supply of laborers, the previously deeply-rooted peasantry began to be released, or expelled, from traditional ties to the land, to face the flexibility
and vulnerability of wage labor. Some industry, particularly in the production of cloth, developed, absorbing workers and contributing to both the
concentration of population into towns and the increase of far-reaching
trade. The circulation of specie increased, made of metals gained from new
mines and from plunder of western Europe's Islamic communities, but
also particularly from liquidation of the accumulated riches of monasteries. To accommodate trade, towns and markets grew. Travel became more
common and easier for merchants, not least because of the increased so-
phistication of banking which allowed deposits made in one city to be
withdrawn in another. This increase in trade meant that merchants and
bankers became a more numerous and influential class. Thus, money took
on greater centrality in this new order than ever before, even in rural areas
as traditional rents and duties began to be transmuted into cash payment
by lords interested in the purchase of luxury goods such as cloth and wine.

24. Mollat, "Pauvres et pauvreté," 305-23. See also Couvreur, *Les pauvres ont-ils des
droits?*

25. Little, *Religious Poverty and the Profit Economy*; Georges Duby, *Rural Economy and
Country Life in the Medieval West*, trans. Cynthia Postan (Columbia, S.C.: University of
South Carolina Press, 1968).

Scholars too were drawn into a new order, both as administrative leaders of institutions and as moral leaders, gradually recognizing that in the market, the combination of many approximations produced a market price, and that this common estimation worked as an impersonal force uncontrollable by the authority of church or crown.[26] The well-documented history of debates over usury through the Middle Ages demonstrates the recognition and gradual permission (granted well after the fact, like an unwilling father blessing the marriage some years after the honeymoon) of a market for money as a productive force.[27]

The development of thought on usury demonstrated two disturbing features of the new economy: first, that the authority of the church could not control the market by proclamation; and second, that the individual wills of the persons engaged in the market likewise could not control it. The moral structure governing exchanges of property came tumbling down, as, long before Adam Smith, merchants and theologians alike realized that the widespread use of money created the possibility of self-regulating markets in which transactions took on a quasi-mechanical impersonality.[28] The fiat of a king to set a low price in time of need was found to have the effect of increasing scarcity, for merchants in a competitive market could not necessarily keep to a set price and stay in business. Where was the operation of traditional virtues, not least of all obedience,

26. Joel Kaye, *Economy and Nature in the Fourteenth Century: Money, Market Exchange, and the Emergence of Scientific Thought* (Cambridge: Cambridge University Press, 1998), Introduction; 222-29.

27. Among important sources on this subject are John T. Noonan, *The Scholastic Analysis of Usury* (Cambridge, Mass.: Harvard University Press, 1957); R. H. Tawney, *Religion and the Rise of Capitalism: A Historical Study* (New York: Mentor Books, 1954); and Odd Langholm, *The Legacy of Scholasticism in Economic Thought: Antecedents of Choice and Power* (Cambridge: Cambridge University Press, 1998) and *Economics in the Medieval Schools: Wealth, Exchange, Value, Money, and Usury according to the Paris Theological Tradition, 1200-1350* (Leiden: E. J. Brill, 1992). By "gradual permission," I mean not that guarded allowance given by Calvin upon which such emphasis has been placed, but the earlier process recognizing external titles to interest, as distinguished from usury. A title to *lucrum cessans*, which Thomas refused to permit but those soon after him began to allow, is in essence a recognition of a market price for productive capital.

28. Kaye, *Economy and Nature*, 97-100, offers an illuminating account of Thomas Aquinas' teaching about just price, which has been variously interpreted. Kaye suggests that Thomas was unwilling to leave the just price to the impersonal adjudication of the market, in spite of his awareness of this process. To do so would mean the removal of rational moral ordering from the economic sphere.

in such an economic world? If greed alone had been the problem in earlier times, astute observers of markets began to suspect that alongside greed a new and deeper problem was at hand, threatening the very idea of moral teaching on exchange of property and use of money.

The traditional bearers of the virtue of voluntary poverty, monastic orders, were themselves deeply enmeshed in the new economy as holders of both land and accumulated riches, goods which in an earlier era had been understood as suitable to their commitment to the worship of God. Poverty of a sort had always been characteristic of monastic vocations and the more perfect following of Christ, and the poor had long before been called the treasure of the church. The monasticism of the early Middle Ages was characterized by a poverty that was less material deprivation than a status of social vulnerability, a lack of political and military power. Drawn largely from the "warrior class," the monks' self-understanding and contribution was defined in relationship to warring, not to the market. Early in the tenth century, a monastery could be described as "a place full of virtue, remarkable for miracles, overflowing with riches, excelling all in the practice of religion."[29]

But in the midst of this economic and cultural ferment, wealth took on a different import. As in the catalogue of vices the preeminence of pride was overthrown by the upstart avarice, so in the virtuous practices of religious life, the renunciation of arms and family came to be seen as an insufficient adherence to poverty. Wealthy monasteries, even if otherwise devout and ascetic, began to appear problematically enmeshed in the disreputable world of money. The reach of the money economy throughout the church roused profound anxiety. Alain de Lille preached,

> The Christ cannot dwell in the homes of prelates that simony inhabits. He is refused refuge in the homes of knights who shelter pillage. There is no abode for him in the homes of the bourgeois, for usury is settled there. He is rejected by merchants whom deceit governs. In the commons, he does not have his place, because theft reigns there. Where then will the Christ live? Only in the homes of the poor of Christ, of whom it is said, Blessed are the poor in spirit.[30]

29. John of Salerno, cited in Little, *Religious Poverty*, 66.
30. "Le Christ ne peut pas faire sa demeure chez les prélates que la simonie habite. Refuge lui est refusé chez les chevaliers qui abritent la rapine. Il n'y a pas de logis pour lui chez les bourgeois, car l'usure y est installée. Il est rejeté par les marchands que domine le

Thus the imitation of Christ became strongly linked with poverty, meaning now the lack of money, particularly when that lack was taken on as an act of devotion.

It was a stormy shift of perspective. Critiques of wealth and repression of those critiques sometimes took on lethal furor.[31] Where the Fathers had preached about the lack of generosity and justice in the rich, new reformers lived among the poor and turned their preaching not merely against the wealth of hypocritical individuals, but against the institutions of property and power, including in some cases the wealth of the church. As older orders had defined themselves against and within the honor code of warriors, so the new religious movements which emerged from this ferment were drawn chiefly from, and understood themselves in relation to the success of, merchants and bankers. Their poverty took the form of the new outsider, the displaced urban poor. Francis and Alexis both renounced wealth and social status in favor of a life of dependent poverty. But where Alexis had joined the silent and almost invisible masses of destitution, Francis became a traveling salesman, a street-corner hawker of poverty.

Francis's own calling bridges the shift from a military to a market context for religious life. An adventurous and romantic youth, Francis wanted to be a knight, but according to his biographers soon found himself called to a different sort of chivalry. His dream of service to the great king led him, gradually, into generosity, experiments in poverty, and love of lepers. In 1208, he heard a Gospel reading including Matthew 10:9: "Do not keep gold, or silver, or money in your girdles, no wallet for your journey, nor two tunics, nor sandals, nor staff; for the laborer deserves his living." From that point he became a barefoot mendicant preacher, and a group of followers gathered around him. The Friars Minor were born, the most famous and notorious Christian voluntary beggars.[32]

---

mensonge. Dans le commun, il n'a pas sa place, parce que le vol y règne. Où donc habitera le Christ? Seulement chez les pauvres de Christ, de qui il est dit: Bienheureux les pauvre d'esprit." Mollat, "Pauvres et pauvreté," 319. Cited from Sermon "De Cruce," in M.-Th. D'Alverny, ed., *Alain de Lille* (Paris, 1965), 283.

    31. Lester K. Little, "Evangelical Poverty, the New Money Economy, and Violence," in *Poverty in the Middle Ages*, ed. David Flood (Werl: Dietrich-Coelde-Verlag, 1975), 11-26. Little documents the social upheaval and lethal violence involved in the shift of the church's attention toward evangelical poverty.

    32. The quest for the historical Francis is, as one would expect, something of a scholarly morass. Although many manuscripts exist and a number are accepted as truly written

Rather than escaping in the night like Alexis, Francis put off the wealth of his family and inheritance before many witnesses. It is one of the most famous of Franciscan episodes: having angered his father by giving away the proceeds of a sale, Francis took off all his clothes in the public square and gave them back to his father, the irate cloth-merchant. By all accounts, Francis did not have to beg in that moment. His vulnerability called for a gift without his saying a word, and the bishop covered Francis in his own robe. Francis's poverty, from the beginning, was about publicly calling for gifts which reveal Christ's church. The metaphor of religious life had shifted from a renunciation of war that witnesses to Christ's peace toward a renunciation of profit-taking that witnesses to Christ's plenty.

Francis expected the friars to work in menial jobs, receiving in-kind payment. The Rule of the Franciscans, which we have both in its canonical form approved in 1223 (the Regula Bullata, or RB) and in an earlier version (the Regula Non Bullata, or RNB) dated approximately 1221, teaches the friars to work, and Francis's Testament is adamant on this point. The earlier rule even permits them, as an exception to their strict poverty, to keep the tools of their work, and advises them to accept whatever they need in return for their work. But when they need more — and for the poorest in their society, payment was often enough insufficient — they are admonished not to be ashamed to beg.[33] They can accept any alms, except one: money.

Francis created a new genre of vocation that swept like wildfire across Europe. His genius, for good and ill, is tied up with the rise of the money economy. In this new social order, where wealth had loosened its

---

by Francis, the influence of other writers on the final products and the historicity of various tales told about Francis, given the polemics of Franciscan life in the thirteenth century, are difficult, where not impossible, to delineate. M. D. Lambert understood this to mean that scholars must continue with caution to discern the outline of Francis himself with reference to all of the sources about him. See *Franciscan Poverty: The Doctrine of the Absolute Poverty of Christ and the Apostles in the Franciscan Order, 1210-1323* (London: SPCK, 1961), 30. As my lack of expertise in such a venture is rivaled only by my ambivalence as to its value, I will not attempt to find a distinct historical voice identifiable as Francis's alone.

33. RNB, 7-9; RB, 5-6. In citations, I will be using *Francis of Assisi: Early Documents,* vol. I, *The Saint,* and vol. II, *The Founder,* ed. Regis J. Armstrong, J. A. Wayne Hellman, William J. Short (New York: New City Press, 1999 and 2000), hereafter abreviated FA: ED I and FA: ED II, respectively. I have continued to refer also to Marion Habig, ed., *St. Francis of Assisi: Writings and Early Biographies: English Omnibus of the Sources for the Life of St. Francis,* Fourth Revised Edition (Quincy, Ill.: Franciscan Press, 1991).

connections to land, heredity, tradition, custom, and even work, becoming instead focused in portable specie subject to the impersonal forces of the market, Francis's horror for coin is worth noting. He forbade the friars not only to earn it, but even to touch it. Though he expected them to work, he tried to keep the friars out of the money economy. They were to live in the city, among the laity and the merchants with whom they were so closely linked — but they were to proclaim in the midst of it a different kind of economy, focused on gift.

Almsgiving, it is often pointed out, coexists happily with the work of the market, allowing those who ordinarily follow only the laws of supply and demand a peripheral location for their benevolence. But this truism should not lead us to forget that almsgiving can also fragment the logic of profit. Biographers agree that Francis's own conversion to a life of poverty had one of its sources in an appeal by a beggar. Francis first sent the beggar away empty-handed, but repented of it, called him back, and gave a generous alms, resolving that as he would never turn away a nobleman who approached him, so he would not turn away anyone who begged for the love of God. That is, a beggar (whose name we do not know) broke into Francis's internally coherent business and successfully challenged its sufficiency, forcing him to measure it by a foreign standard, charity. Francis's categorical rejection of money and the importance of begging in his thought are reactions against and creative resistance to the new economic order shaping his culture.

While it was not unheard of at that time for religious to be permitted to beg *in extremis*,[34] the permission for Franciscans to beg is more broad and its tone is warm rather than regretful. RNB teaches that Jesus, his apostles, and his blessed mother all lived on alms. RB omits that scripturally-unfounded claim, but associates the brothers' begging with being "strangers and pilgrims" (1 Pet. 2:11) and with Christ's poverty. It called alms an inheritance that Christ had won for the poor. His biographers claim that Francis begged, even when there was no strict material need, because he did not want to give up that inheritance.[35] He teased knights who could not find food to buy, and under his tutelage they

---

34. The Grandmontines permitted begging in emergencies. Lambert, *Franciscan Poverty*, 42, n. 3.

35. RNB 9, FA: ED I; II Cel. 72-74, FA: ED II. Parallels can be found in the Legend of Perugia, Mirror of Perfection, and Bonaventure's Major Life.

learned to collect plenty by asking for alms.[36] Creating the opportunity of giving was itself the gift of the friars' begging, although Francis did not intend this charism to excuse them from work.

A particularly striking episode of Francis's begging as instigation of gift is a story from Thomas of Celano's original *Life of Saint Francis,* the earliest biography of Francis. One day, the story runs, as Francis and another friar walked to Osimo to visit the bishop there, they passed a field in which a lamb was grazing in the midst of a pack of goats. Francis was moved at this sight to the thought of Jesus surrounded by his accusers, and he cried out to his companion that they must find a way to remove the lamb from this bad company. The two friars had nothing but their tunics and so could not buy the lamb, but a merchant passing by bought it for them as an almsgift. Francis and the other friar went on their way to the bishop rejoicing. On their arrival, they had to explain the lamb they had with them, and the bishop found this a testimony to Francis's purity. But Francis of course would not keep the lamb. He gave it to the sisters at San Severino, who cared for it and used its wool to make Francis a tunic. They sent it to Francis during a general chapter, and he received it with joy, kissing it reverently and inviting the other friars to rejoice with him.[37]

It is not merely a matter of sentimentality that drives the Francis of this story to remove the lamb from the goats. For Francis, nothing is simply itself. All things refer to Christ, even the animals by the roadside. Francis recognizes this lamb as participating in Christ's redeeming work, and it is through Francis's recognition that the lamb's participation can unfold. The truth about this lamb is not that it cost some amount or that it belonged to such a one or would produce so much wool per year, but that it was an image of the innocent Christ's sacrifice and a gift of the One who suffered crucifixion. This quality, not the lamb's potential for consumption, is what the poorly-clothed and -fed Francis sees, as only one very richly endowed with a love of poverty could.

But quickly Francis's sacramental vision meets a challenge: a cold, hard cash shortage. Providentially the merchant passing by purchases the lamb for the friars. The author tells us nothing about this merchant and his motivation, although he has an essential role to play in the unfolding story, a purchase that the friars and the lamb need. His purchase is an

---

36. II Cel., 72, 73, 77, FA: ED II.
37. I Cel., 1, 77-78, FA: ED I.

almsgift, and it is, like the lamb itself, an image of redemption. The merchant hears Francis's certainty that with this lamb, it is not wool or meat that is at stake, but the story of salvation. In response, he fragments his own practice, profit-making, in order to give a gift to a poor man for the love of God. Through Francis's intervention, the merchant gets a role in the story, not selling Christ to his enemies for silver, but paying the price of redemption. Francis himself would be likely to congratulate the merchant on making a very savvy deal and earning a nice profit for himself where it counts, in heaven. Even the merchant, in the presence of Francis's instigation, takes on a sacramental reference to the economy of salvation.

The story is only beginning. Francis does not want the lamb so that he can set it romantically free on the hillsides. He first delights in its humility and patience, then takes it with him to visit the bishop. The bishop, seat of much temporal as well as spiritual power, recognizes through Francis's intervention the virtue of seeing through all things to their center in Christ. In fact, given Francis's frequent admonitions to friars to respect and obey bishops, it seems that he brings one image of Christ to visit another: Christ the humble sacrifice and Christ the high priest and teacher stand together for a delightful moment in Francis's eyes. But there is no recrimination in this picture. The bishop recognizes and finds joy in Francis's love of the humble Christ, and Francis trusts the wisdom and power of the bishop to serve that humility rather than to be offended by it. The bishop sees enough to know that Francis is not being naïve, romantic, or sentimental.

Francis, of course, will not keep the lamb. He never understood himself to be its owner, because the lamb is not property but a proclamation of the gospel and a sacrament. But the lamb is also a lamb, in need of certain sorts of care and ready to give certain benefits to those who will go to the trouble to gather them. Francis turns the lamb over to the care of the sisters at San Severino. Through their devotion to Christ and their vow of poverty they know how best to honor the lamb's gifts. So it is that at General Chapter the sisters send to Francis a white wool tunic they made for him from the lamb's wool. Francis accepted it "with great reverence and joy of spirit, and, embracing it, he kissed it and invited all who stood by to share his happiness." Having given the humble witness of redemption to the sisters, Francis endowed them with an alms, a gift they received as from God. This gift meant work for them, and fruitfulness for the Christ-lamb so that the sisters and the lamb together send to Francis a white garment of salvation. Thus Francis who recognized and begged for the gift of the lamb gave the lamb freely to do its work of self-gift, and now the lamb in turn has offered to Francis a sign of salvation.

In this tale, the beggar's appeal for a gift is neither manipulation nor an appeal for heroic and futile intervention. It is creative. The beggar instigates an order of gift-giving, searching out those who will join in a cycle of gift which does not exclude work or exchange, but orders them to serve the good of proclaiming Christ. The referent, the measure through which this gift exchange continues, is Christ. But for all Francis's love of literal, biblical imitation of Christ, it is the sacramental Christ, who is both gift and giver in the *sacrum commercium* of the Eucharist, who is essential to his begging.[38]

In Francis's devotion, as we meet it in his letters, the Eucharist holds place of honor, followed closely by the Word.

> And I act this way [respecting all Catholic priests] because, in this world, I see nothing corporally of the most high Son of God except His most holy Body and Blood which they receive and they alone administer to others. I want to have these most holy mysteries honored and venerated above all things and I want to reserve them in precious places. Whenever I find our Lord's most holy names and written words in unbecoming places, I want to gather them up and I beg that they be gathered up and placed in a becoming place.[39]

38. On literal imitation of Christ characteristic of Franciscanism, see Giles Constable, "The Ideal of the Imitation of Christ," in *Three Studies in Medieval Religious and Social Thought* (Cambridge: Cambridge University Press, 1995), 192-93. Francis's concern for the nakedness of Christ is also pertinent at this point, as the vulnerability of Christ in the manger and on the cross calls out, without explicit begging, for compassion. See Lambert, *Franciscan Poverty*, 61ff. The claim in RNB that Christ and his mother and the apostles begged seems to the modern mind a bit bizarre, although it is in fact no more ridiculous than the common present-day idea that Jesus was a carpenter, a non-biblical inference which suits the modern respect for independent craftsmen. The antifraternalist Fitzralph made this claim in the fourteenth century. I do not, however, know its full pedigree. On Fitzralph's use, see Lawrence M. Clopper, *"Songes of Rechelesnesse": Langland and the Franciscans* (Ann Arbor: University of Michigan Press, 1997), 60.

39. FA: ED I, 125. Similar passages can be found in the first Letter to Custodians and the Letter to the Entire Order. Care for the Eucharist and for the Word, especially by friars who are priests, is the dominant theme of the Letter to the Entire Order. Curiously, Francis puts little emphasis on this matter in the Rule, urging reverence toward the Eucharist only briefly in RNB (ch. 20) and not at all in RB. It appears that Francis has made his own the concerns of *Sane cum olim*, of Pope Honorius III (November 22, 1219).

Because of this profound reverence for Jesus present in the Eucharist, Francis teaches reverence for priests who make Christ present through their ministry — regardless of their personal worthiness. But slackness in eucharistic ministry is deeply offensive to him.

> Let all those who administer such most holy mysteries, however, especially those who administer them illicitly, consider how very dirty are the chalices, corporals, and altar-linens upon which HIS Body and Blood are sacrificed. It is placed and left in many dirty places, carried about unbecomingly, received unworthily, and administered to others without discernment. Even His written names and words are at times left to be trampled under foot; *for the carnal person does not perceive the things of God.*
>
> Are we not moved by piety at these things when the pious Lord puts Himself into our hands and we touch Him and receive Him daily with our mouth? Do we refuse to recognize that we must come into His hands?[40]

Francis sees Christ's poor body, dishonored and neglected, not only on the crucifix, but also in the tabernacle, where the sacramental body is at the mercy of worshipers who often despise it. "Behold, each day He humbles Himself as when He came *from the royal throne* into the Virgin's womb; each day He Himself comes to us, appearing humbly; each day He comes down *from the bosom of the Father* upon the altar in the hands of the priest."[41] His desire to honor the poor and vulnerable Christ, rejected by the world, creates this practical syllogism: Christ was cast out and rejected. His name is to be praised and loved and honored. Therefore, whenever we see the name or words of Christ ignored, left in the dirt, we must care for them reverently. This is the God praised by Francis for humility, when he says of the Eucharist, "O sublime humility, O humble sublimity." And it is in relation to this wonder that Francis honors priests and theologians and sees the justice of richly adorned churches.

Thus the material and political power surrounding the Eucharist need not be at odds with the poverty of Christ and the humility of the Eucharist. Boundless riches and glory belong to the one who waits on human mercy, the One whose power was manifest in taking on weakness. The fail-

40. Exhortations to the Clergy, Earlier Edition, 4-9.
41. The Admonitions, I.

THE FEAR OF BEGGARS

ure of humans to see how humility and power can be reconciled is a case of the gospel being "foolishness to the Greeks."[42] Where the vulnerable wait for and invite a gift of love, there Francis sees God.

This is not, however, the same as saying that God is in these moments destitute, as though God could cease to be God. God is still the source of all riches, and the vulnerability of the sacramental Christ, giving himself and calling for the return gift of love in the faithful, is divine power. Thus the paradox — Jesus, the beggar who is at the mercy of his people, appeals for an opportunity to pour out riches on them. In fact, the opportunity for us to show mercy to him is in some sense the opportunity to receive the greatest riches of all, the love of Christ. This is precisely the paradox Francis sees played out by his brothers' begging: although they are the ones asking, it is the donors who receive the real riches by giving their gift. The friars' poverty and begging are at one and the same time their misery and their glorification, as suits an imitation of Christ on the cross, lifted up in shame and in victory.[43]

Franciscan poverty is not, therefore, passive. The friars do not wait on alms; when in need, they go door to door asking for them. The friars' poverty was to be an active apostolate, carried out door to door. Francis classed their permission to beg as a way for them to serve others, or, in his play on commercial language, to offer others a great deal. In his mind, the almsgiver certainly got the better end of the trade, since the friar only received food or perhaps clothes or wood for a fire, while the almsgiver received — by participating in it — the love of God. The begging of the poor is an invitation to true riches. It is as though their mission is to beg, and they must carry it to those who most need it, to those who do not recognize Christ in the poor. This boldness in begging characterized the apostolate of the friars, to delight publicly in being the most perfect and the highest, by being the lowest and least esteemed in the world.[44]

---

42. I was reminded of this matter through David Aers' comments on the threat of Wycliffite theology of the Eucharist to the power structures of the Church. *The Powers of the Holy: Religion, Politics, and Gender in Late Medieval English Culture* (University Park, Pa.: Pennsylvania State University Press, 1996).

43. Cathy Cory explores this image in John's gospel. "Wisdom's Rescue: A New Reading of the Tabernacles Discourse (John 7:1–8:59)," *Journal of Biblical Literature* 116:1 (1997), 95-116.

44. This inversion of wealth and the language of trade had particular significance in Francis's day, with the increase in commerce that so constituted his society. But it is not pe-

We can begin to see how Franciscan poverty remained orthodox in an era rife with unorthodox poverty movements. Francis's vision of Christ's poverty, first, was so profoundly tied to the practices of the Catholic Church and to the Eucharist in particular, that through Christ's poverty he understood himself bound to honor all clergy, no matter how unworthy they were, and to urge the sacrament be kept in richly ornamented places. His devotion to the poor Christ of the Eucharist allows him to maintain a coherent if awkward commitment to a wealthy heirarchy. Second, this notion of Christ's poverty presumes a dynamic and communal version of holiness, although this was not articulated well in early Franciscan writings. The paradox of humble, bold begging could, and did, slide into manipulation and simony when they lost that sense of reciprocity.

As Penance

Beggars make their living, such as it is, without earning wages, and for this they are often classed with criminals and sinners, as manifestations of some social or personal disorder. Nevertheless, voluntary beggars commonly speak of begging as not crime or sin, but penance from crime and sin. *The Way of a Pilgrim* includes the tale of a pilgrim-beggar who on his deathbed admitted he had been a prince. Tormented by guilt for his violence and lust, wasted by nightmares and anxiety that no physician could treat, he turned to pilgrimage as a life of penance. He confessed, freed all of his serfs, and took to wandering through Siberia doing menial labor and begging. "I wanted, because of all my sins, to become the humblest servant of people of the very lowest station in life."[45] He turned to a life of penance to enact justice on himself by making "satisfaction." He had beaten others; he placed himself in a position to endure abuse and to have no means to defend himself. He had lusted; he turned to hunger, loneliness, and filth, knowing himself an object of distaste to those who meet him. As soon as he repented and resolved to enter into that life, he was cured of his ail-

---

culiar to Francis. Paul's rhetoric in 2 Corinthians 8–9 argues similarly that true wealth is liberality. "He who sows sparingly will read sparingly, and he who sows bountifully will also reap bountifully" (2 Cor. 9:6). For a detailed discussion of this passage, see Sondra Ely Wheeler, *Wealth as Peril and Obligation: The New Testament on Possessions* (Grand Rapids, Mich.: Eerdmans, 1995).

45. *Way of a Pilgrim*, 92.

ments and found joy. The penance was both punishment and, it turns out, cure for the hell his guilty soul was already enduring.

This points at the surprising nature of penance in the lives of the saints. Penance is unpleasant, even painful and repugnant. Nevertheless, the unpleasantness of penance is not its purpose.[46] The substance of penance is the turning from sin. This is obviously the case in therapeutic penance, as the penitent avoids pleasurable occasions of sin and disciplines unruly appetites. But it is also the case in forensic penance, in which the penitent suffers in order to enact retribution for sin. Although this kind of penance is pointless if the penitent does not suffer, still the suffering itself is secondary to the enactment of justice, the longing for reconciliation, and the hope that grace will abound to the overcoming of the guilt.

Very well, then, penance implies suffering and there is no surprise in this. The surprise is that saints claim to find joy in penance. This is not a question of masochism; the joy of penance is not that the self is abased, but that it succeeds in drawing closer to its truth and its love, going through confrontation with its failure and weakness to find that abounding of grace and mercy.[47] The joy of penance is that the more the saint finds the self weak and untrustworthy, the more the saint encounters the strength of grace making the self part of the body of Christ. Weight loss, no matter how dramatic, is not in itself evidence of sanctity; only when mortification produces charity is it taken to be evidence of a life of grace. Stories of saints such as Anthony whose fasting produced a body glowing with health and

46. I am speaking here of penance in its best practice. There are cases of penitential disciplines that have won approval from the church that seem rather to be about enjoyment of pain, particularly as a manifestation of love for and from a God in whose sight we are always failures. The pain becomes evidence of the love. These disorders do not prove, however, that penance itself is a theological perversion. For a disturbing analysis of Rose of Lima and other women penitents, see Sara Maitland, "Passionate Prayer: Masochistic Images in Women's Experience," in *Sex and God: Some Varieties of Women's Religious Experience*, ed. Linda Hurcombe (New York: Routledge & Kegan Paul, 1987), 125-40.

47. Maitland expresses this well, when she acknowledges that alongside those canonized saints who hungered for blood and death, there are others "who pursued bold and joyous courses through life and met death merrily on their way to do something else; . . . high-principled people, whose understanding of the destruction of selfhood that comes about through not telling the truth caused them to look death straight in its mean eyes and find it preferable to capitulation. . . ." "Passionate Prayer," 130. I remain uncertain, however, that I can always tell the difference between these kinds of penance.

vigor indicate the necessary direction of Christian penance — not to self-destruction, but to a dying that gives way to new life.

Francis often spoke of penance, and not necessarily in reference to a particular sin. The rules of the order contain provisions for penance in the limited sense of making satisfaction after some serious sin, but one of Francis's characteristic phrases describing the life he called his followers to is living "in penance" or having "fruits worthy of penance." The "third order" of Franciscans began as an order of penitents, and in addressing members of that order, Francis claimed that those who die in penance will be saved and those who die not in penance will be lost. Being "in penance" is actually a way of life appropriate to all Christians, in every state of life and grace.

According to some accounts, Francis's first act of penance was almsgiving. As mentioned above, he refused a beggar, but thereafter repented and resolved that he would never again turn away someone who asked him for alms in the name of God. Still Francis found almsgiving to be a dangerous form of penance. Vainglory lurks within the generosity of the giver, he discovered. Although he never abandoned almsgiving, he first toyed with and then adopted begging as part of his life of penance.

In what sense, then, was begging a penance for him? It was first in the horror of what people gave as alms. Francis found eating the leftovers that were dished together in his beggar's bowl repugnant, although his biographers said as he ate he discovered it to be wonderful. The flesh shrinks from penance at first, but discovers joy in it later. More than a discipline of the taste buds, though, begging was a social penance, striking at pride by displaying the loss of self-sufficiency before others. Francis drew back, when begging oil for the lamps of a church, from approaching a group of his old associates. Discerning in this a sin, he made himself go back, ask them for alms, and confess his fault.[48] Why would Francis have felt shame to beg under these circumstances? He had neither failed in business nor become feeble in mind or body; his poverty as a matter of following Christ need not have been a source of personal shame. Nor would begging for the sake of lighting a church have the same humiliation attached to it that begging for food would imply. Yet the biographers tell us that Francis was ashamed, and many readers instinctively sympathize. Evidently, the shame attached to begging does not have to do with the cause for which one begs.

48. II Cel. 13, FA: ED II.

It is rather a function of acting out dependence upon others for any cause, of feeling oneself to be a nuisance and a burden to them. Francis was not ashamed that he had become poor, nor that the church was in need of oil. He was ashamed to have to ask for a gift.

Lacking the means to initiate an exchange of rights, which is to say, lacking money, he approached his old friends without that which their world holds to be necessary. He had a foot in both worlds, recognizing on the one hand that they would see this begging of his as evidence that he could no longer pay his way, and therefore that he was no longer fit to take the field, economically. On the other hand, he had come to believe in a different kind of wealth and power, the excellence of a God who became humble and who invited his followers to do the same. His shame is evidence that he still socially belonged to the first world, and it is for that reason that he saw this shame as sin. He needed not only to reform himself in mind and in body toward his beloved poverty. He had to enact it socially.

But all of this means that the humiliation of begging and its potential as penance is a function of a certain kind of society, one in which a person who asks for a gift outside the circle of family and friends is seen as fulfilling no socially useful function, and perhaps as engaging in something proximate to crime. It is only when a society sees a beggar as a burden and when the beggar him- or herself has internalized that notion that begging can be a penitential discipline against the pride of social standing.

This is how we can understand a characteristic and peculiar phrase of Francis's from the section of the RNB on begging: "Alms are a legacy and a justice due to the poor that our Lord Jesus Christ acquired for us." This line (along with Francis's claim that Jesus, Mary, and the disciples were all beggars) was dropped in the RB and replaced with the more moderate teaching. The earlier claim, odd as it is, gives us a window into Francis's more idiosyncratic thought. The friars are not to accept the social role of beggars as failures and dependents. Seen through the lens of the life of penance, alms are a *legacy,* that is, a possession of the poor on account of their predecessor, Christ. For his sake, and not for the sake of their own worthiness or human rights, beggars should be given alms. In fact, because of Christ almsgiving is a matter of *justice,* rendering what is due, and not a matter of supererogation. Those who have no rights in the mercantile world are those with the most secure rights in God's kingdom: "Blessed are the poor, for theirs is the kingdom of heaven." Given the teaching of Matthew 25, in which Jesus himself identifies with the "least," almsgiving is giving to the One to whom all things belong, the true Owner. In this kind of vision, social claims of possession, rights, and dignity take on a radically different cast. Francis saw begging as a case of God's sense of justice being dramatically at odds with the justice of the up-and-coming of Assisi. His penance consisted of standing in the breach between the two, receiving the scorn of the worldly-minded (even within himself) while attesting to the social order of Christ's teaching.

This explains a fundamental contradiction in Francis's approach to begging. He teaches the friars not to be ashamed to beg, as they are following the example and teaching of Jesus and as they are in fact offering a bargain, in the more lasting economy of heaven. But some stories also attest to Francis's approval of those who blush when they go to beg. These stories may concern the controversies about bold begging, as critics claimed that Franciscan begging was a demonstration of pride, not humility. Regardless of their status as *ipsissima verba* of Francis, however, they do capture the subtlety of Francis's position: although in the kingdom, the poor and humble are favored by the One who administers all riches, still if those poor and humble use that knowledge to become proud and demanding, they thereby lose their claim. Insofar as the kingdom of God is not yet present, one should blush to beg; but insofar as the kingdom already is among us, one should beg anyway, with confidence.

Penance has therefore an eschatological quality, as it aims to turn from the not-yet and establish the habits and mind of the already. In this way, penance is a pilgrim's work. The direction, means of travel, and adventures on the road have a character determined by the eventual culmination of the journey.[49] In the fourteenth-century poem *Piers Plowman*, the right practice of penance is taught by a figurative character named Patience — and Patience is a pilgrim and beggar.[50]

The protagonist of the poem, Will, is invited by Conscience and Clergy to dine with Reason (Passus XV). There Will meets both a friar who is a theological scholar (a "master") and Patience, who begs a meal or

49. This metaphor can cut differently, considering that pilgrimages were often topics of moralists' concern, as occasions for revelry and licentiousness, as well as simple escape from work and authorities, although these complaints do not necessarily indicate a lack of devotion. Pilgrimages often had, and have, more complex ends than moralists would like.

50. I rely on Derek Pearsall's edition of the C-text (Berkeley: University of California Press, 1978). Verse translations are from George Economou (Philadelphia: University of Pennsylvania Press, 1996).

some money from them. This Patience is not Franciscan (for he accepts money),[51] but he is a pilgrim and beggar knowledgeable about the good life. Langland intends Patience to be the voice of true Christian insight. The virtue of patience elsewhere in the poem appears as that by which Christ brought his Jewish opponents' power "to pure naught" (XVII, 308); the clothing of Peace (XX, 171); and a virtue much needed by popes and bishops (XVII, 236, 284). Even Mohammed ruled through patience, combined with "secret guile" (XVII, 242).[52] Patience is the power of merciful endurance. Given what we have seen about the effect of a beggar on passersby, the sense of power combined with endurance is well-suited to the figure of a beggar, and just ambiguous enough to be a tool for Mohammed as well as Jesus.

The poet introduces the pilgrim Patience in a scene that juxtaposes two distinct genres. The master, the guest of honor at the meal, is a satirical caricature of scholarly friars, and he may even represent a specific Dominican with a reputation for arguing in bad faith.[53] Conscience, Reason, and

---

51. This seems to me a fundamental obstacle to the reading offered by Clopper in "Songes of Rechelesnesse." Clopper argues that Langland is better read not as an anti-fraternalist, but as a reforming Franciscan. As a component of this argument, Clopper claims that Patience and the Master represent scandalous and virtuous Franciscans. The scene echoes that of the Mirror of Perfection, when Francis poses as a beggar in order to show up the failure of humility in the brothers. Without disregarding that possible reference, we can argue that Clopper's failure to consider the non-Franciscan appeal for money in Patience and to set aside the apparent reference to the Dominican Jordan in the Master indicates an excessive desire to read the scene as concerned with an intra-Franciscan debate. The evidence resists reading such a debate as the primary topic. Nor does Clopper wrestle with Patience and his begging as allegorical; the importance of penance in his discourse; or the notion of enemy-love as Do Best. Recognizing Langland's appreciation for primitive Franciscanism and his characteristic critiques of friars does not warrant discounting evidence that he is casting a larger net.

52. In the B-version, Pacience is the name of the tree of charity (B XVI, 8), but in C the name is changed to Ymago-dei. The change may have been made to sharpen the precision of the initial picture-allegory of the tree, rather than with any particular concern for the pilgrim Patience.

53. The use of "iurdan" (chamber pot) as a description of the master may be a pun on the name of Brother William Jordan, a well-known Dominican scholar with a reputation for exaggerated argument conducted in bad faith. M. E. Marcett, Uhtred de Boldon, Friar William Jordan, and "Piers Plowman" (n.p., 1938). The dispute between Uhtred and Jordan (approximately 1366-68) reveals Jordan as a contentious debater, called by one contemporary "adversarium molestissimus."

Patience, all attending the same dinner, are figurative (though by no means flat) characters. Patience sits at a side table and enjoys a delicious meal of scriptural words associated with penance. The master, meanwhile, gorges himself at the head table on meats and puddings, unabashedly gobbling "meat of more cost," which is not only unsuitable to the life of penance but also provides through "what men miswon," donations of filthy lucre.

Langland milks this juxtaposition of figurative and realistic characters for all its satirical worth. The mendicant friar and the pilgrim beggar live in different genres, different worlds, even when they are dining in the same room. For Patience, the words of Scripture regarding repentance and forgiveness are real, reliable, and satisfying. Like the word of God with the power to create and save (and in a lesser way, the words of Langland's poem), the words served to Patience are the stuff of reality and the fulfillment of his desire. They are the end of his begging, which seeks above all else right conversion to God.[54] For the master, no words, particularly words of penance, are half as satisfying as a good meaty stew. He misuses food as he misuses words, and his begging, when he engages in it, will be oriented toward filling this wrong appetite. Patience's first lesson on virtuous begging teaches that what you ask for matters. The religious beggar who is out to fill his belly has missed the right significance of begging, the appetite for penance.

This banquet with the master and Patience crackles with eschatological tension. Patience is not merely allegory; he is a character in a historical scene, someone who testifies to the un-fleshy truth of the good life. His taste for penance is a triumph over disordered appetites, turning him freely toward the enjoyment of virtue. Juxtaposed with the master, he becomes the model of one who in the midst of a society of gluttony and ambition, of the twisting of goods, enjoys the continual turning toward the true good in penance. He is no angel watching this struggle from above, nor merely a voice of criticism. He exists within the world of the master as a beggar, one lacking in power as the master would understand it. His triumph, however, is certain, both in the fleshy world (where the master soon suffers from "penance in his paunch," indigestion) and in the spirit, as Conscience recognizes his pre-eminence over Clergy's books.

Patience wins Conscience over by speaking of love of enemy, declaring that he could conquer all France without bloodshed, because

54. The author has Patience offer a lesson on sacramental penance at XVI 25-32.

"*Pacientes vincunt*," the patient conquer. This intersection of begging, pilgrimage, patience, and love of enemy is highly suggestive. For beggars, after all, patience means especially waiting on almsgivers, and Patience makes painfully explicit the kind of misery such waiting entails.

> But beggars about midsummer sup without bread
> But winter is worse for them, for they go wet-shod,
> Thirsty and hungry and foully rebuked,
> By worldly-rich men, so that it's pitiful to hear. (XVI, 13-16)

As the word "patience" includes the sense of endurance and suffering as well as waiting, this image of a beggar, one all-too-familiar and realistic, brings out the connection of patience to enemy-love. The beggar has enemies to spare; every person who has what the beggar needs and passes her by is an enemy of her life.

The teaching of Patience, a beggar who endures the company of the hypocritical master without rancor, invites love of enemy even at great cost to oneself. Such a teaching runs dangerously close to a pious muzzling of the just complaints of the poor, especially given Patience's interest in heavenly rewards. The poor are, Patience claims, unencumbered in their progress, pressing ahead toward heaven with only a backpack instead of the weighty piles of wealth that hold the rich back. They claim by justice more reward in the next life than those who have had a life of comfort already. Since the reward is eternal, temporary suffering in order to attain it is a good trade. "If you live according to his lore, the shorter life is the better" (XV, 260). Some such vision of future reward is necessary for Patience to excuse himself from the monstrosity of welcoming misery. Though the author describes the suffering of the poor realistically, he still advises them to endure it patiently, even if it is unjust. They will in this way be certain of eternal reward far exceeding their suffering.[55]

---

55. Geoffrey Shepherd, "Poverty in *Piers Plowman*," in *Social Relations and Ideas: Essays in Honour of R. H. Hilton*, ed. T. H. Aston et al. (Cambridge: Cambridge University Press, 1983), describes Will's pilgrimage as the struggle of the *viator* to find a way to live within the present. He notes that Langland treats poverty as "a religious mystery which continues to ask diffuse and complicated questions," related to the paradox of the Incarnation (177). I respectfully demur, however, from Shepherd's conclusion that Will's journey eventually reaches a stoic concentration on principles rather than contingencies, that "the end of the poem suggests a quiet extrication from apocalypse" (189). Conscience sets out on a pilgrimage in the poem's closing lines, which may signal flight from catastrophe, but does not

The misery of the poor is unjust, within the poem's logic, but the solution is not rebellion against the oppressors. Patience condemns the corrupt wealthy with sorrow and wry humor. Asked whether a person who uses riches wisely is not more pleasing to God than the patient poor, Patience responds, "Yes, *quis est ille?* . . . quick, *laudamus eum!*" Should there be such a thing as a rich person who uses wealth righteously, Patience will be the first to throw him a party. He advises the rich on the need to reform and avoid hell, counseling that "Christians should be rich in common, none covetous for himself" (XVI, 43). Then, having given that advice, Patience lives in penance, waiting and suffering within a world of sin, and hoping for better. That hope, however, remains indeterminate, without the political will or imagination to encourage its creation. Eschatological hope here offers a witness, and at the same time advises the poor to accept their lot and allows the rich to get off the hook.[56] Still, this beggar has enough faith to believe that enemy-love will triumph and that justice is not eternally delayed, at least not when the church practices its binding discipline of penance among its members. The beggar, who himself lives in penance, is peculiarly qualified to issue a call for confession and repentance among the leaders of the church — including influential friars.

While Patience is not a literal beggar and his alms do nothing to provide calories, the figurative characterization is not insignificant. The loss of comfort, of health, and of power suffered by a beggar can according to Langland be a witness to a greater recovery of these goods, albeit in a different way. Toward the world, one can forgive, even when exposed to view

---

thereby signal a turn to principles. The contingencies of political material life never disappear, although the ability to read them in relation to the eschaton is crucial. Shepherd's reading of Need and temperance as a return to the central problem of acquisitiveness is likewise instructive, but the claim that this pertains to all people misses the particular danger Need poses to the poor and the voluntarily poor. In general, Shepherd's eschatological reading of *Piers Plowman* tilts eschatology more toward the "otherworldly" than is helpful. If, as he suggests, the author had a stoic turn from contingency to principle in mind, he did not succeed: the contingent is too beautifully portrayed.

56. Commenting on patient poverty, David Aers has noted Langland's lack of constructive politics. "Within the terms and preoccupations of a prophetic, self-consciously reforming poem like this one, such withdrawal [imaginative withdrawal from the field of material production as the basis of all human spiritual life as of all human relations] is not a mark of consummate 'faith' but of evasion. And perhaps evasion is the very opposite of faith, whether in religious or secular domains." David Aers, *Community, Gender, Individual Identity: English Writing, 1360-1430* (London: Routledge, 1988), 67.

in the center of a social order of suspicion and ambition, in certainty of the triumph of good. Toward the flesh, one can convert the appetite to love conversion. Within a world of sin, one can beg mercy, repent, and be restored. Begging's association with pilgrimage and vagrancy becomes richly suggestive, for begging is a wayfarer's vocation. It is, par excellence, the life in *status viatoris*, the condition of those on the way to a fulfillment they do not yet fully know but which already holds them and determines their life on the road. In heaven, Patience will be no beggar, but in the world of the master, his triumph may have to appear as weakness. The voluntary beggar claims and displays already the end toward which Christian hope aims, in which full health, freedom, power, and pleasure are gained in the supernatural gift of friendship with God. That rather grand claim is thoroughly chastened by the fact that Langland, who had plenty of live examples of friars to draw on, used instead a figurative character to carry these matters. Langland is understandably skeptical of people who try to enact this witness. Yet he himself appropriates it as a pivotal image.

For Humility

Thomas Aquinas argues that begging is appropriate for religious as an excellent exercise of humility, as the abasement that is "the most efficacious remedy against the pride which they desire to quench either in themselves or in others by their example."[57] St. Benedict, whose rule is the foundation of the monastic culture which shaped our characters, spent a chapter of his rule on the virtue of humility. He treats it as a virtue of wayfarers: humility is a matter of degrees, like rungs on a ladder, and the prize at the top is a love of God in which self is forgotten and fear is overcome. The stages along the rung — dying to one's own will through obedience, destroying love of self by lowering oneself before others, controlling speech and gesture — tell us that humility is the virtue of disciplining thought and movement as well as will. It is the habit of forgetting the self's desires, except the desire to be obedient to God. Humility is a virtue of the appetite, not the intellect. It is not enough to know one's limits; the humble person habitually loves him- or herself less in order more perfectly to love God. For a voluntary beggar, living on scraps, submitting to public view, surrendering a claim of right to

57. ST II-II, Q.187, a.5.

food and clothing, and facing the disapproval of the sophisticated all serve to point away from the claims of the sufficient and controlled self, to a self oriented entirely toward Christ. Within the larger narrative of Christianity, this is not self-destruction, but dying in order to live. It is turning the self, with the help of grace, toward the self's right end. The appetite is not being corrected to enjoy pain or to make hatred of the self a new fascination, but to set all else in the background behind the love of God. Humility, in this sense, is something of the athlete's power of forgetting the self in the pursuit of the goal. It is, therefore, necessary to the wayfarer.

Because in this case the goal is union with the Creator, humility is not only a means to but also constitutive of the end: one who is still looking at herself will be unable to enjoy the vision of God. Further, joining oneself to Christ implies a participation in the Son's humility. The one who proceeds from the Father is entirely directed toward that Source, and so those who are united with the one become directed toward the other. The one who emptied himself and took on the form of a slave brings all humanity into corresponding humility toward the Father.

Francis, reacting against a childhood spent around the trade in cloth, created a narrative world in which claims of right are related to violence while beggars are the image of Christ testifying to God's peace. Suffering in a world of sin, they invite Christians to participate in a different order. Those who would imitate Christ take up this mission, preaching penance and demonstrating the joy of humility. In this way, Francis's followers were to build up the entire church and encourage the Christian social order, by drawing attention to the power of God to work through weakness rather than through the strength of portable wealth. They did not aim for everyone to do as they did. Francis encouraged rulers to rule well, leading their people to praise God; he accepted the ministrations of a wealthy devout woman (Brother Jacopa) and submitted to the leadership of the Bishop of Ostia, without abandoning his own call. In each case, he attempted to bring them into this narrative world within which voluntary begging, rightly done, was a gift to the church. But that world, recreated again and again in Franciscan literature, was out-narrated on the streets and in the markets and proved unstable even within the order, as we shall see in the next chapter.

Strange as it may seem to us, begging has in various ways served Christian devotion, both the devotion of the individuals who renounced self-sufficiency and also that of the communities which supported them. From each of the angles this chapter has considered, begging is decidedly a social vocation. It depends for its sense and even its survival on reception by a community who can recognize the action. Voluntary begging flourished during the emergence of a money economy, in a world where market and the merchant held increasingly central roles. The remarkable growth of the Franciscan and Dominican mendicants testifies to the *sensus fidelium* that holiness did have something to do with the fostering of property relations outside the rules of the market, based not on exchange and competition, but on voluntary sacrifice and charity. These beggars called the Christian community to see the sacred exchange of faithfulness and grace as central to public life by bringing their imitation of Christ into the center of the markets and streets.

This is not, however, to say that these beggars lacked for critics, including devout Christian critics. In fact, the dwindling of religious orders which beg for their survival[58] should lead us to suspect that voluntary begging did not always provide an inspiring witness nor did it always help manifest the church as the body of Christ. Rather, voluntary begging gave rise to a series of scandals and conflicts which finally weakened the moral importance of poverty and strengthened the hold of rights language in political life. The next chapter will explore the instability of begging as a virtuous practice.

58. Fundraising and the "begging letters" associated with it are distinct phenomena which belong to the stewardship era. This is not to say that no religious orders currently beg. The Little Sisters of the Poor still do, although a recent piece on their begging ended with notes about the success of their $18 million fundraising campaign for a new care facility they will run, so that their begging is not strictly for day-to-day survival. Rebekah Scott, "Local Nuns Make a Habit of Begging for Food," *The (Toledo) Blade*, October 14, 2002. Some voluntary beggars of the hand-to-mouth type (those "without bags," as the tradition puts it) have come to my attention recently. Paul Rohde keeps a weblog recounting many tales of generosity and failures of the same among Christians during his adventures as a religious beggar, and he writes about George Walter, a more traditional pilgrim and beggar. See http://www.geocities.com/cimarronline/, especially April-September 2003.

CHAPTER TWO

The Irony of Voluntary Begging

Whatever good we may say about the witness Christian mendicants offered, the flood of devotional beggary that swept across Europe has slowed to a trickle. Scandals, political struggles, and scholarly arguments — both theological and legal — attached to Franciscan poverty both from inside and outside the order, and these battles over the vocation to begging left scar tissue all across Christian thinking on property and gift-giving. Francis's genius in unsettling the category of rights and declaring the excellence of lowliness became, as it turns out, the occasion for a new burst of defenses of property. Ironically, Christian mendicants played a role in fostering a renewed sense of the moral importance of property, the centrality of rights in public discourse, and the market as a pervasive organizational component of society.

Moral Uses of Wealth, Moral Dangers of Poverty

Even before Francis's death in 1226, the fast-growing Order of the Friars Minor was troubled with disagreements about exactly what "Franciscan poverty" meant and what roles begging and work were to play in their vocation. As we saw earlier, the Rule and the Testament taught the friars to work and permitted them to beg, in terms which made the begging spiritually advantageous to them. While the RNB and Testament are clear that the friars should do *lowly* work and shun positions of authority, their mobility and preaching as well as their enormous popularity led the friars into positions of great influence, and the more binding RB does not forbid such work. The Friars Minor welcomed men already trained as theologians among them and did not require them to discontinue their work. In fact, in the interest of improving their preaching, they found good use for such intellectual training. Books and houses of study began to seem necessities and leadership in the church a natural outgrowth of their excellent formation in humility.

Opposition to the mendicant orders began to generate serious debate and a literature in the 1250s. The mendicant orders had succeeded in gaining chairs at the University of Paris and had promptly aggravated the rest of the university by refusing to go on strike with the others in protest at police brutality against students. Their independence became a divisive force in the university system.[1] What's more, their (sometimes lucrative) pastoral work infringed on the offices and income of lay priests given charge of parishes. Although some critics claimed the Franciscans were depriving the involuntarily-poor of their alms, it is at least as likely that they were cutting into the income of monasteries and secular clergy, for as word of their holiness spread, contributions from the nobility and merchant class began to pour in. Accusations of greed, hypocrisy, and expertise in wriggling out of the strict discipline laid down by their founder raged against the Friars Minor.

When the secular masters excluded the mendicants by way of punishing their refusal to strike, the mendicants turned to their friends in high places, the pope and King Louis IX, to defend them. The secular masters, under the leadership of William of St. Amour, mounted a campaign against the friars, attempting to justify their exclusion from the university. The mendicant orders won the battle, but the writings of William of St. Amour sparked a long-running literature of protest against the mendicant orders, attacking them through scriptural exegesis that linked them to the false preachers and the antichrists expected in the end times.

William attacked the friars on various grounds, including their hypocrisy; the heretical teachings of one Joachimite friar, Gerard of Borgo San Donnino, who released his explication of the unfolding a new age in

1. See, e.g., the account of the disputes that erupted in Paris in 1253 found in Penn R. Szittya, *The Antifraternal Tradition in Medieval Literature* (Princeton: Princeton University Press, 1986), 12-17. Also Virpi Mäkinen, *Property Rights in the Late Medieval Discussion on Franciscan Poverty* (Leuven: Peeters, 2001), 21-33.

the middle of the University of Paris debate; and in particular their claim to be living the apostolic life. Since the successors of the apostles are the bishops, and the successors of the seventy-two disciples sent out to preach are the secular clergy, in whose charge is the sacramental ministry of the church, these mendicant friars who take on the same functions are by definition false preachers. That the friars were authorized by the pope presented an obstacle to this argument, but William claimed that the pope could not have intended the multiplicity and confusion of ministerial leadership that was resulting from the large, or as he put it, limitless and therefore unnatural numbers of friars competing with secular clergy for the lucrative ministries of hearing confessions and conducting funerals. The friars' "apostolicity" was creating disorder in the church's ministry. Francis's parabolic assertion that the friars led the highest form of life because they lived the lowliest form of life created an instability in structures of authority. If the friars were leading the highest life, then they were most desirable as confessors and preachers, and Francis's admonitions that the friars humbly respect all clergy notwithstanding, upstart Franciscan sanctity became a threat to the existing ecclesial structures of authority.

William also raised the question of the excess of Franciscan poverty, claiming that their unwillingness to appropriate anything put them in an occasion of sin, particularly in danger of suicide (by failing to care for their own lives) or homicide (by willingly making themselves unable to help the poor).[2] In spite of the long history associating Christian saints with poverty, William sets a limit: possession of some wealth is necessary to the avoidance of sin. The common property of monks was morally superior to this dangerous innovation of absolute poverty. Moreover, begging could be an invitation to laziness and simony. William argued from scriptural passages that enjoined labor, especially Paul's refusal to take his support from those to whom he preached, and from the apostles' ownership of a common bag. Far from being an element of evangelical perfection, begging was only allowed to those in need who could not work, as in the Acts of the Apostles, where goods laid at the apostles' feet were distributed among the needy. For a preacher to beg was not only appropriation of goods intended for the disabled, but also simony, in the line of Elisha's servant Gehazi, who demanded goods from Naaman the Syrian after his cure and was punished with his own case of leprosy (2 Kings 5).

2. Mäkinen, *Property Rights*, 34-43.

Francis's own words urging the friars to work supported William's critique. Francis had no difficulty both encouraging work and warmly recommending begging without shame when necessary, as we have seen previously. But as the order moved away from menial labor — a life in which work and occasional begging often went hand in hand — and into teaching and preaching, Francis's embrace of both activities became more problematic. Even assuming good intentions among all the friars — a generous assumption by any account — the continuance of begging after the order ceased to be identified with the poorest of society left them open to charges of bad faith. In William's thought, not poverty or dependence but faithfulness to the work of the church as taught in tradition and scripture was the mark of excellence. The "humility" of the friars was only a new face of pride.

William of St. Amour established the main lines of anti-fraternalism as they were to be repeated and developed long past the University of Paris struggle. One famous exchange, salient for our purposes, in this debate was Gerard of Abbeville's *Contra adversarium perfectionis christianae* (written early in the conflict, but released during a papal interregnum in order to avoid immediate papal censure) and its rebuttal in Bonaventure's *Defense of the Mendicants.* The debate between the two demonstrates that the Franciscan version of holy poverty ironically contributed to the development of the strongest direct defense of wealth Christianity had yet seen.

Gerard is of particular importance here because he directly attacked the Franciscan doctrine of poverty and argued for a Christian excellence that did not depend upon absolute poverty. Not stopping with the observation that poverty is an occasion of sin, he developed the idea that possessions contribute to the excellent life by making good work possible. According to Gerard, the association of poverty with perfection is fundamentally in error. Christ and his disciples had a purse, which they used for good purposes. Likewise, the church's perfection requires possession of goods in order to take prudent precautions regarding the future; to do justice to its ministers in return for their service; to offer charity to those in need; for mutual support in love; so that ministers may imitate Christ in relieving the needs of the poor; and so that the church, having all things in common, may be conformed to the life of heaven. All this is true of the church *absque imperfectionis macula,* without spot of imperfection, and indeed as integral to the imitation of Christ. Possession of wealth is not the problem; greed is. Gerard accused the Franciscans of trying to replace the church's perfection with one of their own making.[3]

The key point here is Gerard's defense of possession of wealth not merely as permissible, which orthodox teaching had never denied, but as perfect. As in Matthew 19:21, Gerard and his contemporaries assumed that one could have eternal life by following the commandments, but that perfection meant more than this, an imitation of Jesus' own life without private possession and without family. Ordinary Christians could have good hope of salvation, but those called to the life of perfection embraced practices beyond what was strictly necessary, out of love of Christ. This is not to say that Gerard or Bonaventure thought renouncing property implied individual sanctity. The question concerns only the perfection of the *state* of life, as an ideal of the church. Nor, as they understood the argument, was it a question of lay people's property, but of the practices of various religious orders. Is it more perfect to be poor as the Franciscans were or to be rich in common as were, for example, the Benedictines?

Gerard claims that practices of sharing, gift, charity, and justice all presuppose possession of property, and therefore the highest Christian excellence requires control of material goods, if not individually, then at least in common. Renunciation of goods destroys the power to accomplish work necessary to the life of the church, work extolled by Scripture and tradition and practiced by Jesus. Franciscan pretensions to the highest state of life were therefore false.

Furthermore, Gerard argued, the consequence of Franciscan claims to the highest life was to place them in theory above the pope and the bishops (not to mention non-fraternal university faculty). Gerard claimed that they implicitly put the papacy in a lesser *(minor)* state of holiness because of its responsibility for the care and distribution of goods, and *"Si vilescit nomen pontificum, omnis status Ecclesiae perturbatur,"* speaking ill of the papacy, they disturb all the church. This twist was politically savvy, as the papacy had tended to side with the Franciscans against the Paris seculars. How could Christian excellence be in competition with church authority per se? What kind of humility would claim the highest place?

---

3. Odd Langholm, *Economics in the Medieval Schools: Wealth, Exchange, Value, Money, and Usury according to the Paris Theological Tradition, 1200-1350* (Leiden: E. J. Brill, 1992), 278-79. See "Contra adversarium," ed. P. Sophronius Clasen, *Archivum Franciscanum Historicum,* 32 (1939): 100-117.

In his *Defense,* Bonaventure's major complaint is that his opponent has confused the notion of "perfection" by equating imperfection with failure to follow Christ, and therefore with sin. Gerard has cut out the category of innocent imperfection, into which Bonaventure would place most Christians, including those who hold goods in common. If perfection requires poverty and anything other than perfection is sin, then inevitably Bonaventure is reduced to the heresy of claiming the church itself to be damned. Maintaining carefully that perfection comes in many varieties, that imperfection can certainly be innocent, and that being in a state of imperfection does not imply an individual soul's damnation anymore than being in a state of perfection implies an individual soul's salvation, Bonaventure could claim poverty as a key element in the perfect state of life without having to condemn the wealthy as a group or as individuals. Poverty is a significant aid in working out one's salvation, but it is not a *sine qua non.* In order to defend the Franciscans, Bonaventure as minister general had to defend possession of property as innocent and useful, even as he maintained the excellence of poverty.

This debate provides a historical window into the anxiety that adopting holy poverty means abandoning certain duties. The poor, and the humble along with them, are explicitly understood to be incapable of the certain virtues. The advocates of poverty themselves had to become protectors of the innocence of wealth, in order to distance themselves from heresy. It also demonstrates the problems humble poverty created in ecclesial politics. As long as contemplatives were counted as living the "highest life," meaning they lived the life already closest to heaven, no political problem arose. They were honored, consulted, and sometimes dragged into episcopacies, but as a group, their example posed no systemic threat. But when friars claimed to live the highest life while rubbing elbows with the new urban world, they gained ecclesial power, which is to say political and economic power. When a claim to the "highest" holiness loses its eschatological framework, it can become a new rhetoric of domination and have a profoundly unsettling effect on justification of authority.[4]

Even given all of the forces working to discredit dependent poverty, Bonaventure, in his *Defense of the Mendicants,* thought he could defend it

---

4. The case of Celestine V, the famed ascetic Pietro del Morrone, who lasted in the papacy only five months before resigning, provided a sobering example to those who were certain that poverty and solitude were the best preparations for leadership.

through a *reductio ad absurdum*. In response to Gerard's justifications of possession of wealth, Bonaventure comments,

> These arguments are also ineffective, for they apply as well to a married layman who would be justified in keeping his possessions so that he may, with prudence, justice, mercy, and charity, take care of those who serve Christ; that he may preserve his peace of mind and give examples to others while conforming with the heavenly court, in which there is a lavish sharing of goods. Either such a man will be perfect, or the said arguments are worthless.[5]

Bonaventure agreed that a wealthy and generous layperson could be innocent and holy, following in the long tradition that recognized the wealth of Abraham, Job, and Joseph of Arimathea to be an element of their holy life. But if one grants that those orders that hold property in common are as perfect as those that have none, then this implies that a wealthy layperson who gave generously to the church could also be considered to be in a state of Christian perfection, and that conclusion appeared to Bonaventure manifestly ridiculous. He offers no argument to demonstrate this point. He did not think he had to. If most contemporary readers find nothing absurd in the proposition that a generous layperson can be in a state of perfection, they only demonstrate how far the church's commonplace wisdom has changed since Bonaventure's day.

Rights without Benefits, Duties without Rights, or Holiness Outside the Law

It is one of the peculiarities of Franciscan poverty that because Francis refused to accept any property as his own or as belonging to the friars, the *right* to property, as distinct from use of it, becomes enormously important to early Franciscan identity. RB 6 states, "Let the friars appropriate nothing for themselves, neither a house nor a place nor anything else." Franciscan biographies tell of Francis tearing down houses the friars had built or forcing friars to abandon houses that had been assumed to belong to them, not because he insisted on their sleeping outside, but because he

5. Bonaventure, *Defense of the Mendicants, The Works of Bonaventure*, vol. IV, trans. José de Vinck (Paterson, N.J.: St. Anthony Guild Press, 1966), 178.

would not have them claim or appear to claim the places as their property. One of the common stories has Francis's friend Hugolino and/or representatives of the commune intervene as Francis was pulling tiles off of the roof of a house to destroy it. They convinced Francis to let the house stand by claiming that he had no right to tear it down since it belonged to them. The argument succeeded: Francis acknowledged that he had no right to demolish the house and he agreed to allow the friars to live there, as long as everyone knew that the house did not belong to them. They could live there, as long as they did not have a right to it. They were to be as "strangers and pilgrims" in the world.

Francis resisted possession of rights, according to another pericope, as a particular obstacle to Christian charity. A collection of Franciscan tales that billed itself as a return to the true spirit of Francis has a bishop say to Francis, "It seems to me that your life is very rough and hard, especially, in not possessing anything in this world." Francis replied, "Lord, if we had possessions, we would need arms for our protection. For disputes and lawsuits usually arise out of them, and because of this, love of God and neighbor are greatly impeded."[6] As in the injunction to welcome even robbers, Francis's idea of poverty is not only about asceticism, but about loving one's economic competitors. Rights are the assertion of self-interest against others, and for this, Francis insisted that the friars have none.

In particular, they were not to have money, the efficient sign of rights in the newly emergent economy of Francis's Italy. Francis's aversion to money is well-documented. Friars could receive wages or alms in kind, but they were never to touch money, even if it were lying on the ground in front of them for the taking. A brother who touched a coin was, according to one story, told to put it in his mouth and carry it that way to a dungheap, where he could, as it were, deposit it. Another brother who found a moneybag in the road and was tempted to take it to help the poor learned its true nature when, rather than money, he discovered a snake inside. The question was not how much money one could have or how it was gained. Money was categorically forbidden.

Extravagant as Francis's rejection of money apparently was, we should not assume that hatred of coin was merely an idiosyncratic or superstitious principle. In early twelfth-century Italy, the widespread use of money had already begun to revolutionize economic relations. The con-

6. FA: ED II, Legend of the Three Companions, 35.

demnations of usury so widely produced in the high Middle Ages took the traditional line: money is a measure of wealth, but it is not itself wealth. One cannot eat money, or huddle under it on a cold night. Money is not productive, as land or animals or labor is, and so for money to produce more money is unnatural. Francis, coming out of a merchant family, seems to have understood that in this new economy, although money is not the same as wealth, it is also not simply a measure of wealth and it does more than facilitate exchange. He saw that money functions as the concrete, portable form of the right to command wealth. To use sacramental language, coin is an effective symbol of the right to command property. It bestows a legal power according to an exact measure, independent of personal relations or the common good. To pick up a coin is in this sense to hold a right divorced from charity, to sever Christian fellowship. Francis's term for money, "flies," may come from his sense that the power of money is parasitic. Money does no work itself, being empty. It profits from the work of others. For Francis, a sack of coins was this freestanding, impersonal, portable power, the right to command others. As such, it could not be part of the highest Christian holiness.

The frequency with which the stories of Francis tearing a house down appear reminds us that early in their history the Franciscans had begun to make use of sometimes substantial wealth, and they themselves were concerned about how this fit into their vocation. Francis's Testament, circulated after his death, included a strongly-worded call to the friars to remain poor and lowly, never to seek protection or privileges from the church hierarchy. Meanwhile Brother Elias was constructing in Assisi a basilica in Francis's honor. Francis's friend Hugolino, now Pope Gregory IX, intervened to clarify the Rule and to set the consciences of the order at ease with regard to the goods they used. In a bull entitled *Quo elongati*, Gregory himself accepted possession of the basilica in Assisi, and he taught that the Franciscans had not *proprietas*, but only *usus* in the goods they held. Ordinarily in donations to the friars, property right was expected to stay in the donor, although the Franciscans could be given perfect freedom in use. Later papacies built on this precedent. In 1245, Innocent IV in *Ordinem vestrum* declared all the goods given to the Franciscans to be part of the papal *dominium* (a term that indicated the range of personal authority of a lord, including various rights). Franciscans through this declaration could coherently claim to have only use of goods, without having dominium or a particular property right. Two years later, the pope authorized the Francis-

cans to appoint agents to sell and legally defend this papal property at the
friars' pleasure. Thus the Franciscans, through their own agents, had complete control over the goods purportedly held in the pope's right.[7]

Under obedience to the papacy and in spite of the continual retelling
of stories such as Francis's desire that a scholar renounce even his learning,
so as "to offer himself naked into the arms of the crucified," the Franciscans were able with clear conscience to step into the life of scholarship, sacramental ministry, and favored status within the church, with all the uses
of property those works implied. They could have books and buildings
that would allow for study and preservation of manuscripts as well as portable altars and eventually their own churches, without accepting them as
their own property.

This attempted reconciliation of poverty and property was challenged from two directions. First, a group of Franciscan dissenters, hud-
dled around the work of scholar Peter Olivi, mounted an internal critique,
declaring that regardless of who actually held the property right to the
goods, Franciscans were required to live in the style of the poor. Before
Exiit was issued, Olivi had already written about what he called the *usus
pauper*. According to Olivi, the vows of the order had to include adoption
of "poor use." Even if the pope claimed ownership of every pea eaten by a
Franciscan, the vow of perfect poverty was not honored unless the use of
goods remained suitable to poverty. Persistence in ignoring the *usus pauper*, Olivi taught, was a mortal sin for a Franciscan.

Olivi himself was careful to respect authorities within the church
and the order, but because of his views on several matters, notably the doctrine of the ages which he adapted from Joachim of Fiore but including the
usus pauper, those texts were suppressed and later rehabilitated within his
lifetime, and again questioned under Clement V and John XXII. Some of
those influenced by him and associated with the Spiritual movement
among Franciscans refused to moderate their position on poverty under
the direct order of the pontiff and were eventually judged to be heretical.
Olivi had associated Francis's rediscovery of Christ's absolute poverty with
the coming of a new age in the world. To his adherents, this perfect poverty

7. Another ironic effect of Franciscan poverty is that the sense of the word
"dominium" itself evolved within these debates, moving toward the more abstract property
right in isolation from social duties or status. See Mäkinen, *Property Rights*. This account of
the affair is chiefly drawn from M. D. Lambert, *Franciscan Poverty: The Doctrine of the Absolute Poverty of Christ and the Apostles in the Franciscan Order, 1210-1323* (London: SPCK, 1961).

of Christ was an element of the gospel that no human authority, not even the pope, could challenge.

Olivi's views troubled many Franciscan consciences, but a second critique, this time external, actually brought down the Franciscan edifice built on Christ's absolute poverty. Gerard of Abbeville demonstrated the papal dominion of Franciscan goods to be legally incoherent. How could one have only the *use* and not *dominion* of that which is consumed in its use? Legally, a right to use something belonging to the dominion of another was granted for a limited time and required that the substance of the thing be preserved. I may use your horse, but I must return it to you in good condition and on time. How can that kind of "use" apply to food, which cannot be returned? If the Franciscans could not defend their poverty when confronted with the necessity of eating food, how could they defend it when they were freely disposing of houses and even lands and annuities?

Franciscan defenses took several lines over time. Bonaventure claimed that the Franciscans lived according to the same laws which allowed minors and servants to use and consume goods belonging to their parents or masters. Use does not require dominion in that case, but neither is it unreasonable or illegal. The Franciscans, as minor sons of the papal household, did not have legal standing, but they committed no wrong when they consumed goods under the pope's dominion. Bongratia later argued that Franciscans lived without legal rights, but they had, like all poor people, a natural right, apart from any legal or contingent arrangement, to goods necessary for their survival. He invoked this prior right to justify Franciscan use without legal possession.[8]

But after eighty years in which the papacy claimed ownership of Franciscan goods and the Franciscans claimed to follow Christ's perfect poverty while disposing of large amounts of goods through agents under their own control, Pope John XXII claimed the power and responsibility to change the teaching of *Exiit*. Drawing on the legal principle that dominion and use cannot be separated in perpetuity, John XXII ended the papacy's reception of goods on behalf of the Franciscans. In the terms of later Christian speech about property, the pope declared that the Franciscans could not claim to be mere stewards of goods which they consumed and exchanged without any reference to the purported owner. Such an arrangement was a legal fiction. If those who use, consume, and dispose of

---

8. Mäkinen, *Property Rights*, 66-67, 185-87.

goods freely do not own those goods, then they are thieves. Christ, not having been a thief, must have owned the goods he consumed and exchanged, and he therefore was not absolutely poor. Ownership could in no way be contrary to the imitation of Christ and therefore the Franciscan claim that they were the closest imitators of Christ was false.

In this way, the Franciscan attempt to create a public zone operating apart from assertion of rights failed, the Franciscans themselves having appealed to the rules of rights — civil and natural — in a last attempt to preserve it.

Franciscan pericopes that oppose rights were aimed at fostering a kind of economic non-resistance in the friars, as called for in Matthew 5:38-42:

> You have heard that it was said, "An eye for an eye and a tooth for a tooth." But I say to you, Do not resist one who is evil. But if anyone strikes you on the right cheek, turn and offer him the other also; and if any one would sue you and take your coat, let him have your cloak as well; and if any one forces you to go one mile, go with him two miles. Give to him who begs from you, and do not refuse him who would borrow from you.

The friars went out into the world without any legal defense. They might use a place or some goods, but as soon as someone else demanded them, Francis's followers were to turn them over without complaint. But what about everyday practice, in which no one was demanding anything from the friars, and on the contrary, donors were lining up to make contributions? What did the refusal to appropriate imply about maintenance and liability for goods the friars used and about the *usus pauper*? The refusal to have property rights began in Christological humility and ended in an occasion of gross hypocrisy and a legal fallacy that gave scandal.

But more than that, fraternal and anti-fraternal thought on rights anticipated the modern notion of freestanding rights, independent of corresponding duties. The attempt to renounce all rights severed, from the side of an apparent excess of virtue, the connection of rights and duties, as though one could carry on duties without rights. That is, Franciscans insisted that they had duties as preachers, for example, but that these duties implied no rights to the goods needed to carry out those duties.[9] The papal

---

9. RNB shows some awareness of this when it explicitly allows friars to keep the tools of their trade, and no Franciscan source claims that all people should practice the same poverty.

dominium over Franciscan goods implied a right of property without any corresponding duty. Ironically, the attempt to make the economic world more charitable created a precursor of economic individualism.[10] Franciscan poverty, as the height of the virtue of humility, upheld as most perfect a vulnerability that weakened the integral virtue of the common good, making the greatest Christian virtue appear simultaneously immoral. Meanwhile its subversion of an economy centered on rights turned into a reaffirmation of rights as the definitive category for ethics of wealth, as even the Franciscans made use of it to describe their behavior.

The Franciscan renunciation of property was shown to be legally incoherent, but the idea that use and property right could be distinguished, that one who uses goods might do so without giving up a kind of spiritual poverty, will have a long and distinguished career. What the pope's dominion could not achieve, God's can.

Mendicants and the Market for Sanctity

Confusion over claims of rights, dissension over received forms of holiness, growing discomfort with various traditional sites of authority: the anti-fraternal debates already have a flavor of the modern world. In fact, contemporaries linked the friars with the new world of the permanent market, a world in which value seemed ever more contingent upon the power of those who knew how to play the market, merchants and lawyers. The ambivalence of Franciscan beggars, as both lowest and highest in the church, paragons of humility and disorderly upstarts, lovers of the poor and friendly to merchants, is grist for the creative mill of William Langland, who as we saw in the last chapter uses beggars as models of holiness and hypocrisy in *Piers Plowman*. He particularly excels at showing the friars' own skill in the market, where they peddled holiness as a hot commodity and thereby themselves undermine the order of trust and truthfulness that might have characterized Franciscan gift-exchange.

10. The problem of rights currently reads quite differently than it did in this debate, because rights are now somewhat more potently invoked in defense of the poor. Idealizing renunciation of rights in such a context creates a possible backlash against those who would fight for the protection of decent wages and working conditions. This was not the case in the era under consideration, and no contemporary source I have read criticized the Franciscan refusal of rights on that basis.

In the first of a series of dreams that make up the bulk of the poem, the dreamer sees England as a "field of folk," in which money has succeeded in insinuating a market mentality into relations far beyond mere trade — notably into the church. The poem characterizes the friars as successful hawkers of holiness, and all the more prone to simony because of their practices of poverty and begging.

> I found there friars from all four orders,
> Preaching to people to profit their gut,
> and glossing the gospel to their own good liking;
> Coveting fine copes, some of these doctors contradicted authorities
> Many of these masterful mendicant friars
> Bind their love of money to their proper business.
> And since charity's become a broker and chief agent for
>   lords' confessions
> Many strange things have happened these last years;
> Unless Holy Church and charity clear away such confessors
> The world's worst misfortune mounts up fast.

The close association of friars and merchants was no secret, nor should it be a historical surprise.[11] The leaders of traditional monastic orders had seen themselves against the backdrop of a warrior class of nobles. The monastic identity both sharply contrasted with (in its vulnerability to attack) and imitated (as spiritual warfare) the class from which they emerged. The friars, in the new economic context, bore a parallel relation to the emerging business class, merchants (such as Francis's father) and entrepreneurs. Their poverty was defined against the backdrop of the new economy, but their life in other respects shared certain qualities with that of the merchants. Their mobility, their engagement in argument and persuasive speech rather than manual labor, their spiritual logic with its attention to payment of debt and reception of gift — all of this is in stark contrast to earlier monasticism and situates the friars within the world of the urban market. Certainly the energy friars put into considering the ethics of the money economy is another indicator of their close ties to the lives of merchants and bankers. The "bargain" of mendicant labor is only one example of this kind of thought. The Franciscan fascination with the scrip-

11. The following analysis is indebted to Little, *Religious Poverty and the Profit Economy in Medieval Europe* (Ithaca: Cornell University Press, 1978).

tural Jesus is strangely paired with a novel religious order that was not tied to the land or overly interested in silence. We need not be surprised that both the attack on the mendicants and the defense of the mendicants bear the marks of a changed economic world. In 1261, Pisa made St. Francis their patron saint of merchants.

The two commodities critics claimed the friars were peddling were preaching and confession. In their preaching, they, like lawyers, sold their words in exchange for alms, instead of speaking the truth. By means of glosses on texts, they shifted the meaning of words to suit the market, creating a useful liquidity in their asset. Mobility, intellectual and moral as well as geographical, so essential to the market, was the enemy of traditional social order.

Langland was particularly concerned with their perversion of the sacrament of confession. Early in the work, the lovely lady Meed (whose name means reward or profit, but also money) confesses to a friar when he promises absolution in return for a horse-load of wheat. He requests payment from her to work against Conscience on her behalf in the king's court, and wheedles a bit more out of her in return for having her name engraved on a window in the friars' church. To complete the pun, he assures her that "In mass and in matins, for Meed [profit/money] we shall sing" (III, 53). In the ending of the poem, demonstrating the "world's worst misfortune," Langland casts the friars' practices of confession as the betrayal that catastrophically weakens the church from the inside during its siege by the Antichrist. Need advises Conscience about the friars: "They'll flatter rich folks in order to get by./ . . . For he lies more often who must beg for a living/ Than he who works for a living and shares it with beggars" (XXII, 235-239). When Contrition is lulled to sleep by the ministry of Friar Flatterer, Conscience decides to "become a pilgrim,/And walk as wide as the world reaches/To seek Piers the plowman . . ." (XXII, 380-82). Langland shows the begging of the friars as an occasion of sin for them and a disaster for the whole church as they misuse the sacrament of penance.

In fact, the rectors of London in 1309 complained that *they* were reduced to begging because so much of their usual revenues were being given to the friars instead of the secular clergy.[12] Because the friars answered to the pope, rather than to a diocesan bishop, they claimed to be

---

12. Wendy Scase, Piers Plowman *and the New Anti-Clericalism*, Cambridge Studies in Medieval Literature #4 (Cambridge: Cambridge University Press, 1989), 20.

proper confessors for any place. With this argument, they left bishops who preferred to exclude them with the option of appearing resistant to representatives of the pope, thereby undermining his authority in the local church. The mobility of the friars becomes an incursion which violates the local order, sows dissension, and permits penitents to treat the sacrament of penance as a market transaction, an impersonal transfer of the commodity absolution. The association of "contributions" with this transfer, particularly contributions made in lieu of restitution, turns the entire process into a sale, justice and the common good no longer holding sway. The portability of the friars' ministry parallels the mobility and portability of wealth in their economy, and this is at the center of the corruption the friars wreak upon contrition.

Relative to the social cohesion considered under the heading of "To Instigate Gift-Giving" in the last chapter, this turn makes begging deeply ironic. The alms invited are no longer a testimony to social cohesion, to the unity and mutual care of the church centered upon Christ. Rather, alms have taken on a quality of bribe or even straightforward payment. Those who beg for such gifts are marketers, and their humility is a clever tactic for appearing particularly holy while attracting large donations. To make their offense worse, the honesty of their marketing was judged, by some, to be suspect. The anti-fraternalist Fitzralph taught that voluntary begging is always false begging, since it could have been avoided.[13] The rightful claim of the "real poor" has been turned into the weapon of the ambitious poor, or worse, of the false religious.

But if public poverty has turned out to be only a new market in which alms are traded for grace and if destitution becomes a face of ambition for honor and power, if, that is, voluntary beggars have become merchants of the holy, then who will become the new icon of humility?

One image of decent poverty from *Piers Plowman* is indicative: poor women in hovels, scrimping and working to exhaustion to provide for their children, and who then "turn the fair outward" because they are ashamed to admit their need. These "truly humble" are commended not only for their hard work and attempt to keep a family intact, but also for their shame. They do not want to be recognized or to instigate gift-giving. They do not implicitly or explicitly criticize the wealthy or claim to have any moral advantage over them. They work hard and make no demands.

13. Cited in Scase, Piers Plowman *and the New Anti-Clericalism*, 67.

In short, they pose no threat to the market as a system nor are they competitors within it. The humble are those who play by the rules.[14]

Note the strange inversion of virtues: the unwillingness to admit need before one's neighbors could be called pride and would appear under that name to be a traditional enemy of Christian society. Yet this pride becomes the test of their innocence. The only truly worthy poor are those whose pride clears them of any charge of humility's social threat, for they do not want the recognition the gospel would offer to them and they do not take up its challenge to the wealthy. Those who hold cultural and ecclesial power, the makers of social mores, have good reason to prefer this pride to the challenge implicit in poor humility, and the historical scandal of the friars lends moral weight to that preference.

In *Sacrum Commercium,* an early Franciscan text,[15] Lady Poverty pours out her sad story to her true lovers, Francis and his brothers. Among her

14. Kenneth Baxter Wolf's work on Francis, *The Poverty of Riches: St. Francis of Assisi Reconsidered* (Oxford: Oxford University Press, 2003), is a sort of latter-day anti-fraternalist polemic. Wolf has claimed that the popularity of the cult of Francis among the merchant class is an indication that his version of voluntary poverty complemented the bourgeois version of property-accumulation. Far from offering a heavenly inversion of wealth and poverty, Wolf argues that Franciscan poverty insulated thirteenth-century burghers from the realities of poverty and any genuine attempts to address the needs of the urban poor. Franciscans functioned as a docile body of artificial paupers, moneyed young men posing as paupers without losing the social habits of their families, on whom the new bourgeoisie could focus their charity without facing any real challenge to the justice of their social order. In fact, argues Wolf, this is not an unintended consequence, but is fully characteristic of Francis's spirit, which was always focused on the personal quest of holiness rather than on relief of the poor. In this, I think that Wolf overstates his case. Francis's practices were not merely personal asceticism and they did provoke concern and controversy, particularly in the earlier period. The popularity of Francis's cult had to do not only with his own gentleness toward the wealthy but with the popularity of his order, whose faithfulness to his example is widely questioned. Nevertheless, Wolf's sense that the result of Franciscan practice was ironically to strengthen Christian rationalization of property and market relations is broadly on target. A useful companion to Wolf's discussion is Talal Asad's work on Cistercian "humility" and its impact on serfs. Talal Asad, "On Discipline and Humility in Medieval Christian Monasticism," *Genealogies of Religion: Discipline and Reasons of Power in Christianity and Islam* (Baltimore: Johns Hopkins University Press, 1993).

15. The dating is contested, but I accept here the conclusion of the editors of *Francis of Assisi: Early Documents* that the style is not consistent with the scholastic debates, and if we reject the date on some manuscripts of 1227, we may accept external evidence that it was written by Caesar de Speyer, in or before 1238.

woes is the trickery of Greed, who goes by the names Discretion or Foresight to win followers away from Poverty. People under the influence of Greed known by these names make seductive arguments: "It is good to continue in works of piety, to have time for good, fruitful deeds, to provide for the needy, and to give something to the poor." And again, "Vice is not in things, but in the soul, for God saw all that he had done and it was very good. To the good, everything is good, everything is useful, and everything is made for them." Poverty's answer, even as written by her advocate, is weak:

> I am not contradicting the good that you have said, brothers, but I beg you: *look at your calling.* Do not look back. Do not *come back down from the housetop to take something from the house.* . . . For it is inevitable that those who are again entangled in these affairs will be overcome and *their last state will become worse than their first,* for under the appearance of piety, they withdraw from that which was given them by holy commandment.[16]

Even Lady Poverty admits that practicing humility in the production, collection, and use of goods impedes other excellent achievements. We have seen in this chapter the problems such humility posed for the mendicants, both as a practical liability and as an occasion of sin. In caring for the poor, an efficient use of wealth seemed necessary. Public responsibility and accountability required that those who use, control, and alienate goods also accept title to them. Resistance to the incursion of the market into the practices of absolution and preaching required, given the weakness of most people when held hostage by their bellies, a certain prudent provision for religious leaders. And in each of these cases, we want to know how their practice of poverty affected those who had no choice but to be poor. Are they to welcome early death, to forgo asserting their rights? Should they willingly give up effectiveness in order to continue in humility? Should they, or should they not, publicly confront the wealthy? In the end, we must ask ourselves, given all this, can the embrace of poverty be moral?

With the rise of the money economy, the meaning of wealth shifted such that religious orders that held land, buildings, artwork, and so on

---

16. FA: ED I, The Sacred Exchange between Saint Francis and Lady Poverty, 39, 40, 45.

looked suspiciously hypocritical in claiming to maintain a vow of poverty. The Franciscan explosion redefined religious poverty as material destitution and life without rights, without the protection of common property, and their founder also tied that poverty closely to the sacramental life of the church and respect for clergy. Francis put a finger on the violence implicit in this emerging economic order and turned the vulnerability of the eucharistic host and the nakedness of the cross and the manger into the economic vulnerability of the beggar. Placing oneself on the dependent or receiving end of almsgiving could be humility because it was a matter of submitting to someone else's mercy within the new order of power. But putting oneself on the receiving end could also appear as — and in fact become — sloth, greed, irresponsibility, and callousness toward those who were poor but did not choose to be so. The Franciscan love of poverty, which drew its meaning from the rights-based relations of the market, became, within the logic of that market, either just another business or else a sin. Its role as meek critic or as counterwitness within that society collapsed into the very world it arose to challenge. But the tradition of holy poverty, so esteemed among Christians, will have to be rehabilitated, somehow, so that respect for beggar-saints can be reconciled to a world in which property, impersonal exchange, and individual rights have become the building blocks of economic morality.

CHAPTER THREE

Stewardship: The Rehabilitation of Humility

We have seen how the attempt of the Franciscans to separate their use of goods from the rights of ownership collapsed under the weight of hypocrisy. Yet the idea that one might morally use goods without being their owner is commonplace in present-day Christian thought, under the rhetoric of stewardship. Stewardship, the notion that goods belong to God but are given into the management of human beings for use according to God's will, resolves the instabilities and excesses of virtuous begging by reconciling the ideal of poverty with the importance of responsible and effective use. Leaving questions of legal property rights to their own logic, stewardship reinterprets ownership from a spiritual side. The moral requirement to obey God's law is enacted through the use of property entrusted to the Christian. Humility has little to do with renunciation of wealth, but much to do with accepting responsibility for wealth. Some fragments from the history of stewardship, however, will suggest that the power of stewardship to "resolve" the problems set by voluntary begging is self-deceptive.

Stewardship: Where Did We Get This?

Stewardship "came of age," according to Douglas John Hall, with the Christianity of North America, where churches were disestablished and had to rely on the personal commitment of members to pay salaries and maintain buildings and carry out missionary efforts. That is, as the churches of the U.S. lost their proximity to establishment power and wealth, they learned to articulate the modest and lay-centered use of personal power through the biblical metaphor of the "steward." In Hall's account, the idea of "stewardship" lay dormant in Scripture until disestablishment roused awareness of its importance. North American churches were ahead of the international curve on disestablishment, and for that reason they have been given the charism of stewardship as an insight to share with the rest of the world, as Latin Americans were given an understanding of liberation, for the up-building of Christians everywhere. The humble image of the steward speaks directly to the situation of post-Christendom churches, as Hall understands it. Christians now carry on their office as servants, not owners, and in this they come to appreciate their self-sacrificial calling as stewardship.

This argument, developed in Hall's influential *The Steward: A Biblical Symbol Come of Age,* emerges out of his life's work of issuing a wake-up call to American congregations that cling to the delusion that they are still in charge.[1] He argues that stewardship is not merely a codeword for donations. Instead, it describes the position of Christians within a world they do not own and do not control, but in which they must nevertheless act responsibly. He says stewardship is "the gospel in miniature," a metaphor that has "come of age."

Hall could learn from Janet Soskice's work that a favored metaphor continues to function "in virtue of its own applicability certainly, but also because the history of its application makes it already freighted with meaning."[2] The metaphor lives in a linguistic community for whom its history of use is constitutive of its significance. For this reason, the history of the metaphor can be crucial to a proper understanding of it. Hall's claim, then, that stewardship arose in the U.S. among disestablished churches as they grew in humble service posits a certain content to the metaphor that can be historically contested. In fact, the stewardship ethic arose among holders of substantial wealth and power, and it has repeatedly been used to reinforce their property rights, even as it calls for generosity and responsibility. Recognizing its history helps us to name the present

1. *The Steward: A Biblical Symbol Come of Age,* Revised Edition (Grand Rapids: Eerdmans, 1990). Hall's work will be examined in more detail in Chapter Five.
2. Janet Soskice, *Metaphor and Religious Language* (Oxford: Clarendon Press, 1985), 158.

function of the term. "Stewardship" signifies a turn from the material and political presence of the church as an economic community capable of material sharing toward the church as a spiritual association of individual property holders with primarily motivational rather than organizational impact. The problem is not that the image of the steward is too thin a metaphor to bear the weight of Christian teaching on wealth. The problem is that "steward" already bears a heavy burden in ecclesial habits of speech and structure, habits cultivated historically, and Hall has not adequately recognized that function.

This chapter disputes Hall's hypothesis and displays the possibility of a different history of stewardship, attending to historical moments overlooked by Hall and his predecessors. Far more historical work will be needed to nuance, correct, or deepen this account. My hope here is at least to demonstrate the need for such work and to indicate the direction in which it should begin.

Stewardship's Emergence in English

The excellence of the prudent use of wealth and the idea of God's ownership have lengthy histories before the emergence of modern stewardship, centering around the terms *oikonomia* in Greek or *dispensator* in Latin. Strangely enough, though, "stewardship" as presently used in ecclesial jargon, is peculiar to English — peculiar enough that the U.S. Catholic Bishops' document on stewardship had to use the term "corresponsibilidad" in the title of its Spanish version and had to indicate with asterisks the terms in Scripture selections that were all "steward" or "stewardship" in English, since in Spanish no single term translated all of them.[3] Germans use *Haushalter* but have on occasion preferred to germanicize the English word.[4] The International Catholic Committee on Stewardship has now dropped cognates of "co-responsibility" in romance languages in favor of "administration of the gifts of God." It appears, therefore, that the term in its present valence is most at home in English. Although Reu-

---

3. See Marina Herrera's note on the copyright information page of the Spanish language edition of the text. *Oikonomos,* usually translated as "steward" in English Bibles, is in Spanish variously *mayordomo, administrador, encargado, dispensador, guardián,* and *servidor.*

4. Hall, *The Steward,* 4.

mann[5] has offered a fine study of *oikonomia,* the Greek word sometimes translated by the English word "stewardship," and Hall makes some comments on its origins, the history of the English term remains largely unexplored. Before proceeding, therefore, it will be useful to consider briefly the issues raised by that history.

In its scriptural and patristic uses the Greek *oikonomia* most frequently referred to God's providence, even miraculous providence, for Israel and the church. On its own, *oikonomia* often referred to the Incarnation as the central act of God's providential care. *Oikonomia* could also refer to the administration of the sacrament of the Eucharist, or occasionally to the giving of alms, but it most frequently referred to God's action rather than to human action.[6] A tour of the *Oxford English Dictionary* shows that a number of early uses of "steward" in English follow this pattern. The *Ancrene Riwle* (c. 1225) comments that "Love is heaven's steward, on account of her great liberality, for she retains nothing for herself, but giveth all that she hath, and even herself, otherwise God would not esteem any of the things that were hers."[7] "How the good wife taught her daughter," in *The Babees' Book* (1430), teaches, "Gladly give thy tithes and thy offerings both,/to the poor and the bed-rid — look thou be not loth./Give of

5. John Henry Paul Reumann, *Stewardship and the Economy of God* (Grand Rapids: Eerdmans, 1992).

6. Reumann, *Stewardship,* 27-29. Reumann does not research the Latin word "dispensator." My own search for the uses of the term in Augustine, Leo I, and Gregory I suggests that it was used among Latin authors to refer to human ministry in the church, as in *dispensator verbi* or *dispensator sacramenti.* However, I have also encountered texts in which the right use of material possessions is considered as a matter of *dispensanda* for which one will be required to give an account to God. See, e.g., Leo I, "Sermon X: On the Collections," in which the good *dispensator* is contrasted both to misers and to lovers of luxury. Augustine considers the *dispensator* of money as one who may be tempted to pride, but should recall that he was "taken up destitute from the dust, and lifted from out of the mire." *Enarrationes in Psalmos,* Ps. CXIII, in *A Select Library of the Nicene and Post-Nicene Fathers of the Christian Church,* Vol. VIII, ed. Philip Schaff (Grand Rapids: Eerdmans, 1979). While the economic ramifications of such usages and the ethical context in which they appear will be quite distinct from those of modern stewardship rhetoric, still a study of the matter would be a useful contribution.

7. *The Nun's Rule, being the Ancren Riwle* modernized by James Morton, with Introduction by Abbot Gasquet (London: Chatto &Windus, 1926), 293. In the Ancrene Wisse, the passage runs "luue is heouene stiward. For hire muchele feolec. For heo ne edhalt na þing. Ah geueð al þ ha haueð — ec hire seoluen. Elles ne kepte godd nawt of þet hiren wére." *Ancrene Wisse,* ed. J.R.R. Tolkien (London: Oxford University Press, 1962), 197.

thine own goods and be not too hard,/for seldom is the house poor where God is steward."[8] As late as 1594 Alexander Hume, having raised the question, "why the Lord, seeing all things are at his gift and disposition, doeth so hardly intreate his servants in this life?" replied, "That the Lord is a wise & discreet stewart, and dispensator of his benefites: and seeing he hath created and made vs, hee knows our strength and weaknes, what is most meete for vs, and howe able wee are to beare, and vse his giftes and benefites."[9] Margery Kempe, as well, wrote that Christ promised to "be a trewe styward" of all she entrusted to him.[10] In this sense, "steward" chiefly designated the office of one who distributes goods. The question of who owns the goods, the point which becomes critical to the use of "stewardship" later, did not arise in these early theological uses. The image of God as owner leaving affairs in the charge of a steward does however appear in a poem of Hoccleve's, "The Emperor Jereslaus's Wife" (c. 1422). The poem ends with a prose "moralization" which takes the two stewards in the story to represent the human who has charge of his body and continually tempts the soul, and the other, "pride of life, which is the Styward of this world by whom many folk been deceyued and begyled. . . ."[11] Stewardship was as likely to imply evil as good.

The word "steward" could denote a wide range of positions. It particularly refers to someone given charge of a household, especially providing for meals, and it has been used since the fifteenth century to describe the office of one in charge of providing for the needs of travelers, whether by ship or later by train or plane. But already in the late thirteenth century "steward" had been appropriated as the English equivalent of the Norman *seneschal,* and under that title Simon de Montfort made himself the effective, if short-lived, ruler of England. A similar office in Scotland (originating in the twelfth-century *senescallatus Scotiae*), collapsed into the crown itself when Robert the Steward became Robert II and founded the house of Stewart (later Stuart). The office of Lord High or Great Steward indicated

8. *The Babees' Book: Medieval Manners for the Young, Done into Modern English from Dr. Furnivall's Texts by Edith Rickert* (London: Chatto & Windus, 1923), 32.

9. *The Poems of Alexander Hume,* ed. Alexander Lawson (Edinburgh: William Blackwood & Sons, 1902), 147.

10. *The Book of Margery Kempe,* ed. S. B. Meech (London: Humphrey Milford, Oxford University Press, 1940), 157.

11. *Hoccleve's Works: I. The Minor Poems,* ed. Fredrik J. Furnivall (London: Kegan Paul, Trench, Trübner & Co., Limited, 1892), 176.

pro temp authority during a coronation or a trial of a peer after the time of Henry IV, and "steward" commonly indicated from the fifteenth century onward the nominal care for royal lands entrusted to nobles. Thus "steward" took on a connotation of royal power and authority in its use as equivalent to *seneschal*. In this sense, Falstaff imagined himself "Fortune's steward" when he received news of Henry V's accession to the throne (*Henry IV, Part 2*, 5.3). Although royal stewards sometimes still had a ceremonial responsibility for meals, the office in fact signified deputation of sovereignty, including the authority to oversee great wealth and the administration of punishment and reward in the name of the ruler.

In the writings of followers of John Wyclif this English term met the tradition of argument about poverty and property, which had traveled through the Franciscan Ockham and the anti-fraternalist Fitzralph.[12] In Wycliffite writing on "dominion" we begin to see the logic of stewardship unfold in English, and in quite a different direction than modern readers would expect.[13] While in his early Latin writings on dominion Wyclif energetically advocated clerical poverty as appropriate imitation of Christ, he also developed a theory of property rooted in the claim that God is the true owner of all things and that earthly owners have a contingent right to their property.[14] But where twentieth-century arguments use the trope of God's true ownership rhetorically to undermine claims of absolute ownership in the interest of increasing contributions to ecclesial causes, Wyclif's "dominion" strengthens the rights of lords to refuse to give to the church. Wyclif did not emphasize God's dominion as a contrast to an individual owner's rights; he used it to oppose the theory that papal plenitude was the source of property and authority. To those who claimed the pope, as Christ's vicar, held the highest human authority over property, Wyclif answered that God, not the pope, is the chief lord of all creation, and it is to God that the human lords owe allegiance. Their dominion coming from God, they are obliged to exercise that authority according to God's will,

12. Ockham was a member of the Michaelist opposition to John XXII. See Joan Lockwood O'Donovan, *Theology of Law and Authority in the English Reformation* (Atlanta: Scholars Press, 1991).

13. It is recognized now that Wyclif's own vernacular writings were destroyed. Selections that follow are Wycliffite writings from Thomas Arnold, ed., *Select English Works of John Wyclif*, vol. 3 (Oxford: Clarendon Press, 1871).

14. *De Dominio divino* (1375) and *De Civili dominio* (1376). See *Advocates of Reform, from Wyclif to Erasmus*, ed. Matthew Spinka (Philadelphia: Westminster Press, 1953).

notably against ecclesial corruption. "The reward of salvation, peace in the realm, and, to speak practically, temporal profit should move them to this."[15]

Wyclif only concedes right possession to those in grace, since right possession of any property is a gift of God. This principle is not very useful, however, since Wyclif also is a proponent of the invisibility of the true church, the elect. No one could, on the grounds of failing to be in grace, be deprived of property.[16] On the other hand, Wyclif insists that clergy should hold no property, not because of their sin, but because of their calling to imitate Christ. Although the doctrine of Christ's *absolute* poverty had been rejected as contrary to reason and law, still the poverty of Christ's life was widely assumed, and some adherence to that poverty was expected of those who imitated him most closely. Following the anti-fraternalists before him, Wyclif saw that to accept the sanctity of poverty implied a censure not merely of hypocritical Franciscans, but of all clergy who had not adopted such poverty. Wyclif, however, embraced this conclusion. If the clergy will not do it voluntarily, he taught, it is incumbent upon the laity to dispossess them, for the good of the clergymen's souls. The dominion given by God to the kings and lords requires them as God's good servants to save the clergy from their wealth. And if, "to speak practically," this worked to their profit, so be it.

God's true dominion and the stewardship entrusted to humans is in Wyclif's work therefore a tool for denying rightful ownership to the clergy and to the church as a body. This is not to say that human holders of wealth had *carte blanche*, once they had dispossessed the clergy. Wyclif did write of the righteous dominion given by God to those in grace as evangelical dominion, in which property is held commonly without protective distinction between mine and yours, without appeal to rights. But he also recognized the legally held property of secular lords and encouraged them to use that property defensively so that they and the nation would not be impoverished by clerics who thought only of their bellies. In particular, they were not to alienate their property in perpetuity, as in grants to the

15. Wyclif, *On Simony*, trans. Terrence A. McVeigh (New York: Fordham University Press, 1992), 35.

16. This is not peculiar to Wyclif. This problem can be found originally in Augustine, and it was to address it that Ockham distinguished *ius poli* (such as Franciscan use without the claim of property rights) from *ius fori* (legal property rights, which should not be undermined without due cause). O'Donovan, *Theology of Law*, 14-15.

church which clergy were forbidden to release. The laity should not themselves enter into evangelical possession, but use their civil possession to hold clergy accountable to it. The virtues of poverty and ownership, dependence and independence, were inscribed the one on priests and the other on the laity and temporal powers. Alongside these ideas of right property, and in fact inscribed within them, was the presumption that the purity of the spiritual involved poverty and submission to temporal political power.

The term "steward" itself appears in moralizing discussion of church polity in Wycliffite writings, although again in unexpected ways. In response to the idea that Christ is gone "on pilgrimage" and has left the pope as his "steward to rule his house,"[17] the pope is claimed to be "not Christ's steward, but steward of Antichrist."[18] Rather than keeping Christ's house in order, he has let it be overrun by corrupt priests, and that in greater and greater number, culminating in the friars. As for those good servants who use gifts of God in accord with God's will, "gentlemen of the world should serve their God through gifts that he has given them, and especially in this; that they defend God's law by power of the world."[19] Thus the theological notion of a responsibility to God for right use of God's gifts did appear in English in the wake of Wyclif — as rhetoric against the pope and for secular reform of the church.

The Wycliffite English translation of the New Testament did not use the word "steward," preferring in the gospels to use "procurator," "dispender," or "bayli." In fact, several words are used in the Greek and in the Vulgate. In Matthew 20:8, the "steward" of the vineyard is *epitropos* and *operarios* or *procuratio*. The parable of the talents in Matthew 25 concerns three *douloi* or *servos*. Pilate's assistant in Luke 8:3 is an *epitropos* or *procuratoris*. Only Luke's parables of preparation (12:42) and the shrewd servant who changed records of debts (16:2) use the term *oikonomos*, the one now commonly taken as the Greek equivalent of "steward." In the Vulgate, the former is *dispensator* while the latter is *vilicum*. The Vulgate follows the Greek in the epistles, where numerous uses of *oikonomos* almost always become *dispensator* in the Vulgate, and the Wycliffite translation employs cognates of the Latin (see 1 Cor. 4.1; 9:17; Gal. 4:2; Eph. 1:10; 3:2;

---

17. "The Church and Her Members," in Arnold, *Select English Works*, 343.
18. "The Church and Her Members," in Arnold, *Select English Works*, 346.
19. "On the Seven Deadly Sins," in Arnold, *Select English Works*, 145.

3:9; Col. 1:25; 1 Tim. 1:4; Tit. 1:7; 1 Pet. 4:10). The term "stewardship" evidently did not suggest itself for these uses.

Tyndale's 1534 translation of the New Testament used "steward" to translate *oikonomos* only once, in the parable of the shrewd steward (Lk. 16:2), also adopting it to translate *epitropos* in Matthew 20:8 and Luke 8:3. "Minister," "governor," "disposer," "chamberlain," and "servant" translated other instances. "Steward," that is to say, was used only in its literal sense. Likewise, "stewardship" was not used outside Luke 16, *oikonomia* being rendered throughout the epistles as "office," "ministration," "ordinance," or "fellowship." Tyndale's Bible, the Great Bible, and the Geneva Bible all use "ministering/ministers" to translate *diakonountes/oikonomoi* in 1 Peter 4:10, creating a parallelism in English not warranted by the Greek. Again, no one English word easily came to mind for *oikonomos*.

The Great Bible, which is chiefly attributed to Coverdale, extended the meaning of "steward" metaphorically, paralleling *oikonomos*. In addition to the passages in which Tyndale used it, the Great Bible uses the term "steward" also in Luke 12:42 (preparedness); Titus 1:7 (regarding bishops); and 1 Corinthians 4:1 (on Paul's office). The Great Bible had on its title page an illustration usually attributed to Hans Holbein showing God blessing the king, who is in turn distributing the Bible to Thomas Cranmer and Thomas Cromwell. Although the passage is not cited, this illustration is evocative of 1 Corinthians 4:1, which in this translation calls Paul, Apollos, and Cephas "stewards of the mysteries of God." This vernacular edition was published in 1539, an auspicious year in the history of church property, as it saw the enforcement of the dispossession of religious houses by the government. It is estimated that lands worth an annual income of more than £136,000 as well as portable wealth of as much as £1 million to 1.5 million was confiscated and given to propertied laymen in an era in which the crown's annual income from land never exceeded £40,000. This loss of property brought with it a dramatic loss in political as well as economic power for ecclesial bodies.[20] At the same time secular lords were exercising the duty described in Wycliffite literature as stewardship over

---

20. Christopher Hill, *Puritanism and Revolution: Studies in Interpretation of the English Revolution of the Seventeenth Century* (New York: St. Martin's Press, 1997), 30-45. Regarding this estimate of the value of confiscated property, Hill refers to A. N. Savine, *English Monasteries on the Eve of the Dissolution* (New York: Octagon, 1974), 100. The distribution of monastic properties was not an unmixed blessing to the aristocracy. It was, however, a decided loss to the church.

against papal dominion, the term "stewardship" made significant strides in use as the English translation of *oikonomos* in Scripture.[21]

The first widespread use of the word *steward* with its modern theological connotations of ethical use of money as a gift of God seems to have occurred in Archbishop Sandys's sermons, which he hoped to have read throughout England for the edification of the newly Protestant people.[22]

> The rich man is a servant to the poor, to relieve and comfort him as he is able; for that is right, and to that end God hath made him rich, that he as a faithful steward might bestow those rich blessings upon the family and household of God. . . . This service is of us very slenderly and slackly done: Christ's impotent and miserable members are sent away not relieved. To suffer him in his members so to beg, who hath given thee all that thou hast, is horrible ingratitude. . . .[23]

Sandys cites no Scripture explicitly here. In this section on righteousness in various states of life, he uses "steward" only to refer to right administration of wealth. Since the same sermon includes a sizable diatribe against usury, a topic he addressed frequently, his comments do not indicate that he thought of *all* property as a gift of God. To which circumstances, then, does the term apply? Stewardship, here, has a flavor of class to it: Sandys uses it principally when speaking to or about the court. When, on the other hand, Sandys exhorts his regular congregation (not this time including the Queen) to generosity, he uses the term "sacrifice."[24] Perhaps it was chiefly the inheritors of great wealth that Sandys had in mind when he spoke of those whom God had made rich. Being born into these wealthy families could be taken as evidence of divine endowment. Such an office would clearly be distinct from the possibly usurious fortunes of bourgeois merchants. If this conjecture is correct, it seems that the choice

21. As a point of reference, the RSV translates *epitropos* and *oikonomos* as "steward" in the gospels, and uses "steward" for almost half of the occurrences of *oikonomos* in the epistles. The importance of vernacular English, and particularly of the English translations of the Bible, can hardly be overestimated in the larger scheme of English history. See Christopher Hill, *The English Bible and the Seventeenth-Century Revolution* (London: Allen Lane, 1993).

22. *The Sermons of Edwin Sandys*, ed. John Ayre (Cambridge: Cambridge University Press, 1862).

23. *The Sermons of Edwin Sandys*, 193.

24. *The Sermons of Edwin Sandys*, 413.

of the word "steward" has more to do with the connotation of deputized royal authority than with household management or table service. Echoing the implications of the Holbein illustration in the Great Bible, Sandys wrote of Queen Elizabeth as an overseer of the vineyard of God in England[25] and along with David, Solomon, Jehoshaphat, Asa, Ezekiel, Josiah, and Moses, as a nurse of the church,[26] although a nurse who in function as magistrate should trap the enemies of the church through punishments of death, exile, confiscation, and incarceration.[27] He refers to the Queen in a sermon delivered in her presence as ruling through God's power, as God's servant, who has been given much and of whom much will be expected and who therefore must give glory only to God, for "Thou art but a steward of his goods, which will call thee to a strict and a hard reckoning for every mite."[28]

The association of ministry, royal office, and the term "steward" appears to have been in the air in the sixteenth century. All of the earlier uses of "steward" in the New Testament passed into the King James Version, which made the significant and final addition of 1 Peter 4:10. "As euery man hath receiued the gift, euen so minister the same one to another, as good stewards of the manifold grace of God." In a sermon by Sandys on 1 Peter 4, this scriptural *oikonomoi* had been translated "disposers," in keeping with his association of stewardship with the nobles. In this sermon, Sandys discusses the call of all Christians to stewardship, but his class presumptions are intact, as he claims that St. Peter has in mind particularly "two sorts of high and principal stewards, at whose hands an especial reckoning of the graces of God will be required; the magistrate and the minister . . . whose gifts are the sword and word."[29] The attribution of stewardship to the laity trickles down from the claim that the sovereign and the nobility have stewardship over power and wealth, to defeat heretics and care for the poor. The flavor of the term in English comes rather from its connection to *seneschal* than to the lowly table servant.

The forces at work in the term are many, including at least an interest in translating the Scripture into English accessible to all and still faithful to the Greek, so that the limits of the term "stewardship" would be pushed by

25. *The Sermons of Edwin Sandys*, 57.
26. *The Sermons of Edwin Sandys*, 70, 84.
27. *The Sermons of Edwin Sandys*, 72-74.
28. *The Sermons of Edwin Sandys*, 102, 105.
29. *The Sermons of Edwin Sandys*, 401.

relating it to the New Testament's metaphorical uses of *oikonomia*. But its place in these sixteenth-century sermons and Scripture translations suggests that it also played a role in the reconfiguration of church and state in England whereby the sovereign becomes not the first of all the church's subjects, nor the leader among the ordained, but the chief steward of God, entrusted with the welfare of the nation, as overseer of commerce and protector of the faith alike, and incidentally as redistributor of large amounts of ecclesial property.

The division of labor between church and state as developed by Marsilius of Padua, Wyclif, and the sixteenth-century Anglican reformers defined boundaries of "material" and "spiritual" differently but agreed in theoretically ascribing care of the material to the state and care of the spiritual to the church.[30] The importance of the theory and its practice in the sixteenth century at least offers a context in which "stewardship" could begin to be particularly the domain of powerful and wealthy laity. It was precisely in the years in which the crown was confiscating monastic property, between 1534 and 1540, that the most conspicuous increase in the use of "steward" occurred in translations of the New Testament. This coincidence hardly establishes causal relations, much less defines them. Nevertheless, the association is pregnant. The idea of a service to the church that combined care for material goods with a deputation of royal authority had a very concrete illustration in the English Reformation.

During the course of the sixteenth century, "stewardship," with its connotations both of royal authority and of humble, material service, began neatly to combine the qualities necessary in the secular lords as they took charge of ecclesial and monastic property. Under the leadership of the king, they were to use and distribute prudently, both for the aid of the poor and to assist the clergy. This powerful office was entrusted to them by God, so that the more lofty spiritual work could be conducted without scandal or temptation by the clerics. In agreeing to take on the care of the material side of Christianity, they also had to exercise vast secular power, under the rubric of faithful service. The stewardship ethic was christened in a period that needed a name for the dubious but necessary function of

30. In the background of my thinking here is William Cavanaugh's remarkable study of this division of labor in twentieth-century Chile, *Torture and Eucharist: Theology, Politics, and the Body of Christ* (Oxford: Blackwell Publishers, 1998). I am also indebted on this point to O'Donovan, *Theology of Law and Authority.*

managing the church's wealth. The steward metaphor had, to borrow Douglas John Hall's phrase, "come of age," some four hundred years earlier than Hall estimated.[31]

In 1719, nearly 150 years after Sandys's heyday, a sermon preached at St. Paul's in London by Joseph Smith uses the term "faithful stewardship" in the context of raising funds for families of deceased members of the clergy.[32] In this sermon, God's stewardship has entirely dropped out of the scene. The author emphasizes instead the trust implied in human stewardship and the necessity of faithfulness in light of a final accounting before the God who gave gifts. For the clergy, this is faithfulness to their people, to the church, and to themselves, which is to say, to their own teaching. For the laity, this faithfulness demands the duty of respecting the clergy, of using their trade or other sort of calling according to the "just Expectations of their Almighty *Donor*," and of contributing their "*Share* of the several *Gifts* to the Honour of *Him* that gave them, and to the Publick Good of that *Body* whereof the Owners of them are *Members*. . . ." "The *Wealthy* Circumstances, which your own *Parts,* and your own *Industry,* have advanc'd most of you to, are an Evidence of your *Good Use* of the *Talents* God has given you. . . ."

Among the various trusts that Smith admonishes his listeners to use wisely, the last is "Riches."

> They open a very Large & Noble Field of Action to the several Possessors of them, to render themselves highly and universally Useful, and Beneficial to Mankind; there being scarce any *Wants,* any *Dis-*

---

31. Hall, *The Steward,* 11. I am omitting, in this account, the wealth of material on Puritanism and attitudes to the poor in the sixteenth and seventeenth centuries. In particular, the Calvinist and bourgeois rationales for opposing indiscriminate almsgiving and endowing industry and thrift with key moral significance are an important piece of the story, and might challenge the way I emphasize stewardship's function in the upper classes. The separation of economic power from the church need not be seen as purely derived from movement within the nobility. Certainly the Puritan ethic of frugality and vocation with its opposition to the idle rich, mistrust of the Catholic festal calendar, and disgust toward the idle poor contributes to the ethic of responsible stewardship. In the interest of demonstrating the mistakes of Hall's narrative, I have emphasized the role of court and crown, but this is not intended to deny that much more could be added to this tale.

32. Joseph Smith, "The Faithful Stewardship. A Sermon preach'd before the sons of the clergy, at their anniversary meeting in the Cathedral-Church of St. Paul. December 10, 1719" (London, 1720).

tresses, any *Calamities* whatever, incident to Human Nature; but what the Beneficence of the *Wealthy* may minister relief to. They may be *Eyes to the Blind,* and *Feet to the Lame, Fathers to the Fatherless,* and *Husbands to the Widows.* They have *Bread* to give to the *Hungry, Clothing* to the *Naked, Education* to the *Ignorant,* and the Subsistence of a *Trade* to poor *Orphans* in Distress.[33]

To these hearers who, in memory of the service of their fathers in the clergy, offer financial assistance to poor families of deceased clergymen, the temporal and spiritual blessings of their fathers' ministries will be "secured and perpetuated" for themselves and their family, and they will go to the final judgment with hope of eternal reward.

Here already in pre-Methodist England we see stewardship much as we encounter it in the twentieth century. It is that line of thought which takes as the normative ethical agent a layperson who owns disposable wealth and most likely is engaged in profitable business; which grounds the right use of money in the fundamental presupposition that all things belong to God but must be administered by individual humans to honor God, particularly by caring effectively for human needs; and which considers growth or increase characteristic of that effectiveness. Frequently associated with these principles is the expectation that the person who uses wealth in accord with God's intentions will be rewarded with an increase in wealth. But even where that corollary is not pronounced, stewardship's attribution of ownership to God makes renunciation and voluntary poverty unnecessary and excessive. In fact, since persons do not own goods but are given charge of them for efficient use, renunciation is a refusal to take up the moral responsibility God has given people. Effective, productive administration which cares for the needs of the poor is the righteous use of property.

John Wesley and the Seam in the Stewardship Ethic

More than any other single figure, it is John Wesley who gave the word "stewardship" its functional equivalence to money management in church language. Methodist circles had officers called "stewards of the society"

33. Smith, "The Faithful Stewardship," 28-29. Emphases in the original.

who had charge of weekly income and expenditures. In his sermons, Wesley frequently used the term "steward" to urge the faithful to put all of their wealth at the service of the true owner, God.

> Who gave you this addition to your fortune; or (to speak properly) *lent* it to you? To speak more properly still, who lodged it for a time in your hands as his stewards; informing you at the same time for what purposes he entrusted you with it? And can you *afford* to waste your Lord's goods, for every part of which you are to give an account; or to expend them in any other way than that which he hath expressly appointed? . . . You have, therefore, no more right to gratify the desire of the flesh, or the desire of the eyes, now than when you were a beggar. O no! Do not make so poor a return to your beneficent Lord! Rather, the more he entrusts you with, be so much the more careful to employ every mite as he hath appointed.[34]

In Wesley, stewardship is primarily a matter of the conscientious use of money. He calls money "that precious talent which contains the rest,"[35] associating good stewardship with the works of mercy from Matthew 25. Regardless of whether he knew Smith's sermon, he echoes it in his own when he claims that using money, "an excellent gift of God," people "may be a defence for the oppressed, a means of health to the sick, of ease to them that are in pain; it [money] may be as eyes to the blind, as feet to the lame; yea, a lifter up from the gates of death!"[36]

The repetition of this sentiment only emphasizes the importance of stewardship as a rhetoric of money. In the right economy, all needs can be reduced to a lack of money. All necessities can be bought. In fact, they may need to be bought, since those who provide the goods and services in question must earn a living somehow. Someone has to pay for them, and therefore the wealthy donor becomes the focal point of the works of mercy. Money, being nothing in itself, has the power to be all things. It is a blank, formless power, until the hands of the wealthy man decide what it will be: luxury, a store for the future, or eyes to the blind and feet to the lame. The

---

34. Sermon 126, II.5. All citations from Wesley's sermons are taken from the online collection of the General Board of Global Ministries of the United Methodist Church: http://gbgm-umc.org/UMhistory/Wesley/sermons/.

35. Sermon 51.

36. Sermon 50.

will of the disposer is determinative, and therefore the will of the disposer becomes the object of greatest concern.

> Do you that possess more than food and raiment ask: "What shall we do? Shall we throw into the sea what God hath given us?" God forbid that you should! It is an excellent talent: It may be employed much to the glory of God. Your way lies plain before your face; if you have courage, walk in it. Having *gained,* in a right sense, *all you can,* and *saved all you can;* in spite of nature, and custom, and worldly prudence, *give all you can.*[37]

Wesley was adamant that this excellent gift of God could become a curse.[38] The temptations to luxury and frivolity, to setting one's heart on wealth, and to the false prudence of storing wealth up without using it were strong. Nevertheless, the wealth itself is not to blame. It is empty, formless. Only the will of the one who uses it gives it shape, and that intention is tested and magnified as it creates out of formless money either good or evil.

The proper intention is to meet the needs of oneself, one's household, the household of faith, and as many others as possible. As a guideline for determining what to use on oneself, Wesley teaches people to consider themselves simply the first in a number of poor they must care for. Hence, a Christian should care for himself or herself as for the poor, by tending to necessities and nothing beyond. In doing so, the believer is giving all things back to God. Not only that which is given to the poor, but even that which is used frugally to maintain oneself and one's household is returned to God and can be called "sacrifice."[39] In this way, faithful stewards make a return of all they have, without reducing themselves to dependence. The kind of renunciation that would make a person a beggar is considered reprehensible, for one's first duty is to (frugal) self-preservation. As Wesley noted, admitting himself to be rich, it is not possessing wealth, but possessing more than is employed according to God's will that is the problem. In fact, the faithful must be eager and dedicated to gaining wealth, but only to meet their own needs and to distribute to others. "Gain all you can, save all you can, give all you can." The issue is, as

37. Sermon 87, II.8.
38. Sermon 126, 2.
39. Sermon 50, III.2, 5, 6.

it was with beggars, not merely possession or poverty as static states: property is that which can be given, and right appropriation is having the privilege of giving effectively. In this way renunciation and even a kind of asceticism are tied to accumulation.

The core of the rhetoric of stewardship as used by Wesley and spread far and wide in his wake is that when earned honestly (an important caveat that Wesley, to his credit, did not neglect), wealth is given by God in order to be "given back" through using it for the necessities of oneself, one's family, and all others. While Sandys may have had in mind inheritance when he spoke of wealth that was "given by God," Wesley is not talking to a court of royalty and nobles. His hearers earned their money through hard work and entrepreneurship. What does it mean to affirm this money, then, as "given" by God? The making of fortunes is not merely a matter of hard work, but is also dependent upon timing, unforeseen coincidence, and that sudden insight that might be called inspiration. Divine providence, apparently, has a hand in the creation of wealth. The idea of money earned as a gift of God may also suggest that industry and conscious labor come from God. That is, if earning money is a gift, then God is at work in human voluntary action. Labor is not merely human achievement, but is simultaneously grace. If this is what Wesley meant, then he would more precisely have had to say that work or health or action are gifts of God. Money is merely the outcome. It is the first sense, a recognition that prosperity is not predictable in relation to labor or ability but appears sometimes as a kind of sheer grace, that most accounts for the claim that wealth is a "gift."

But the language is not consistent. Wesley insists, in keeping with his predecessors, that God is "proprietor" and that nothing created can be alienated from God's possession. If this is so, and humans are only stewards, then wealth should be called not "gift" but "loan" or "trust." In fact, Wesley insists that these "gifts" are only loans. How can this be? The two terms are not compatible: gift requires a change of possession from one person to another. This "gift" is to be given back, and on analogy with the parable of the "talents" (Mt. 25:14-30) is to be given back with increase to one who will weigh the accounts and make reward and punishment contingent on its use.[40] A giver of gifts hardly comes back to "settle accounts"

---

40. The meaning of this "increase" is variously interpreted. Wyclif, Rheims (1582), and the Authorized (1611) all read "with usury." When Sandys cites the parable, he claims that the right use of talents is that "no man should seek his own things, but the things that

with the recipients later. How can God continue to be the owner of something given to a person?

The convention of affirming both "gift" and "God's ownership" in Wesley's terminology is a visible seam running through the legacy of stewardship rhetoric. The social necessity of stable property rights has to be reconciled with the Christian (recurrent, though sometimes contested) teaching that in cases of need, all things are common. Stewardship does so by conflating the two claims: only God is the true owner, yet the wealth is a gift given to a person, who therefore has an uncontestable right to dispose of it. The gift is given for the good of others and is to be used in accord with divine teaching. It is, however, a gift, not a loan. Therefore, any threat to that ownership can be rebuffed by the insistence that it was given by God. Divine law is thus invoked to strengthen property claims, in the same sentence in which those claims are nominally undermined and hedged about with stringent demands for generosity.[41]

---

make for the profiting of another" (401). Wesley, in Sermon 87, II.5, uses the parable to argue that the faithful servant must distribute his wealth rather than merely store it for himself. In fact, "steward" is not used in any translation of the scriptural text, which calls those entrusted with talents "servants."

41. Among the many unanswered questions surrounding this history is the possible relevance of Weber's thesis on the theological nature of industrious asceticism in the "spirit of capitalism." *The Protestant Ethic and the Spirit of Capitalism*, trans. Talcott Parsons (New York: Charles Scribner's Sons, 1958). Stewardship, an oddly ascetic and industrious use of wealth, might be seen as another manifestation of that same phenomenon. I have no stake in disproving Weber's position on how the anxiety characteristic of certain forms of Calvinism encouraged such industry, and I am willing to allow that his account has some explanatory power over the shift from beggars to stewards as models of economic excellence, at least among those whose faith is accurately characterized by Weber's version of Calvinism.

I do not draw on Weber because his contribution includes some mystification of its own, particularly in his assumption that the intersection of economics and theology is one of practice and ideas. Weber was interested in the intersections of the theological and economic, but he also reinforces their essential distance from each other, making the Puritan moment an intervention of a theological interest into the underlying "this-worldly" provision for appetite. See for example Max Weber, *Economy and Society: An Outline of Interpretive Sociology*, ed. Guenther Roth and Claus Wittich (Berkeley: University of California Press, 1978), especially "The Original This-Worldly Orientation of Religious and Magical Action" (399-401). Weber does not subscribe to a myth of economic origins (70), but the very fact that he displays such caution regarding economic practice while he does provide a generalized version of the emergence of religion out of "this-worldly" concerns indicates the priority. Weber's insight into the complexity of social forces prevented him from simple accounts of them. But underlying all his cautions and caveats is the notion of religion as a sec-

Stewardship in Nineteenth-Century America

The rhetoric of stewardship had already begun to be developed in the second half of the sixteenth century and had been well-articulated before it was adapted to the American context. Nevertheless, in that context it flourished as never before. Sermons, tracts, and even books on stewardship become abundant in mid-nineteenth-century Protestantism in the United States as a way for clergy to raise support for missions and for their own churches, gradually replacing demands for tithes (which had been enforced by the civil government) and pew rents. This period, called by some "the great stewardship awakening," has been pinpointed in several works on stewardship as the emergence of the modern use of the term.[42] Its earlier development already shows stewardship as a useful language for bringing together stability in property rights, a recognition of God's prior claim on wealth, the necessity of effective use of wealth, and the formless neutrality of money as the center of material life in modern society. If the rhetoric of stewardship was already developed in England, why is it typically considered a contribution of U.S. American churches?

Luther P. Powell claims that although

> it would be blind provincialism to imply that stewardship was a movement identified with, or characteristic of, American churches . . . [and] presumptuous to assert that the principles of stewardship are products of the nineteenth and twentieth centuries, . . . there has been a definite movement of Christian stewardship in the last one hundred and fifty years and the churches in America have shared in it.[43]

---

ondary interpretive layer (the other-worldly) over the primary necessary layer (the inner-worldly). The present discussion of stewardship, by contrast, does not exemplify theological influence on economics, but demonstrates how the financial and the theological are not distinct forces contending on turf neutral toward each, an other-worldly demand on an inner-worldly reality. Rather, church and crown are two contending proprietors, crossed in complex ways by various economic practices and theological habits. The important question, which I cannot answer here, is whether the idea of a sphere of economics and politics that could theoretically function independently of theological truth is itself a peculiar theological conviction arising out of a contingent political and intellectual history.

42. Hall, *The Steward;* George Salstrand, *The Story of Stewardship in the United States of America* (Grand Rapids: Baker, 1956); and Luther P. Powell, *Money and the Church* (New York: Association Press, 1962) all agree on this point.

43. Luther P. Powell, "Stewardship in the History of the Christian Church," in

In spite of this caveat, Powell does not elaborate on other historical forces at work in establishing the principles of stewardship. Appeals to stewardship and reliance on voluntary contributions are, in his narration, characteristic of the primitive church tradition and of those communities that embrace separation of church and state in the United States. Powell tells the story of church donations under the rhetoric of stewardship as a rebirth of pristine Christianity through the witness of disestablished Protestant churches in the U.S. Nevertheless, his study provides a fascinating survey of church tactics for raising money in the United States, through government-enforced tithes, pew rents, church farms, and so on.

George Salstrand's account concurs in general that stewardship is a contribution of American Protestant churches, which developed it as a result of disestablishment. Salstrand's work is intentionally limited to the history of churches in the United States, a history which he treats in admirable detail, but without any reference to its antecedents. Even more than Powell, Salstrand accepts stewardship language as a natural expression of a Christian's responsibility to adhere to the will of God, particularly through financial generosity. Salstrand's particular read of the development of stewardship, however, is its close affiliation with missionary efforts.

> Missions and stewardship are partners. One cannot be missionary minded without thinking of life and possessions in terms of stewardship. On the other hand when a person embraces the tenets of stewardship he will likewise develop concern for the needs of a dying world and see the duty of investment to meet that need if at all possible.[44]

Salstrand recounts many stories of ministers and businessmen who increased their giving as they increased their wealth, contributing large

---

Thompson, *Stewardship in Contemporary Theology* (New York: Association Press, 1960). The fact that Powell's little book was cited by Hall as the most recent work on the history of stewardship itself demonstrates Hall's point that we gravely need a serious history of stewardship. Powell's book, while useful for tracing means of support of the churches in the United States, is sorely inadequate. He claims that the medieval church, or even the patristic church, distorted the gospel by emphasizing merit and selling indulgences, and Protestantism has restored the original voluntary character to the church, particularly in the development of the separation of church and state in the United States. Stewardship, as he sees it, is the appropriately voluntary but serious requirement of Christians to support their churches, missions, and benevolent societies.

44. Salstrand, *The Story of Stewardship*, 25.

sums and sometimes large portions of their income or savings to churches and missionary work. Wesley's appeal for Christians to know that not one penny should be wasted on oneself continued to have an effect on some people, who burned with a passion for good works, fueled particularly by the great preachers of the 1840s and 1850s, Horace Bushnell, Abel Stevens, Lyman Abbot, and Josiah Strong (author of the comment, "It is the duty of some men to make a great deal of money"). Their words inspired what Salstrand calls "the great stewardship awakening."

This "awakening" grew on one hand out of the churches' need for income, both to support domestic ministry and to sponsor missionary work. But it was also influenced by a line of thought exemplified by Pharcellus Church in his *Philosophy of Benevolence*.[45] While maintaining the moral importance of indiscriminate giving and the call of Christian societies to accept precarity and continual dependence on the willing donations of pious people,[46] Church argues in favor of concentrating donations into larger quantities to take on the great ventures that modern science is making increasingly possible with the facilitation of travel around the world. The "light of the knowledge of the glory of God will fill all lands," as the combined donations of Christians make possible the spread of the faith.

> Yea, what is more, the establishment of civilization within the present precincts of barbarism, will open new marts of trade, and so will pour back into the coffers of the nation from which the influence emanated, an amount perhaps more than equal to what she sent abroad upon this errand of mercy. Who can calculate the extent of commerce that would be thrown open to human enterprise, by overspreading Africa, for instance, with the institutions of civilization? Who can estimate the increase of those articles of trade for which we now depend upon nations in a state of nature, or a state little better, if those nations were to feel the impetus which a pure Christianity gives to the human mind?[47]

45. Pharcellus Church, *Philosophy of Benevolence* (New York: Leavitt, 1836).

46. Church, *Philosophy of Benevolence*, 256 and 336-45. Note that Church encourages Christian organizations not to expect security and independence, but to take risks boldly. Toward individuals, however, he is clear that one's first duty is to avoid becoming dependent on others.

47. Church, *Philosophy of Benevolence*, 321-22.

The right use of riches is "the use by which they will be made instruments of the greatest good to their owners and to general society."[48] Good business, the march of civilization, and missionary efforts mutually reinforce one another when property is used in accord with God's will, and the judicious investment in projects featuring economy of scale and offering the hope of profit is therefore simply part of the work of God. All things do work together for the good of those who love God, after all. In this way, in spite of the righteousness of indiscriminate giving, the wise steward (as opposed to those who are improvident and reckless) will give rather to common funds for large projects than, for example, to beggars. The steward will give systematically, regularly, not in such a way to reduce him or herself to dependence, but aggressively funding the reign of God. Mind will at last overcome matter by putting it to right use instead of either being seduced by it or resorting to monastic flight from it.[49] True spiritual poverty is fully compatible with sound investment policies.

Because this period has been documented by Powell and Salstrand, we can leave it in their hands, pausing only to note a few highlights. First, it is in these American writings that the narrative of the generous man who grew more wealthy after he made a commitment to give generously assumes its mythic importance. The notion that those who give will be given more becomes a conspicuous characteristic. Second, it is also in these writings that the caveat found so often in both Wesley and Sandys, that the wealth must be gained justly, fades from the scene. This is not to say that the authors of this period were necessarily unscrupulous about how a Christian made a fortune. The difference seems to be that they were not wary of the danger that those who were rich had perhaps become so through unjust means. Filthy lucre is a forgotten category among most Christians, and the enthusiasm of the age for grand projects, particularly grand projects that brought the "uncivilized" into contact with Christian (i.e., European) civilization, distracted people from concern for just acquisition.[50] Furthermore, writers of the era hold a strong account of the right

---

48. Church, *Philosophy of Benevolence*, v.

49. Although Church echoes Malthus on this point, he defers to Say in economic analysis. It is interesting to note that contrary to Hall's claim that "hellenistic spiritualization" is the opponent of the more "earthy, Hebraic" idea of stewardship, a number of proponents of stewardship have been strong advocates of a spiritualized Christianity.

50. This history has been traced most recently by Odd Langholm in *The Merchant in the Confessional: Trade and Price in the Pre-Reformation Penitential Handbooks* (Leiden: Brill,

to private property and unquestioningly take the use of that property to create more wealth as a social good, particularly when the increase is used to alleviate poverty and spread the gospel.[51] The caution that one is only a steward of wealth *gained in just ways* drops out of play.

Slavery and Right Use of Wealth

That apparent lack of concern about the justice preceding stewardship has a particularly grim history in the Christianity of the American Confederacy. For arguments about the Christian use of property in the United States in the nineteenth century, there exists a vast literature contemporary with the stewardship awakening which has been overlooked in existing treatments of the history of "stewardship": defenses of slaveholding. How did Christian slaveholders think about rightful ownership of slaves?

The proslavery arguments of the Confederacy were not peculiar to that society, having a long history in slave-owning cultures. Nor was racism per se the constant core of such arguments.[52] Studies of proslavery writings find that the first wave of proslavery advocates for the South was composed more of clergy born in New England, New York, New Jersey, and Pennsylvania, with a substantial contribution from some born in Europe, than of those from the South. Many of these writers were educated at Yale and what later became Princeton. An oversupply of Congregational clergy in New England led to the migration of educated and ambitious proslavery clergymen to the South. These apologists for slavery in the early nineteenth century share the view that just slavery is an instrument of social ordering. They need only condemn its abuses and commend its philanthropic possibilities. Ownership of slaves has been known in all societies and is assumed in Scripture, and therefore it is not inherently unjust, they argued. A member of the Anglican Society for the Propagation of the Gospel, Thomas Thompson, wrote in 1772, that absolute freedom could not exist in a law-governed society, and various degrees of bondage clearly existed for the common good. Thompson did not argue explicitly on racist

---

2003), who emphasizes the significance of changing notions of consent within theological discussions, rather than the marginalization of theological discussions.

51. Church, *Philosophy of Benevolence*, 89.

52. Larry E. Tise, *Proslavery: A History of the Defense of Slavery in America, 1701-1840* (Athens: The University of Georgia Press, 1987).

grounds, but justified slave trade as "conducted upon true mercantile principles." Slavery, he wrote, is necessary for social order and for business, and therefore, "not contrary to the law of nature."[53]

While some slave owners treated their slaves badly, so the typical argument ran, such abuse was not itself evidence that slavery itself was wrong. Owners might just as well have treated their slaves excellently, raising them out of their barbarity, caring for them more personally than capitalists ever did their wage laborers, and instructing them in Christianity. George Fitzhugh makes the case in characteristically flamboyant terms in *Cannibals All! Or Slaves without Masters.*

> It is said in Scripture, that it is harder for a rich man to enter the kingdom of heaven than for a camel to pass through the eye of a needle. We are no theologian; but do know from history and observation that wealthy men who are sincere and devout Christians in free society, feel at a loss what to do with their wealth, so as not to make it an instrument of oppression and wrong. Capital and skill are powers exercised almost always to oppress labor. If you endow colleges, you rear up cunning, voracious exploitators to devour the poor. If you give it to tradesmen or landowners, 'tis still an additional instrument, always employed to oppress laborers. If you give it to the really needy, you too often encourage idleness, and increase the burdens of the working poor who support everybody. We cannot possibly see but one safe way to invest wealth, and that is to buy slaves with it, whose conduct you can control, and be sure that your charity is not misapplied, and mischievous.[54]

In fact, Fitzhugh argues in this book that the English problems with mendicancy are the result of freeing slaves, who do not know how to use their freedom and become hordes of deceptive slackers.

Fitzhugh was given to particularly dramatic images of the vice of the North, but the argument that slavery is philanthropy is hardly unique to him. As early as 1773, Richard Nisbet, a West Indian living in Philadelphia, argued not only that slaveholding but that the slave *trade* was a "generous disinterested exertion of benevolence and philanthropy, which has been

53. Tise, *Proslavery,* 27-28.
54. George Fitzhugh, *Cannibals All! Or Slaves without Masters,* ed. C. Vann Woodward (Cambridge, Mass.: The Belknap Press of Harvard University Press, 1960), 219.

the principal means of heaping wealth and honours on Europeans and Americans, and [of] rescuing many millions of Africans, *as brands from a fire,* and even compelling them to the enjoyment of a more refined state of happiness, than the partiality of fate has assigned them in their native state."[55] And as the slave trade was found to be just and even philanthropic, some writers argued that when a Christian master kept slaves and Christianized them, his efforts would be rewarded with great material profit. The slaves would actually become better slaves, more obedient and more industrious.[56] The profitable business was Christian, and Christianity would prove to be profitable business.

Yet proslavery writers did not deny that slavery involved evils, particularly in the wake of the Revolution and its enthusiasm for human liberty. They argued rather that slavery offered certain goods and that its moral disadvantages were less than those of barbarism, wage labor, an egalitarian society, the demise of the southern economy, or the release of uncivilized and unintelligent blacks. One leading advocate of slavery as a positive good wrote that "the condition of our whole existence is but to struggle with evils — to compare them — to choose between them, and so far as we can, to mitigate them."[57]

As the nineteenth century wore on, faced with much evidence of "abuses" and growing recognition that Christianizing slaves produced not more obedience but greater danger for the masters, the slaveholding South knew little dissent over the permissibility of holding slaves, but substantial argument around what constituted rightful slaveholding.[58] Dominion over

---

55. Cited in Tise, *Proslavery,* 29.

56. Morgan Godwyn in 1680, Cotton Mather, and Stephen Hales in 1734. Tise, *Proslavery,* 19-20.

57. William Harper, cited in Tise, *Proslavery,* 36. This is a characteristic move of economic thought, to say that we are always choosing among evils. But it is not an opportunity-cost account, such as we find in the "proportionalists."

58. Eugene Genovese, *A Consuming Fire: The Fall of the Confederacy in the Mind of the White Christian South* (Athens: The University of Georgia Press, 1998). In post-Revolutionary thought, the slave-trade, however, was subject to greater condemnation. Many religious figures in this period treated slavery as an evil to be opposed, but only to be eliminated gradually, given its importance in the economy and the supposedly still-barbarian state of enslaved Africans. Catholic views on this matter have received new attention within John McGreevy's study *Catholicism and American Freedom: A History* (New York: W. W. Norton & Company, 2003). McGreevy's nuanced history indicates that widespread Catholic opposition to the abolition movement was due rather less to racism or even competition among laboring classes

slaves was commonly described as a "trust" given by God which could be re-voked if abused. While the term "stewardship" was not commonly used, the logic by which God's possession generates a defense of civil property was.

As is characteristic of this strand of stewardship thinking, the prior questions about the justice of the possession and the means of acquisi-tion were by now excluded. Genovese documents, however, a substantial theological argument conducted over the right use of this trust. In par-ticular, the sanctity of slave family bonds, the necessity of literacy for the Christianizing of slaves, and the viciousness of sexual abuse of slave women were frequent topics of sermons and church statements. Since the South claimed moral superiority over the North precisely on the grounds that slaves and masters were connected by such bonds that the cold use of labor as a commodity characteristic of Northern capitalism was impossible in the paternalistic, Christian economy of the South, these calls from clergy for masters to respect the families, souls, and chastity of their slaves had to be taken seriously. To dismiss them would be to admit that the slaves were the commodities proslavery rhetoric de-clared them not to be.

This is not to say that the appeals succeeded in the way their authors intended. Reform, as they imagined it, was impossible. Their success was in revealing the fallacy of the premise: in fact, slaves *were* commodities. Masters could not teach slaves to read and could not place family ties ahead of economic need while remaining competitive. Preachers argued that as long as slaves were treated as persons, the owner was God's deputy acting in the necessary markets of the world. But slaves could not be treated as persons and remain at the same time slaves. What the "sacred trust" rhetoric masked, the demands of some clergy on their Christian congregations threatened to reveal.

In the aftermath of the war, one of the most prestigious theologians of the Confederacy, whose systematic theology remained in use well into the twentieth century, spoke revealingly of the importance of recognizing God's ownership, particularly in a culture of accumulated and inherited wealth. When Robert Dabney in his *Lectures in Systematic Theology* dis-

---

than to the association of abolitionism with liberal individualism, and therefore with anti-Catholicism. Many Catholics subscribed to versions of the argument that slavery was not sig-nificantly more reprehensible than the misery of wage labor, not because they wanted to de-fend the privilege of slaveholders, but because they maintained the importance of hierarchi-cal ordering within a truly free society.

cusses the moral right of possession, he rejects labor as the basis, since many have a "perfect" right to that for which they have not labored.

> Now the truth is, that there is but one perfect source for a right of property, creation out of nothing; and consequently, but one natural proprietor, God the Maker. The only rational solution of the existence of a right of property in man is also the scriptural one, that contained in the second and ninth chapters of Genesis, God's gift of the world and its contents to man, as His tenant. Our individual interests in the gift are, then, based on the Golden Rule, and properly regulated in detail by the laws of civil society. This position is vital to our security. For on any lower theory of right, an invasion of property may be plausibly justified whenever the majority persuade themselves that it is most politic.[59]

Dabney explicitly states that only the claim of God's true ownership ensures an undisturbed right of possession for the tenants. The Golden Rule (reciprocity) and civil laws order the uses of wealth, but ownership itself is only made inviolable through the gift of God. It follows, therefore, that if God has given charge of goods to certain people, then those people have both the right and duty to maintain that wealth. Renunciation is impious.

Humility's New Home

The evolution of stewardship from referring to God's care for humans; to the authority of the nobility over the church's property; thence the responsibility of the prosperous Christian is not in itself evidence that claims made in the name of stewardship are always evil, and certainly it is not evidence that the term somehow itself is to blame. As we saw, advocates of slavery rarely used the term "stewardship," but freely perpetuated the worst versions of its subtle duplicity. The story of this term is rather a cautionary tale about the danger of theological vocabulary run amok. Without a defining grammar which binds a notion such as God's ownership to a larger set of specific goods and model practices, the claim that wealth is a gift loses contact with the scriptural cautions which claim wealth is a danger

59. Robert L. Dabney, *Lectures in Systematic Theology* (Grand Rapids: Zondervan, 1972), 415-16.

97

and the discernment of a community that even in the Confederate south recognized that persons could not be commodities.

Christianity does have room for right uses of wealth. That matter has been resolved several times in Christian history, as in debate with Pelagianism and with the apostolic poverty movements. The central problem with these teachings on stewardship is not that they say one may innocently possess goods but that they maintain that philanthropic use of wealth is properly the *center* of Christian economic ethics, and in doing so elide a number of other issues. The momentum of the history of stewardship shifts the center of gravity within economic ethics, the daily disciplines and language of preaching, toward the presumptions that the key moral agent, the model disciple, has disposable wealth and that existing property rights are underwritten by God. Holders of property are not only more numerous than the voluntarily poor, but are the standard in relation to which the poor will be understood. The order of virtues seen in *Blanquerna* has shifted: it is no longer that certain wealthy people can participate in the virtue of the poor through almsgiving or secret asceticism, but that even the poor can participate in the virtue of the wealthy through prudent use of their modest means. The nature of rights is no longer the ground of the moral contest; now the question is only how to make use of whatever rights the civil law recognizes.

The effect of this shift in the center of gravity is visible around the topic of humility. That one must be humble is not questioned at any point in this history. But the material specification of excellent humility changes. The humility associated with obscurity, penance, contemplation, the crucified Christ, and dependence gives way to the humility of a successful owner who disciplines his uses of wealth in order to provide for the needs of others. Subject to God's dominion rather than that of the pope or any mere human authority, the good steward accepts the political and economic order in which he finds himself as the backdrop against which he works out his salvation. His possessions are a gift from God, whatever the means of delivery in the economic realm. In Charles Taylor's terms, his salvation is a matter of adverbs: *how* he employs his property, rather than where it came from or what it is.[60] The prosperous businessman maintains a spiritual poverty which may be a stringent discipline and may produce

<hr>

60. Charles Taylor, *Sources of the Self: The Making of the Modern Identity* (Cambridge, Mass.: Harvard University Press, 1989), 211-33.

financial support for many good works. But the notion that true economic virtue, and in the wayfarer's sense, true economic power, belong to Christ's poor is incompatible with the steward's ethic.

Nevertheless, stewardship has been popular and, in a sense, useful language in Christian communities. As compared with the disturbing excesses of beggarly humility, the humility of the steward is cautious and practical. It requires no disruption of social structures, endows no romantic spiritual excellence on the poor, leaves the order of property rights largely uncontested, and yet makes room within that order for a critique of selfishness, for a stern demand for attention to the needs of others, for an obligation to generosity. The language of "sacred trust" among slaveholders proved double-edged, requiring of those authorized owners that they behave in ways finally incompatible with having property rights over a person. Furthermore, the relative absence of questions about how money is earned in modern stewardship discourse is a function of larger changes in Christian teaching. Christianity's widespread inability to maintain its teaching about usury and the just price within a society characterized by market relations meant that ethical guides were less likely to talk of "filthy lucre" and tended to shift their attention to other matters. Knowing their responsibilities and limitations, the prosperous were to be humble through generosity. This shift in attention is tied into and draws on the use of stewardship as authorization of lay power and judgment in matters of wealth, without the interference of church leaders.

This story of how moral authority shifted from beggars to stewards within ecclesial language leaves us with insight into only half of the contemporary problem, however. We turn now to the work of classical economists, whose accounts describe an economic order no longer plagued with the problem of economic humility.

CHAPTER FOUR

The Insolence of Human Wretchedness

Without explicitly denigrating voluntary poverty, even by exalting it in a limited sense, the stewardship ethic offers a kind of humility free from the complications of dependence and the social confusion bred by excellent lowliness. "Spiritual" poverty takes pride of position, especially when combined with possession of large enough amounts of material wealth to produce effective reductions in human suffering. Still, that tale is only one contribution to the modern stewardship ethic, and at least one other influence bears investigation. It is one thing to make the benevolence of the prosperous businessman the normative center of one's ethic; it is quite another to remove the beggar from that ethic altogether. Complaints that beggars lied or were dangerous to the morals and safety of a community are no modern invention, but modern Europe, in its efforts to create prosperous, healthy, and rationally centralized nations, threw new and enlightened energy into the quest for a "final solution to the beggar problem." Classical economic system-making wrote beggars out of the rational society, and the enclosure movement attempted to purge them from the body social. Yet even in the midst of the efforts, crowds acclaimed another Christian pilgrim and beggar as a saint and the very image of Christ.

Smith and the Market for Sympathy

Rational thought about property and exchange long predates the work of Adam Smith. But Smith serves as the landmark thinker in the emergence of economic analysis because of his role in developing a rational system that accounts for all property relations through the model of negotiation between strangers.[1] In the context of lectures on the history of astronomy, Smith explained that systems are made to soothe the restless imagination, but this comment rather underplays the power of a persuasive system.[2] As the imagination accepts its account, the all-encompassing system actually reshapes the world it narrates, and Smith's elegant system is a case in point. As a basic building block, that system depends on predictable exchange between strangers, and beggars disrupt that venture. Beggars had to be subsumed under the logic of exchange, and in both the material and moral sense, Smith was up to the challenge.

The so-called "Adam Smith problem" of relating *The Theory of Moral Sentiments* (hereafter TMS), which pivots around the notion of "sympathy," to the *Wealth of Nations* (hereafter WN), which often uses competition as the organizing principle of human relations, has been demonstrated to be based on poor readings of both works.[3] The notion of sympathy in TMS is by no means opposed to a sort of egoism in the competition of WN. On the contrary, sympathy describes the real nature of human egoism, and more importantly, demonstrates how humans can be noble and society robust even though a certain kind of egoism is intrinsic to human nature.

Sympathy, in Smith's work, names that function of human psychol-

1. Smith was, of course, not an economist but a philosopher in the broad antique sense, and what came to be called political economy was originally part of Smith's lectures in moral philosophy, under the heading of jurisprudence. Joseph Cropsey has spoken of the "deflection" of economics away from political philosophy in Smith's work, as Smith's commitment to common sense over rarified philosophy led him to bring the resources of philosophy to bear on pragmatic matters.

2. Ian Simpson Ross, *The Life of Adam Smith* (Oxford: Clarendon Press, 1995), xix.

3. See, e.g., Raphael and Macfie's introduction to *The Theory of Moral Sentiments*, ed. D. D. Raphael and A. L. Macfie (Oxford: Clarendon Press, 1976), which claims that the "so-called 'Adam Smith problem' was a pseudo-problem based on ignorance and misunderstanding" (20). Peter Minowitz, in *Profits, Priests, and Princes: Adam Smith's Emancipation of Economics from Politics and Religion* (Stanford: Stanford University Press, 1993) insists that Smith's work is full of contradictions, not only between TMS and WN but within each work. Most notably, Minowitz demonstrates that TMS and WN differ markedly in their rhetoric about God and religion. While it does appear that TMS is happily deistic while WN is in places decidedly atheistic, the "sympathy" of TMS is not at all contradictory of the competition assumed throughout WN. Both are, I'll argue, manifestations of Smith's focus on negotiation among strangers as the normal ground of life.

ogy by which I imaginatively, even against my will, enter into other people's situations, including the situation of observing me. I cannot actually feel another's feeling because my sensations are sealed within my own body. But I am profoundly affected by other people's feelings in my imagination. This sympathy is therefore the source of both compassion (as I imagine another's feelings) and vanity (as I imagine another looking at me). A man may sympathize, Smith argued, with a woman in labor, by imagining how she feels.[4] But her pain is for him always only imaginary, as it is impossible for his body ever to know it. He is self-enclosed, even as that enclosed self is deeply moved by its imagination of the woman's sensations.

Sympathy means that we are each alone, and that we are never solitary. Even my moral knowledge of myself is logically secondary to my observation of and sympathy with others. Smith imagined that raised in isolation from others, a human would only notice and care for "the objects of his passions, the external bodies which either pleased or hurt him."[5] He would not notice his own sentiments as either worthy or despicable any more than he would notice the attractiveness of his nose. Only when he comes into some society and begins to judge others through his power of imagining himself in their places would he realize that others do the same to him. At this moment, he would learn to see himself through their eyes and to judge his own actions. Or rather, his innate sympathy with others leads him to see himself from the viewpoint of an imagined impartial spectator. Moral discernment is the process of negotiating between his feelings and the way an idealized informed stranger would see him. This "outside" or impartial view causes him to moderate the expression of feelings and to act in a way others could approve. Achieving this approval, a harmony in sentiments, is the goal of human relations.

Society is in this way absolutely necessary to mature morality in Smith, but it is a society of mirrors in which I am reflected again and again in the faces and situations of others. I depend entirely upon others, but they can only be different versions of myself, as reflected to me in the mirror my sympathy with them creates. Smith hoped to provide a rich enough account of sympathy to avoid a self-enclosed moral epistemology, but ultimately sympathy only makes my isolation more complex and more ines-

4. TMS, VII.iii.i.4.

5. TMS, III.i.1.3. Since Smith uses "he," I will retain his usage. It is not surprising, but worthy of note, that the impartial spectator was assumed to be male.

capable. In this peculiar social world our human existence is constituted by our social relations, and yet we can never touch each other.

Some people, however, seem to think that they can, in fact, share each other's feelings. Lovers become a particularly problematic case.[6] Observers can sympathize with the generality "being in love," but in its particular extravagant attachment to one person, it often appears disproportionate or even ridiculous. Knowing this, the lovers' impartial vision may still cause them to control the expression of their love in front of other people. But between the two themselves, common feeling is so strong that no impartial view intrudes. While typically sympathy creates a need to consider the particular other as well as the imagined impartial view, between lovers sympathy is so complete that it destroys rather than creates impartiality. I judge my lover without any distance between us. When I see myself in the mirror of my lover, I do not gain in impartiality toward myself. The empty space between people in which the impartial spectator stands is absent between lovers.

This intimacy allows people not to seek recourse in impartiality to govern their dealings with each other. The structure of being in love is the same as fanaticism. According to one commentator on Smith, "Love that cancels the need for sympathy of a spectator is inherently dangerous politically, for it privileges the perspective of the actor over that of the spectator and thereby loses perspective altogether."[7] Still, romance can be taken lightly, as a *private* matter which does not generally threaten any serious harm.[8] But the faculty of imaginatively entering into the feelings and ideas of others is necessary not only for self-control, but also for rational argument. Those who lack or fail to have recourse to the impartial spectator actually become dangerous in some cases, as their inability to consider the position of others from an outside view leaves violence as the most likely route for resolving conflict. Smith, with an eye perhaps on Jacobite battles and the bitter struggles within the Church of Scotland, called this phenomenon "fanaticism." If the self is in fact enclosed and isolated from others, then without something like this faculty of sympathy we are left with a self unintelligible to and unconcerned with others, a self unwilling

6. TMS, I.ii.2.1.

7. Charles L. Griswold, *Adam Smith and the Virtues of the Enlightenment* (Cambridge: Cambridge University Press, 1999), 151.

8. As far as I know, Smith did not consider the dangers of domestic violence.

to consider compromise.[9] Fanatics and lovers (as well as philosophers, in certain respects)[10] fail to recognize their own limits and therefore to participate morally in rational society.

Still, Smith did not agree that these fanatical or merely tedious people had actually breached their isolation. Thinking that they have overcome the need for impartiality is their error. Smith was so committed to the principle of individual self-enclosure that he found it strange that people would mourn the falling of a king even more than they mourn the damage his fall may bring to them.[11] He explains this peculiar behavior as a function of sympathy: the king's misfortune seems worse because he was in the state to which all aspire, a state of universal admiration. The destruction of such a delightful state seems to the observer even more bitter than the observer's own ongoing difficulties, and therefore the onlookers grieve for the king. Smith completely ignored the more plausible explanation, that of the king's corporate personality. When a king falls, a nation is shamed, if not also ransacked and enslaved. The king's misfortune touches other people not only through imaginary sympathy, but also through a shared political body. For Smith, this account of the king was unimaginable, requiring as it does a degree of shared selfhood his system excludes.

Beggars represent the same kind of challenge to Smith's world of mirrors. Although Smith disapproved of prejudice against the poor, he understood it to be necessary for the maintenance of order in society and at any rate almost universal.[12] "We despise a beggar; and though his importunities may extort an alms from us, he is scarce ever the object of any serious commiseration."[13] The wealthy and powerful achieve the highest happiness at which everyone aims — to be looked upon with admiration. This sympathetic gaze guarantees itself. As they seem to be happy, people admire them and as they are admired, they seem to be happy. When forced to look on the poor, by contrast, "The fortunate and the proud wonder at the insolence of human wretchedness, that it should dare to present itself be-

---

9. TMS, III.i.3.43. Writing of those engaged in "faction and fanaticism," Smith claims that for such people, an impartial spectator "scarce exists any where in the universe."

10. TMS, I.ii.2.6.

11. TMS, I.iii.2.3-6, especially the description of the parade of the defeated king of Macedon in #6.

12. In fact, this section on the corruption of the moral sentiments was only added in the sixth edition.

13. TMS, III.i.3.18.

fore them, and with the loathsome aspect of its misery presume to disturb the serenity of their happiness."[14] People despise beggars because they do not want to have to feel any version of their sensations, as sympathy will tend to make them do. Beggars are inevitably guilty of implicating uninvolved others in their unhappiness. In contrast with the stiff-lipped gentleman in straitened circumstances who does not show any regard for his poverty, beggars display their suffering with the intent to cause others to share in it. In this they fail both to show a noble disregard for material comforts and to limit their expressions of suffering to that with which a passerby could reasonably be expected to sympathize. The beggar becomes a classic example of moral weakness.

This case becomes the occasion for a study in the limits of sympathy. Smith commented on certain philosophers who teach people to "feel for others as we naturally feel for ourselves. . . . [These] are those whining and melancholy moralists, who are perpetually reproaching us with our happiness, while so many of our brethren are in misery."[15] Smith found this approach absurd and impossible, and its practice less admirable than heroic disregard for the immediacy of one's own suffering. We inevitably do feel some of a beggar's misery, but we cannot enter into it as we do our own feelings. Sympathy will not extend so far. Beggars who actively appeal for our compassion and those moralists who urge others to have compassion must understand that the only noble solution to the problem of our distance from each other's suffering is for poor persons to conceal their pain so that it is less of an imposition on others, while the rich generously extend themselves, freely rather than under the influence of manipulated sympathy.

Instead of seeking this concord of sentiments, the beggar rouses the sympathy of passersby even beyond the sympathy they would willingly give. "Persons of delicate fibres and a weak constitution of body complain, that in looking on the sores and ulcers which are exposed by beggars in the streets, they are apt to feel an itching or uneasy sensation in the correspondent part of their own bodies."[16] These beggars strive to cause sufficient discomfort in observers that they will give alms to relieve their own sympathetic suffering. Tugging on the cords of sympathy, the beggar can drag the attention of the "weak" to him- or herself. The beggar acts as though the

14. TMS, I.iii.2.1.
15. TMS, III.i.3.9.
16. TMS, I.i.1.3.

passerby should share in the hunger and cold of beggary, as though fellow-feeling should exceed what sympathy can negotiate. "Nothing is so mortifying as to be obliged to expose our distress to the view of the public, and to feel, that though our situation is open to the eyes of all mankind, no mortal conceives for us the half of what we suffer."[17] Beggars, in effect, tackle this problem proactively, working on helping other mortals conceive of their suffering, magnifying it if necessary in order to make them conceive at least half of it. Rather than being ashamed, they use sympathy to control others. It is a kind of extortion. At best, beggars who approach potential donors with the frankness of lovers, assuming commonality rather than independence, will be in Smith's system the kindred of lovers and fanatics. Morally disabled, they lack the ability to see their own situation in proper perspective and therefore posit an impossible relationship with others.[18]

Beggars, to sum up, are morally disordered because they do not attempt to "see" rightly by entering into an impartial perspective between themselves and others; are suspected of weakness and cowardice for not controlling their display of suffering; and may subscribe to the absurd proposition that happy people can and should feel the sorrow of persons outside their family and friends. These conclusions are not the result of an evidently monstrous proposition. Nor are they mere rationalization to avoid the responsibility to provide for others. Smith made generous gifts out of his own wealth, and his aim appears to have been the fostering of virtue, including beneficence. His own writing demonstrates his distaste for the machinations of the powerful against the weak.[19] He hoped by

---

17. TMS, I.iii.2.1.

18. TMS, III.i.3.1-3.

19. In his analysis of the combinations of masters and workers, for example, although he trusts the negotiations of self-interest to keep the workers from starving, he allows that it is naïve not to think that owners are continually working together to keep wages low. Workers' combinations, though always more controversial, may arise from the desperation of those who know they must "starve, or frighten their masters into an immediate compliance with their demands" (WN, I.viii.13). He held the view, in fact, that an increase in wages was no disadvantage economically. "No society can surely be flourishing and happy, of which the far greater part of the members are poor and miserable. It is but equity, besides, that they who feed, cloath, and lodge the whole body of the people, should have such a share of the produce of their own labour as to be themselves tolerably well fed, cloathed, and lodged" (WN, I.viii.36). Citations are from *An Inquiry into the Nature and Causes of the Wealth of Nations*, ed. R. H. Campbell and A. S. Skinner, textual ed. W. B. Todd (Indianapolis: Liberty Classics, 1981).

placing the stranger at the heart of his moral theory to limit selfishness and the narrowness of self-interest and to limit violence. Nevertheless, these conclusions about dependent poverty merely follow from his system of morality as the negotiation of approval or disapproval of uninvolved others, internalized in such a way as to become approval or disapproval of an impartial spectator. The result of the theory is to make strangerliness normative and frank admission of need a violation or perversion of the moral faculty.

This world of negotiation among strangers is not only a matter of the sentiments. "The propensity to truck, barter, and exchange" in WN is an extension of the same system of human relations.[20]

> Nobody but a beggar chuses to depend chiefly upon the benevolence of his fellow-citizens. Even a beggar does not depend on it entirely. The charity of a well-disposed people, indeed supplies him with the whole fund of his subsistence. But though this principle ultimately provides him with all the necessaries of life which he has occasion for, it neither does nor can provide him with them as he has occasion for them. The greater part of his occasional wants are supplied in the same manner as those of other people, by treaty, by barter, and by purchase. With the money which one man gives him he purchases food. The old cloaths which another bestows upon him he exchanges for other old cloaths which suit him better, or for lodging, or for food, or for money, with which he can buy either food, cloaths or lodging, as he has occasion.[21]

"Even a beggar. . . ." To be a beggar is by definition not to depend on exchange, but to wait for gifts which one cannot control through a claim of rights. As soon as he asserted negotiated exchange among strangers as fundamental to human systems, therefore, Smith had to respond to the obvious exception to his rule, begging and almsgiving. His response to the problem is telling: the beggar as such does not engage in exchange, but no one — he asserts — is merely a beggar. In truth, the beggar, materially as well as psychologically, trucks and barters along with the rest. What beggars want to achieve by their labor is to accumulate stock, and they do with

---

20. Smith associated this propensity with human speech in WN, I.ii.2. He did not elaborate, but it appears that he understood speech as the means through which the isolated self carries on its negotiations.

21. WN, I.ii.2.

their stock the same thing anyone else does: exchange it for better. The beggar "chuses" to do this, a turn of phrase which indicates that the beggar, out of various options open to him, found this to be the most preferable way to accumulate exchangeable stock. This decision is peculiar, but not unintelligible. Begging is just another variation on economic behavior, revealing by that "*even* a beggar . . ." that his attempt is to eliminate any possible exceptions to his account of a world defined by exchange.

Beggars engage in trade, and they can be objects of trade. Smith mentions an account in which an "Arabian chief" sat to eat in "a town where he had come to sell his cattle, and invited all passengers, even common beggars, to sit with him and partake of his banquet."[22] Such hospitality is itself an act of trade. In an economy which does not rely on currency for exchange, surplus wealth must be used promptly, because surplus wealth in such an economy is perishable. Since one cannot use all of the surplus oneself, giving it to others in order to put them in one's debt is the most reasonable use. Almsgiving, then, uses gratitude and debt to achieve the end that currency would eventually achieve more efficiently, the storage of surplus wealth for the future. Beggars, in this narration, are — even prior to a money economy — engaged in a game of predictable and equal exchange, selling their loyalty and future service to those who had a surplus to share with them. They are merely the lowest stratum of labor-for-hire.

Already we can see the shift from TMS to WN. Although the sympathy of TMS and the competition of WN are not opposed to each other, the two works do treat beggars in characteristically different ways. Beggars are by definition ignoble within TMS, but in WN they are part of the luscious richness of commercial life in its endless bustling variations. With the same admiration for the bizarre that a biologist may show in studying tapeworms, Smith details the operation of economic bottom-feeders, noting with pleasure that even they have a place in the commercial world. Whether they will or not, they are drawn into the dance of negotiation. Their begging is less offensive in WN, therefore, because the world of commerce saves them from their own parasitism, making them useful to others. As TMS advises, "even the ordinary commerce of the world is capable of adjusting our active principles to some degree of propriety."[23] The best school of morals for a beggar is the unavoidable demands of doing business with others.

22. WN, III.iv.5.
23. TMS, III.i.3.7.

This human web of trade is particularly helpful in forcing beggars to become productive. In itself, unproductive labor is not necessarily noxious. Clergy and entertainers likewise produce no good which lasts beyond their performance, but they are useful and desirable. Beggars produce nothing and serve for nothing. They want peace and rest, taking for themselves the leisure that kings desire; and who, Smith asked, can call that irrational? Yet Smith's appreciation of this "wisdom" did not lead him to recommend that we all "consider the lilies." The love of rest is a function of the beggar's imprudence, his preference for tranquility over the work of creating security.[24] Beggars are, like prodigals, unproductive, consumers of the sacred trust of wealth created by others, dangers to the wealth of the nation. If their own sympathy does not lead them to seek impartial approbation and change their behavior, then those charged with care of the common good may have to change it for them.

The worst offenders against wealth are those voluntary beggars who deliberately and in the name of some supposed eternal good pervert productive wealth. Smith snipes at them in a subtly worded passage: "It is with them as with the hussars and light infantry of some armies; no plunder, no pay." This incentive drives them to innovative and energetic ministry to "animate the devotion of the common people. The establishment of the two great mendicant orders of St. Dominic and St. Francis, it is observed by Machiavel, revived, in the thirteenth and fourteenth centuries, the languishing faith and devotion of the catholic church. ('Discourses on the First Decade of Titus Livius,' book iii, chap. i.)"[25]

The citation from Machiavelli's *Discourses on Livy* gives away the irony of Smith's admiration. Machiavelli's reading of the revival fostered by the poverty of the friars is that they taught people "that it is evil to say evil of evil, and that it is good to live under obedience to them, and if they make an error, to leave them for God to punish. So they do the worst they can because they do not fear the punishment that they do not see and do not believe."[26] The friars therefore made the continued corruption of the church possible. Attracting the common people through a supposed revival of early Christianity, they duped them into complicity with the cor-

24. TMS, VI.i.1-15.
25. WN, V.1.g.2.
26. Niccolo Machiavelli, *Discourses on Livy,* trans. Harvey C. Mansfield and Nathan Tarcov (Chicago: The University of Chicago Press, 1996), 212.

ruption of later Christianity. In appealing to Machiavelli, Smith was congratulating the friars for their ingenious and successful abuse of the good faith of believers. They share in the propensity to truck, barter, and exchange, and in fact they excel at it. Smooth operators, they work their section of the market very successfully. Smith despised this hypocrisy, but he was no Langland, lamenting the sin and hoping to doctor the church. He intended to illustrate that these apparently counter-economic holy people are neither counter-economic nor holy.[27] In fact, their moral failing is not that they are engaged in exchange, but that they do not embrace the negotiations of sympathy fully, which would lead them to exchange with an eye on the impartial spectator.

Smith did make a more direct attack on the mendicant orders, however, claiming that in Spain, Portugal, and France, people

27. The section in which that discussion occurs provides insight into the difference in Hume's and Smith's views on religion. Smith has just asserted that competition sharpens preaching as it does all other industry. He then cites Hume at length, identifying him only as "by far the most illustrious philosopher and historian of the present age," arguing that the state would do better to give ministers endowments in order to "bribe their indolence" and keep them from stirring up the people. Smith counters that rather than bribing the indolence of ministers of one church, the state would do well to refrain from using religion as a tool of politics and instead allow religious freedom, which will so fragment churches that no one of them will have power enough to do any harm. Smith's cynicism about Christian truth and anxiety about Christian factionalism is hardly less than Hume's in this passage. The difference comes in Smith's final hope, that among these thousands of competing churches which will have to make certain concessions to each other, religious leaders "might in time probably reduce the doctrine of the greater part of them to that pure and rational religion, free from every mixture of absurdity, imposture, or fanaticism, such as wise men have in all ages of the world wished to see established . . ." (WN, V.i.g.8). Truth, which has been appreciated by all the wise in every age and therefore does not require special revelation, is a *reduction* of doctrine, not clarification or amplification of it. Since Smith's natural theology requires no account of the supernatural to complete it, it is reasonable to expect that he means reduction of Christianity to the principles of natural religion along the lines that he had taught. One wonders why people were surprised that Smith found Hume to be as close to perfection as human frailty would permit.

Smith did, of course, maintain a functional Christianity throughout his career. He signed the Calvinist Confession of Faith as a prerequisite to taking his chair at the University of Glasgow, and given that Hutcheson had been acquitted of heresy, he may have done so in good conscience. While Calvin would have had Geneva up in arms against him for characterizing the victory of Protestantism this way, Smith claimed of the Jacobite wars, "Our forefathers kicked out the Pope and the Pretender [to] preserve the precious right of private judgment" (Ross, *Adam Smith*, xviii).

are oppressed with a numerous race of mendicant friars, whose beg-gary being not only licensed, but consecrated by religion, is a most grievous tax upon the poor people, who are most carefully taught that it is a duty to give, and a very great sin to refuse them their charity.[28]

Those who have the audacity to flaunt their dependence on the turn-ing of productive wealth away from further productivity are deeply offen-sive to Smith's program. They lack the sense they should have of their im-position on society. They do not act with the humility proper to those who make a burden of themselves. Quite to the contrary, they teach people to see gifts to them as pious works. They encourage the consumption of wealth that could be put to further productive use, and they do it using all the power of theological rhetoric. In the battle for the hearts of the com-mon people, the friars are Smith's dear enemies.

This underhanded style of business is consistent, for Smith's system, with their Catholic theological commitments. Concern for penitence or right worship of God offended Smith philosophically. In his view, through social interaction we develop a set of laws, an understanding of duty, to which we adhere in order to win the approval not only of actual spectators, but of the impartial spectator, who is less easily deceived. The greatest im-partial spectator, who is never deceived, is God. Smith claims that the moral faculties we develop through this socialization process are given to us by God to bring us happiness, meaning prosperity and the esteem of others. "Humanity does not desire to be great, but to be beloved."[29] That happiness is the reward of our virtue, and loss of it is our punishment. God, first known through the natural process by which humans transfer their own sentiments onto whatever gods toward whom they direct their religious awe and then confirmed by reason and philosophy, gives the law and ensures that just reward and punishment will come to each. Having created the process by which humans learn right and wrong, God becomes the judge of how well we live up to it. Smith believed that by and large, over the long run, people get what they deserve: the industrious will finally suc-ceed in business, and "knaves" will not get away with it forever.[30] Never-theless, when other rewards and punishments fail, God is the enforcer.

With such a view of God and the moral order, Smith saw devotion

28. WN, IV.vii.b.20.
29. TMS, III.i.5.8.
30. TMS, III.i.5.8.

directed at God rather than at cultivation of human well-being as an attempt to bribe the judge, to curry favor instead of honestly submitting to
judgment. The world can rely on religious people only

> wherever the natural principles of religion are not corrupted by the
> factious and party zeal of some worthless cabal; wherever the first duty
> which it requires, is to fulfill all the obligations of morality; wherever
> men are not taught to regard frivolous observances, as more immedi-
> ate duties of religion, than acts of justice and beneficence; and to imag-
> ine that by sacrifices, and ceremonies, and vain supplications, they can
> bargain with the Deity for fraud, and perfidy, and violence. . . .[31]

Ceremonies and sacrifices are foolish and wasteful, since God cannot
be bought. They are, worse yet, an indication of moral corruption, in that
they attempt to circumvent the law and God's impartial arbitration. True
religion, according to Smith, will be to fear God and therefore to cultivate
an objective view, consciousness of the impending judgment but never approaching the bench in a play to sweeten it unfairly.

This association of worship and penance ("futile mortifications of
the monastery")[32] with injustice has its partner in Smith's treatment of
what may be called "gift economies." While recognizing that gifts functioned as a kind of rent in earlier economies, Smith added, "During the
continuance of this state of things . . . the corruption of justice, naturally
resulting from the arbitrary and uncertain nature of those presents, scarce
admitted of any effectual remedy. . . . Those presents, it seems to have been
supposed, could more easily be abolished altogether, than effectually regu-
lated and ascertained."[33] Gift appears always too personal and too gratuitous to be impartial. By freeing people from the bonds of affection or loyalty or obligation that gift can create, salaries improve the likelihood of
justice being impartially done. For Smith, gift is indistinguishable from
bribe. In private relations, where partiality is licit (the family) or tolerated
as relatively harmless (philosophers, members of clubs, lovers), such behavior may have a place. But publicly, it is disastrous.

Nor could it be otherwise, given Smith's understanding that we neither participate in each other's being nor in God. The One, the Great

31. TMS, III.i.5.13; III.i.2.34-35.
32. TMS, III.i.2.35.
33. WN, V.i.b.16.

Judge, gazing down on these monads of humanity, can only judge each distinctly. In truth, any sharing of merit or guilt or grace is impossible, and the pretense of it always cowardly and corrupting. It is no accident that in Smith we find no trace of Trinity, Incarnation,[34] or Holy Spirit. Legislative attempts to impose order and system on people, as though they were pawns on a chessboard "with no other principle of motion besides that which the hand impresses upon them,"[35] become tyranny; God only escapes such condemnation by leaving the pawns (humans) untouched, uninfluenced as they move themselves within the bounds of the game God has structured. The fundamental principle of TMS — that we are, though social, always limited to the discrete experiences of our own bodies — assumes a world in which God is never Gift.[36] In such a world dependence is an economic aberration; and humility, even as an appeal for mercy before God, is a manipulative ploy.

Malthus and the Moral Necessity of Misery

Whereas Adam Smith's TMS revealed the order of gift as unjust through a philosophy of human atomism, Thomas Robert Malthus came to his tragic conclusions about human misery based on an abstract mathematical analysis of social life. It was not a problem of persons, but of population, or more precisely, of the rate of increase of population. Malthus's central proposition is simple and well known: since population can easily increase at a geometric rate while agricultural productivity can increase at — at the very most, and not infinitely — an arithmetic rate, the rate of population growth is continually limited by the availability of food. Where food supplies are growing as they were in the United States in Malthus's day, population can increase freely. Where food supplies are stagnant, as in Malthus's England, population growth is curtailed by disease, starvation, social unrest, and vice. Contrary to the prevailing wisdom that a large population

34. When translating a quotation from the French, Smith omitted the word "Jesus" so that the author seemed not to be referring to specifically Christian belief. TMS, III.i.2.34. See p. 133, n. 15.

35. TMS, VI.ii.2.17.

36. For a history of gift and disinterestedness in Cartesian and Kantian conceptions of the soul and God, see John Milbank, "The Soul of Reciprocity (Part One): Reciprocity Refused," *Modern Theology* 17:3 (July 2001): 335-91.

was a nation's strength, Malthus elevated the specter of the mob from merely an occasional political event to a fundamental threat inherent in human reproductivity.[37] In the wake of the French Revolution, the image of crowds of clamorous poor aroused terror in the upper classes. Unless people, or more precisely the lower classes, were taught to understand and respond to the reality of the limits of population in a stagnant agriculture, Malthus foresaw only misery for the poor and the potential of mob violence against the rest. He rejected Smith's idea that an increase in the wealth of a nation implied a corollary improvement in the lot of the poor. The problem of misery in Malthus is far more fundamental and more physical than Smith had portrayed it, and the welfare of the haves is not simply coincident with that of the have-nots.

In his first exposition of this argument, the 1798 *Essay on the Principle of Population, as it affects the future improvement of Society, with remarks on the speculations of Mr. Godwin, M. Condorcet, and other writers,* Malthus treated results of this pressure of agricultural stagnation against population growth under the headings of misery (starvation, disease, and war, with frequent references to filth and stench for added piquancy) and vice ("promiscuous intercourse, unnatural passions, violations of the marriage bed, and improper arts to conceal the consequences of irregular connections.")[38] In revisions beginning in 1803 and running through 1826, Malthus moderated his argument by allowing that voluntary moral restraint might serve as a virtuous check on population which could greatly reduce and perhaps eliminate the misery and vice caused by unwarranted population growth. But even in this substantially revised and greatly expanded version (titled *An Essay on the Principle of Population; or, a view of its past and present effects on Human Happiness; with an inquiry into our prospects respecting the future removal or mitigation of the evils which it occasions*), Malthus was skeptical of the power of moral restraint to work sufficiently to counteract the mathematical certainty of the rate of population growth exceeding the rate of increase in food supply. Using not moral psychology but the emerging field of anthropology, and the accounts of explorers and of statisticians,

---

37. See Thomas Pfau, *Wordsworth's Profession: Form, Class, and Logic in Early Romantic Cultural Production* (Stanford: Stanford University Press, 1997), 341-62.

38. *The Works of Thomas Robert Malthus* (8 volumes), ed. E. A. Wrigley and David Sonden (London: Pickering & Chatto, 1986), vol. 2, 15. Hereafter cited *Works* by volume number, vol. 1 being the 1798 edition of the Essay, and vol. 2 and vol. 3 being the 1826 edition, with annotation concerning other editions.

Malthus urged his readers to face an inescapable fact of human life: the demands of the many needy others cannot be met because the world cannot nourish all those who might need food.

If he had them, Malthus did not record his doubts about God's goodness. But because the gap between growth rates of population and food supplies is an inexorable reality, Malthus, an Anglican cleric educated by Unitarians, found himself forced to give an account of how these "natural" laws which result in human misery can be a part of a good God's plan. Theodicy is a recurrent concern in his work on population. To complicate matters, Malthus would not attribute phenomena merely to the impersonal design of a now-absent creator. Providence for Malthus means that all things that exist are willed by God, at each moment. That seeds grow into plants is no mere natural necessity; it is an arrangement created by God for human welfare, so that people learn to work in the fields in order to provide for themselves.[39] The patterns which we observe and call *laws* because of their repetition are in fact direct acts of God's will. "It accords with the most liberal spirit of philosophy, to suppose that not a stone can fall, or a plant rise, without the immediate agency of divine power."[40]

The laws of nature are nevertheless reliable because God makes them so. All human knowledge depends on the assumption that such apparent laws can be treated as actual laws. Since God desires human growth in knowledge and ability, he does not frequently intervene in the patterns of creation.[41] The stability of natural "laws" is not a function of their goodness or of God's love, but of their ongoing efficiency within a stable order, approved specifically and at each moment by God. The principle of population, with all the misery and vice it entails, is one such law and therefore can be named at every moment the active will of God.

In his 1798 *Essay*, his first formulation, he made the astounding claim that the misery caused by overpopulation is willed by God as the necessary goad to drive humans toward their goal, transforming "matter into mind."[42] "Man as he really is" is "inert, sluggish, and averse from labour, unless compelled by necessity,"[43] a state which proceeds from "the original

39. *Works*, vol. 1, 361 and 246 n. 2.
40. *Works*, vol. 2, 127-28; vol. 2, 529.
41. E.g., *Works*, vol. 1, 363.
42. David Nicholls, "Population and Process: Parson Malthus," *Anglican Theological Review* (XXVII:3): 321-34, claims Malthus as a process theologian ahead of his time.
43. *Works*, vol. 1, 363.

sin of man . . . the torpor and corruption of the chaotic matter, in which he may be said to be born."[44] Even after having reconsidered his first publication, in his later version of the *Essay*, Malthus asserted that "a state of sloth, and not of restlessness and activity, seems evidently to be the natural state of man; and this latter disposition could not have been generated but by the strong goad of necessity. . . ."[45]

Ultimately, the goad can fall away, because the habits will be in place and all humanity will be at last like the industrious bourgeois, with a taste for work. Such a taste cannot be produced by reason, but must be formed through experience.[46] God wisely established the threat of starvation as the root of that necessary disciplinary experience. Though on this question also Malthus became more cautious in his later versions, he did initially assert that human bodies would eventually be replaced by a new sort of body, "the essence of thought in an incorporeal, or at least invisible, form."[47] Pure energy would triumph over the inertia of matter. Paradoxically, this would happen through the influence of the constant threat of human fecundity.

In the earliest version of the *Essay*, Malthus counted even the existence of vice as necessary to the ultimate production of good.[48] Malthus himself referred to the Fall very rarely, and as in the citation above, without reference to salvation history. But J. B. Sumner, who authored a theological counterpart to Malthus's *Essay*, treats it more fully. The *"O felix culpa"* of the Easter Proclamation recalls the Fall as a happy event because it made humans the recipients of such an astounding redemption; Sumner made the Fall the happy commencement of real human virtue, which cannot grow without being tested and proved in the midst of evil.[49] Vice may not be necessary to virtue, but temptation is. Misery, temptation, and tragedy are the necessary context for human moral maturity.

---

44. *Works*, vol. 1, 353.

45. *Works*, vol. 2, 92. This torpor is apparently even more natural than, or at least prior to, the appetite for sex, which is God's way of shaking us into activity.

46. *Works*, vol. 1, 261-63.

47. *Works*, vol. 1, 246.

48. *Works*, vol. 1, 139, 266, 375.

49. John Bird Sumner, *A Treatise on the Records of the Creation and on the Moral Attributes of the Creator; with particular reference to the Jewish History, or to the Consistency of the Principles of Population with the Wisdom and Goodness of the Deity*, vol. 2, *On the Wisdom and Goodness of the Creator* (London: J. Hatchard, 1816), 217.

In later versions of his work Malthus moderated his claim of a positive role for suffering significantly, asserting that humans by their lack of self-control and prudence bring upon themselves the miseries associated with overpopulation, which God applies as moral correctives. "Natural and moral evil seem to be the instruments employed by the Deity in admonishing us to avoid any mode of conduct which is not suited to our being, and will consequently injure our happiness." As overeating makes one ill and anger leads to acts we later regret, so overpopulation produces poverty and disease.[50] The difference between the two formulations (evil as necessary positive tool used upon some for the benefit of all or as nearly-inescapable corrective applied to some for the benefit of all) is, however, relatively subtle. Even in his revised formulations, Malthus continually asserted that it is the desire of improving our situation and the fear of worsening it that is the "master-spring of public prosperity"[51] and the *"vis medicatrix reipublicae."*[52] The tangible threat of misery remains necessary to the overall good of society.

This threat of misery is, of course, borne by the poorest of society, those for whom Malthus held out little hope of an escape from misery. If fear of starvation is a means of formation, it is most effective in forming the poor upon whom it has the most immediate effect. This too is simply as it should be. Any increase in equality would only cause unwarranted increases in population and require heavy-handed government interference. The "someone" at the bottom of the stack will always have things harder than the rest, though not as hard as before the principle of population was understood. These are those who must personally make the sacrifices required for society to prosper — moral restraint; late marriage or celibacy; and hard work to maximize productivity out of the land. "A labourer who marries without being able to support a family, may in some respects be considered as an enemy to all his fellow labourers."[53] Malthus failed to note explicitly that such a person is not, however, the enemy of the proper-

50. *Works,* vol. 3, 256. These are ill-matched examples, however, since a single case of overeating or a minor incident of anger only results in a foretaste of the more extreme consequences that would come from a more extreme bout of overeating or of anger, whereas overpopulation, by the time it has caused misery and been recognized, is already the full-blown horror that only long-term gluttony or rage could produce.

51. *Works,* vol. 3, 427.

52. *Works,* vol. 3, 90.

53. *Works,* vol. 1, 86.

tied, who may benefit from a reduction in the cost of labor and at most will see him as a reminder to protect their own position.

All of this means that God has arranged a world in which the misery of the poor plays an essential role, and Malthus did not find God guilty of misbehavior on this count. "Notwithstanding the acknowledged evils occasioned by the principle of population, the advantages derived from it under the present constitution of things very greatly overbalance them."[54] "Many vessels will *necessarily* come out of this great furnace in wrong shapes. These will be broken and thrown aside as useless. . . ."[55] In considering young children in Manchester sent from workhouses to labor sometimes all night in factories where they were regularly exposed to fever epidemics and the like, Malthus approvingly cited a Dr. Aikin: "It is the wise plan of providence that in this life there shall be no good without its attendant inconvenience."[56]

As the permission of a "lesser evil" is no defect in God's goodness, so it is no sin in humans. Malthus explicitly and repeatedly took this consequentialist line, claiming we always act by choosing lesser evils and calculating how to achieve the greatest benefits (by which he means an unspecified happiness beyond mere physical satisfaction). "In human life we are continually called upon to submit to a lesser evil in order to avoid a greater; and it is the part of a wise man to do this readily and cheerfully."[57] In fact, he considered utility "the foundation of morals," or "the great criterion of moral rules."[58]

Malthus's wrath is most directed at those who shirk the responsibility to act, who postulate miracles (which are not to be expected, since God honors the rules of creation in order to allow us to develop our minds), or who simply refuse to face the facts.[59] The responsible person cannot afford to be squeamish in the face of some inevitable misery.[60] An element of so-

54. *Works*, vol. 3, 496.
55. *Works*, vol. 1, 246 n. 2. Emphasis in the original.
56. *Works*, vol. 3, 220.
57. *Works*, vol. 3, 322.
58. *Works*, vol. 3, 283.
59. See, for example, *Works*, vol. 2, 294, where he discusses the ability of Swedish workers to bear any suffering patiently, until they were taught by the "vanity and mistaken benevolence of the government and higher classes of society" that they were dependent. The expectation of assistance destroyed independence and patient endurance.
60. Malthus does not bother with the fine points of consequentialism, such as exactly

ciety is always tending to starvation, and, drawing on his reading of anthropological accounts of explorers among "primitive nations," Malthus argues that this scarcity of food leads to war and eventually cannibalism.[61] Peace and plenty are only restored by the establishment of a class of unpropertied laborers and a class of private property holders whose rights are inviolable. The proportions and happiness of the two classes can change for better or for worse, but the existence of two such classes is a necessity if a society is to live in peace and prosperity and inherent in nature as God wills it. The right to private property which makes this division possible must be inviolable.[62]

Contrary to the Christian teaching that in time of mortal necessity all things are common, Malthus holds that only the existence of an inviolable right to property saves us from a free-rider problem so severe that it would threaten us with starvation and a return to a war of all against all. Such a right is recognized, in this primordial myth of economic origins, when a society returns to peace and prosperity (or the possibility of it) through the emergence of two classes — the owners and the workers.

Malthus readily grants that laborers are a commodity, and that the market for labor controls the possibility of their survival. This is not a social construct to be considered, but a fact about a natural order so necessary that Malthus considered a society in which food grows easily to be disastrous for the poor. Since they live and die by demand for their labor, they will die in a land in which food grows without labor, because no one will hire them.[63] Giving them small landholdings or commons on which to farm only increases their population, and since they are still laborers (not small landholders) only worsens an existing glut in the labor market.[64] The

what is meant by good (*Works*, vol. 2, 364), or who makes the calculations about maximizing it. Although he refers to consequentialism as the root of all morality, he does not apply it to, for example, promise-keeping or honesty. He refuses to support any means of birth control other than abstinence, regardless of how useful such means might be for minimizing the size of the "excess population." Such practices injure the dignity of women, he held. He offers no argument to justify women's dignity as more important than increased means of birth control, and he fails to note that his concern to defend women's dignity overrides his concern for population growth, while his concern for the deaths of children working in unhealthy factories does not.

61. *Works*, vol. 2, 48-49. See also vol. 1, 194-97.

62. *Works*, vol. 3, 88, 320, 325.

63. *Works*, vol. 2, 170-71. See also Sumner, *Records of the Creation*, 350.

64. *Works*, vol. 3, 381-83.

work of the poor functions "by the analogy of every other commodity which is brought to market."[65]

> A young person saved from death is more likely to contribute to the creation of fresh resources than another birth. It is a great loss of labour and food to begin over again. And universally it is true that, under similar circumstance, that article will come the cheapest to market which is accompanied by the fewest failures.[66]

Since these divisions of society are a necessary precondition of successful economic life and of human life in accord with God's plan for happiness, efforts to undermine them are usually wasteful and often counterproductive. Malthus recognized that many owners would and did give generously to alleviate the suffering of the poor, but he argued that gifts, if they do not increase the amount of foodstuffs available, only change the identity of the "excess population" without doing anything to reduce it. Charitable work projects, if they do not expand the demand for labor by creating new industries or bringing new land under cultivation, only help the less deserving at the expense of those already employed. In the long run, any aid that promotes the expectation that help will be offered when financial troubles loom will reduce the independence and prudence of the poor, worsening their situation both financially and morally. Large gifts to the poor encourage idleness and vice and therefore potentially reduce the supply of goods produced. In addition, the experience of being obligated and dependent (for the poor) and of holding power over others (for the rich) is bad for both parties.[67] Relationships of fair exchange and balanced interdependence between owners and workers, the owners buying the labor of the workers, is in every way preferable, and for those interested in eliminating misery, apparently necessary.[68]

If the poor will not themselves control their rate of population growth, nothing can be done for them, and it is incumbent on those with enough to refuse to hear any plea, especially a plea based on a claim of rights. People have, according to Malthus, no right to eat, to work, to live, but only the right to own what is legally theirs. This is so, he claimed, simply because there can

65. *Works*, vol. 3, 291.
66. *Works*, vol. 3, 449 n. 6.
67. *Works*, vol. 1, 290-92.
68. *Works*, vol. 1, 292-93.

be no right which it is impossible to honor, and it is impossible to feed all those who are or may become hungry. "[A]s the rich do not in reality possess the *power* of finding employment and maintenance for the poor, the poor cannot, in the nature of things, possess the *right* to demand them. . . ."[69] To argue for parish laws or the like on the basis of rights is therefore in his view nonsense. Attempting to fulfill the obligation created by a universal right to eat will only increase starvation by eliminating the prudential check against population growth. The poor will quickly produce hordes of ravenous children.[70] Imposing a system inspired by a universal right to work only shifts the burden of unemployment onto those who deserve it less, those who have already found jobs under a system of competition. Or, as he noted parenthetically and perhaps sarcastically, if the poor have a right to support, then their wealthy defenders would have to give up their wealth.[71] A right only exists by virtue of a social order that can support it.[72]

In the 1803 version of the essay, Malthus wrote a parable about nature's banquet which captured the horror and fear he felt toward the demands of the poor on the rich.

> A man who is born into a world already possessed, if he cannot get his subsistence from his parent on whom he had a just demand, and if the society do not want his labour, has no claim of *right* to the smallest portion of food, and, in fact, has no business to be where he is.

Such a man has come to the table where nature is offering a banquet only to find all the seats at the table taken. He has no place, and "if he . . . work upon the compassion of some of her [nature's] guests" then immediately other "claimants" will storm in. Plenty turns into scarcity,

> and the happiness of the guests is destroyed by the spectacle of misery and dependence in every part of the hall, and by the clamorous impor-

69. *Works,* vol. 3, 438. See also 319, 453, 459.

70. Malthus called the Roman practice of distributing grain for free to the poor, "a strange and preposterous custom, which, however, the strange and unnatural state of the city might perhaps require." *Works,* vol. 2, 245.

71. *Works,* vol. 3, 453.

72. *Works,* vol. 3, 452, 454. Malthus slips up, saying that the children of the poor have a right to support from their parents. Impossibility is no excuse here, because the existence of the children was caused by the parents. Not possibility, but location of responsibility becomes the issue.

tunity of those, who are justly enraged at not finding the provision they had been taught to expect.[73]

This passage was omitted from later editions. It made its point, perhaps too graphically. No wonder Malthus urged pastors to educate their poor parishioners about the need to control their numbers and to give "proper moral and religious instruction" to keep them from disturbing the peace.[74] He thought it best to make "some kind of compact with the poor,"[75] so that the owner class will not live in fear of that overturning of nature's table and the collapse of civilization, learning, and virtue.[76] "If the hand of private charity be stretched forth in his relief, the interests of humanity imperiously require that it should be administered very sparingly."[77]

Nevertheless Malthus, as a Christian clergyman, could not oppose charity. He reconciled his understanding of population with necessity of Christian charity by claiming that benevolence (in a way perhaps analogous to the gentleness, beauty, and delightful irrationality associated with the feminine) has a dark side and must be controlled. Benevolence is perilous because it so easily undermines the common good.[78] Seeing only the persons in need, it forgets the larger inescapable reality of the principle of population.[79] Benevolence is, in Malthus's categories, a passion, and therefore needs the direction of prudence. As benevolence limits self-love, so prudence — by which he means calculation of consequences — limits benevolence so that the pleasure of indulging one's desire to be generous is directed by a rigorous judgment about the larger consequences of the act. Occasional relief given to those who suffer poverty through some accident (that is, not through lack of industry or foresight) permits some of those

73. *Works*, vol. 3, 697-98.
74. *Works*, vol. 3, 469.
75. *Works*, vol. 3, 464.
76. Malthus repeatedly associates poverty with vice; e.g., *Works*, vol. 3, 298.
77. *Works*, vol. 3, 339.
78. Note the gender-flagging in Malthus's language for charity and benevolence. He says of benevolence that it is not a "great moving principle," but it is the "kind corrector of evils," the "balm and consolation and grace," and the "source of our noblest efforts in the cause of virtue, and of our purest and most refined pleasures." *Works*, vol. 3, 454.
79. *Works*, vol. 3, 361: Benevolence is an emotion which is "general, and in some degree, indiscriminate and blind." Since it is an emotion, it must be governed by utility, just as all other emotions (love, anger, ambition, hunger) are.

who can survive without misery to do so and is therefore true charity, prudent as well as benevolent. But even this kind of charity must not be guaranteed. Charity is — when both spontaneous and carefully calculated not to raise the rate of population — an improvement of the human spirit and the best possible answer to the suffering of the surplus population.

Given the mutual necessity of self-interest, charity, and private property, Malthus proposed the following synthesis:

> Every man has a right to do what he will with his own, and cannot, in justice, be called upon to render a reason why he gives in one case and abstains from it in the other. This kind of despotic power, essential to voluntary charity, gives the greatest facility to the selection of worthy objects of relief, without being accompanied by any ill consequences; and has further a most beneficial effect from the degree of uncertainty which must necessarily be attached to it.[80]

But beggars immediately disqualify themselves from such charity.

> Even in the relief of common beggars we shall find that we are more frequently influenced by the desire of getting rid of the importunities of a disgusting object than by the pleasure of relieving it. We wish that it had not fallen in our way, rather than rejoice in the opportunity given us of assisting a fellow-creature. We feel a painful emotion at the sight of so much apparent misery; but the pittance we give does not relieve it. We know that it is totally inadequate to produce any essential effect. We know, besides, that we shall be addressed in the same manner at the corner of the next street; and we know that we are liable to the grossest impositions. We hurry therefore sometimes by them, and shut our ears to their importunate demands. We give no more than we can help giving without doing actual violence to our feelings. Our charity is in some degree forced and, like forced charity, it leaves no satisfactory impression on the mind, and cannot therefore have any very beneficial and improving effect on the heart and affections.[81]

Malthus made a treaty with charity in the contingent and unpredictable practice of private beneficence, but beggars destroy that peace by con-

80. *Works*, vol. 3, 369.
81. *Works*, vol. 3, 366.

fusing the categories. The silent, grateful poor play by Malthus's rules: they understand that charity cannot be a matter of rights, they feel the shame of dependence, and they aim to earn their way out of it as soon as possible. They accept Malthus's account of property rights. Those who ask for alms lack shame for their dependence and failure to be productive laborers, as though they thought perhaps dependence and being productive laborers were not particularly important. Malthus's presuppositions do not impress such beggars. Nor does his distinction between rights and benevolence: while beggars may not claim alms as their right, neither do they honor the right to private property as Malthus would want them to. They ask in the expectation that a reasonable person may be willing and able to share property. They are, therefore, more threatening to property than thieves, for they are more insidious.

Malthus was so anxious about beggars' power to seduce the rich into error that he compared promiscuous sex, in which a normal human passion escapes the governance of prudence and results in an increase of vice and misery, to indiscriminate almsgiving, in which another normal human passion (benevolence) escapes its prudential governance and results in an increase, not in industrious workers, but in indolence and beggary.[82] Beggars are the bastard children of the prodigal rich whose indulgence in the pleasure of charity created them. Having been born out of a luxurious act of benevolence, the existence of these miserable dependents is the fault of those who most want to make them disappear. Like a Mordred loitering around Camelot, beggars do have a claim on the throne, rooted in the weakness of their betters.

Malthus will not tolerate them. Goodness which shirks the necessity of prudent severity is only cowardice and weakness. But better by far to prevent the situation. Make no gift which recognizes kinship among classes, no matter how small an indulgence it seems to be. If benevolence is appropriately reined, the giver will never face such an ambiguously just expectation of more from the hordes of the needy.

If for Smith, God can never be gift, for Malthus, all the world is God's gift, and the gift will mean misery to many. Both beggars and promiscuous almsgivers refuse that difficult gift, failing to understand that it goads humans for their own good, to force their progress and limit their immorality. Malthus rescues God's charity, but only by describing it as merciless.

82. *Works*, vol. 3, 362-363.

In Smith and Malthus, dependence is vicious — at least for an adult man, the character they took to be the mature human. For Smith, it cannot be otherwise, because dependence is based on the false hope that humans can know some kind of commonality, that their suffering and pleasure can be shared. For Malthus, dependence perverts divinely-ordered nature. The Humean atomism that Smith attempted to moderate in TMS means that any admission of need is an imposition which can only be excused if it is greatly understated. The negotiations of the market become an escape from and discipline on such admission. Malthus's loathing of dependence is far more urgent and visceral: the person in need is like one drowning in deep water, liable to pull would-be rescuers under as well. He does not relish watching them drown, but he refuses to hide from the painful conclusion: a time of trial is necessary, and we must be willing to see some people fail, or starve, along the way in order to achieve God's good end. When these rational worlds based on the human as individual meet up with stewardship's emphasis on the moral importance of property, they lock begging out of the discussion on public, economic morality.

These anthropological claims travel with a corresponding notion of God. Smith and Malthus have distinctly different understandings of God, Malthus insisting that particular events are the immediate expression of God's will for human good, that Jesus plays an important role in salvation, and that ultimately virtue is its own reward. Nevertheless both consider the soul's reward to be a happiness for humans which is overseen or administered by God, but in which God is simply the largest player in the game. What God is not, for either Smith or Malthus, is the one common joy of all humans, the source and end of human freedom, the spirit shared by all the baptized, the crucified and raised one of whom all Christians are members. Participation in the divine is now the work of justice or of effective and prudent minimization of misery, the work of a faithful steward. The beggar-God has become a stranger. The vulnerability of Christ in the incarnation and Eucharist, which spoke to Francis of God's patient desire for fellowship with and among humanity, plays no role in this version of Christian morality. The good Christian must be concerned with how best to make the poor more like the rich, or at least more independent, because that is the only way to reduce their misery and the only way to work out one's salvation.

The Pilgrimage of Benoît-Joseph Labre

These constructions of beggars as twisted traders, parasites, or bastard children of the wayward rich undermine the possibility of a role for beggars as representatives of an alternative economic order. Submerged in a world of trade or utterly excluded from it, the figure of the beggar loses its moral significance. But these textual systems, powerful as they were, only worked out accounts of what European political systems had been moving toward for some time already: the isolation and removal of beggars from the social scene.

Benoît-Joseph Labre, a late eighteenth-century French pilgrim and beggar popularly acclaimed as a saint at his death, was a bit shy about admitting that he begged. He told one priest who offered him a steady source of food "that he obtained his food by begging, very few things being necessary for the conservation of his poor carcass."[83] Various witnesses of his life acknowledged that he did beg, although he did not always thank his benefactors, and several donors reported that they saw him give away the alms they had given him. Yet when Dom Valeri, at the shrine of Loretto to which Labre returned annually, asked upon meeting him whether he begged, "He answered me with an embarrassed air, 'If I find something and if they give it to me.'"[84]

His reticence in answering Valeri is understandable. Begging in Italy and France was not only, as Thomas Aquinas had held, "uncomely," but also a somewhat perilous business. What would it mean, in late eighteenth-century France and Italy, to be a beggar?

> But if foreigners are rather severe on begging, at Rome beggars had, so to speak, the keys to the city in that period. Roman piety didn't reason. Mendicancy is the appeal to the exercise of one of the three theological virtues. Under this title, it was encouraged as an evangelical institution and protected by the police. How could the pontifical government have forbidden or limited it?[85]

83. "qu'il procurerait sa nourriture en mendiant, très peu de chose étant nécessaire pour la conservation de sa pauvre carcasse." Cited in Joseph Richard, *Le vagabond de Dieu: Saint Benoît Labre* (Paris: Editions SOS, 1976), 52.

84. "Il me repondit d'un air gêné: 'Si je trouve quelque chose et si on me le donne.'" Richard, *Vagabond de Dieu*, 48.

85. "Mais si les étrangers sont plutôt sévères pour la mendicité, à Rome, celle-ci avait

This rhetorical question by one of Labre's biographers papers over a more complex story about Rome, the church, and beggars. In fact, the papacy did take steps to deal with beggars through enclosure as early as the sixteenth century. At the recommendation of Charles Borromeo, Gregory XIII established a hospice in which 850 beggars were solemnly enclosed in 1580, although only two years later they were released because funds to support them ran out. But in 1587 Sixtus V, an ascetic Franciscan from a poor agricultural family, renewed the attempt to enclose beggars, as part of a broad and brutal attempt to impose order within the papal states. Begging *was* at that time forbidden in Rome.[86] Sixtus, in fact, compared beggars to "brutes who have no other care than the search for food to quiet their hunger and fill their bellies."[87] His social policies were not, however, popular; upon his death, Sixtus V's statue on the Capitol was torn down by an enraged crowd of Romans.

A new wave of concern with beggars arose with Innocent XII (1691-1700), who converted the Lateran palace into a workshop for the unemployed. It is significant that the same pope ordered the publication of *La mendicité abolié*, by P. Guévarre, S.J., in 1693.[88] The notion of beggars as a social blight was hardly foreign to Rome.

But at the moment of Benoît-Joseph Labre's sojourn in Rome, Rome had become decidedly more tolerant of beggars than his homeland. In France, Christian charitable organizations had long since offered assistance to the poor and to travelers. In 1622, the famous hospital of Notre Dame du Charité in Lyons offered assistance in the form of a place for the poor to be confined. This *renfermement* was believed to be for the good of the donor as well as the "recipient."[89] Similar institutions began to appear

pour ainsi dire droit de cité, à cette époque. La piété romaine ne raisonnait pas. La mendicité est l'appel à l'exercice d'une des trois vertus théologales. A ce titre, elle était encouragée comme une institution évangélique et protegée par la police. Comment le gouvernement pontifical pourrait-il l'interdire ou la limiter?" Richard, *Vagabond de Dieu*, 84.

86. Jean-Pierre Gutton, *La société et les pauvres en Europe (XVIe-XVIIIe siècles)* (Presses Universitaires de France, 1974), 119.

87. "Brutes n'ayant d'autre souci que la recherche de la nourriture qui calmera leur faim et repaîtra leur ventre." Gutton, *La société et les pauvres*, 111.

88. Gutton, *La société et les pauvres*, 128. I have unfortunately been able to investigate only an English translation of Guévarre's work, in which the translator reassures his readers in his introduction that he has removed any papist ideas from the work as he translated it.

89. Romand Coles, *Rethinking Generosity: Critical Theory and the Politics of "Caritas"* (Ithaca: Cornell University Press, 1997).

across France, particularly under the aegis of the "Company of the Holy Sacrament." Louis XIV encouraged measures to care for the poor in hospitals, but only for the deserving poor, i.e., the sick, aged, or children *("invalides")*. The unemployed able-bodied *("valides")* wandering in search of work, on the other hand, deserved not compassion but correction. The General Hospital of Paris was opened in 1656 to imprison such "false" beggars, and in 1661 Louis XIV pronounced begging not only the school of other crimes, but a crime itself.[90] Legislation in 1724 instituted a repression of beggars in France conducted partially at the king's expense. When the project was revived in the second half of the eighteenth century, a centralized bureaucracy which put local hospitals and police under the royal chain of command made possible a nationwide coordinated program documenting and applying various remedies and punishments to vagabonds and beggars. It was during this wave of the policing of beggars that Benoît-Joseph Labre became a permanent pilgrim, starting in France but spending much of his time in Italy with occasional forays back to France, into Switzerland, and perhaps even Spain.[91]

As a young man, Labre had decided to become a monk, but he was repeatedly refused admission at a number of monasteries, sometimes because of the condition of the monastic community, sometimes because of his physical weakness, sometimes because of suspicions that his moral scruples indicated Jansenism.[92] But after three years of traveling to differ-

90. Robert M. Schwartz, *Policing the Poor in Eighteenth-Century France* (Chapel Hill: University of North Carolina Press, 1988), 18.

91. The economic system in vogue at the time of this upsurge in enclosure was Physiocracy. Although Smith's thought was deeply informed by his sojourn in France where he learned from the Physiocrats, I have not treated that school of thought separately. I refer the interested reader to Schwartz, *Policing the Poor,* and Thomas McStay Adams, *Bureaucrats and Beggars: French Social Policy in the Age of the Enlightenment* (New York: Oxford University Press, 1990).

92. Jansenism was a body of thought condemned for teaching that as after the fall the human soul is totally corrupt, only a gift of irresistible grace can save it, by which was meant turning it from the corruption of the natural toward the supernatural. More broadly, Jansenism was characterized by a strong distinction between worldliness and holiness, and, in the generation after Pascal, a kind of anti-intellectualism that led people to understand it as fideistic. Jansenism spread in France perhaps more because of the papal condemnation than on its internal merits. Labre, in his canonization hearings, was cleared of the heresy of Jansenism, but as it flavored much of French Catholicism, it is no surprise to catch a whiff in his devotion.

ent monasteries, somewhere after his eighth attempt to become a monk, Labre determined that his call was not to a monastery at all. His vocation was to pilgrimage and poverty in the world. Labre's favorite spiritual writer taught that Christians must not question the road God chooses for them, but accept it as the one most conducive to their salvation.[93] Labre saw that God had made him a pilgrim, a homeless wanderer. Eventually, Labre took Rome as his base, and from 1777 to his death he remained there, continuing only to make annual pilgrimages to Loretto until his death in 1783. Even after he slowed his travels, he continued to live in extreme poverty. According to testimony in the investigation leading to his canonization, Labre endured his homelessness with patience and great joy, even accepting as penance a severe case of lice. One witness reported, with devotion, seeing him stop to recover an insect which had fallen off of his body so that he could tuck it safely back in his sleeve.[94]

Labre spent his adult life among people on the road, in an era that saw many people displaced by pressures on small farms. Increasing population, higher rents, the growth of manufacture and large pastures, and the enclosure of commons all bore down on the laboring class in France between 1750 and 1780. Unemployed workers were judged to be a blight on the social body, the powers of progress, wealth, and knowledge, and Labre adopted their situation as the site of his penance, his endurance of conflict with the world that rejected Christ. He took what was seen by some as a social problem to be handled by specialists, the strong, propertied, and wise, and turned it into an opportunity to imitate the crucified Christ.

Studies of Labre have not discussed this political context, and Labre himself made no comment on it, not being much given to expressing his views verbally. No records have indicated that Labre was arrested as a vagabond. His status as pilgrim, which his passport verified, probably offered him protection from being lumped permanently with dangerous *mal sujets*. Still, the passport would have needed frequent renewal and could be subject to suspicious scrutiny anytime authorities had doubts. The full

93. R. P. LeJeune, Sermon 27, "Des raisons pourquoi Dieu envoie les afflictions, et de l'usage qu'il en faut faire," *Le Missionaire de l'Oratoire: Sermons du R. P. LeJeune, Prêtre de l'oratoire de Jésus,* Nouvelle edition, vol. 9 (Paris: Louis Vivès, 1873).

94. In fact, Richard dedicates a chapter of his biography to discussing Labre's lice. Having endured prison camp himself, Richard found this element of Labre's life to be far more significant than it might appear at first glance. To have lice is, after all, not only to be uncomfortable, but to be segregated from polite society.

documentation for a pilgrim could be complex, including permission from one's bishop and certificates from local authorities and the chief magistrate. If the possibility of arrest was small, the likelihood of harassment, official and unofficial, was high, both for Labre and for those who gave shelter or alms to him. Labre's companions on the road certainly knew the underside of *renfermement* well enough. The life of this silent ascetic inevitably impinges on the politics of managing the wandering poor.

We do not know whether Labre's attraction to Rome was in part due to the hope of minimizing his trouble with police. He may have simply wanted to be in the city of Peter. For whatever reason he chose to spend most of his time there, he did not and could not entirely avoid confrontation with authorities. He did make return trips to France, and pious families risked irritating local police by taking him in. While Labre was staying with a family in Moulins, neighbors planted fears of theft and careless fire-setting (the most common accusations against vagabonds) in the minds of the daughters. The local lieutenant reportedly "couldn't stand" Labre.[95] Rather than draw the family into more conflict, Labre moved to another location. In Rome, the pastor of the church Labre frequented preached from the pulpit that both those who gave and those who received alms in the church committed sins. Labre, who did not verbally beg in the church but did accept alms offered to him, thereafter relocated. He did not move out of the church, but he did move out of the path of that priest.[96] The silent and "otherworldly" saint became a modest figure of resistance and a participant in a popular game of opposition to those church leaders who joined in hostility to travelers. Labre is hardly a typical social reformer, but his imitation of Christ placed him squarely in the center of a political and economic ferment, where he quietly reinterpreted poverty and dependence as a privileged location for Christian reflection.

Labre's contemporaries who served as witnesses for the cause of his canonization reported that they saw in Labre Christ, the rejected stranger walking through the world as a foreigner, unrecognized, but all the while united to God, though in prayer rather than in the hypostatic union. A Franciscan sister told of seeing Labre in Rome — the city so friendly to beggars — surrounded by a group of eight or ten people of various ages

---

95. "ne pouvait souffrir." Richard, *Vagabond de Dieu,* 40.
96. Richard, *Vagabond de Dieu,* 89-90.

who pulled at his beard, hit him with fists, threw his hat to the ground, and knocked him down, continuing to insult and hit him. Labre made no move and spoke no word against them. Another witness tells of seeing children throwing stones at Labre, shouting *"Gabbamondo!"* (Hypocrite!). Watching Labre pass through this "avalanche" unperturbed, this witness commented, "Such a spectacle provoked in me feelings of compassion and I believed I was seeing the image of Christ Our Lord among the soldiers of the Praetorium who mocked, abused, injured, and struck him."[97] Père Temple, to whom Labre put himself under obedience in 1776 at Loretto, remarked that

> . . . when I consider attentively this great servant of God, so poor, so exhausted and at the same time so joyful, but with a heavenly joy . . . I seem to recognize in him, in due proportion, the most perfect portrait of the Crucified, coming from the fact that he had constantly in his spirit the divine model, the imitation of which the eternal Father has deigned to inculcate in us.[98]

At Labre's death in Rome, crowds in the street took up the cry, "The saint is dead!" and the disorder around his corpse was so great that soldiers were called in to protect it. The reserved Eucharist had to be removed from the church in which his body lay before burial because of the mob trying to get close to it. This strangely extravagant ascetic seized the theological imagination of his contemporaries. He had touched a nerve.

Given the accounts of economic life we have seen in the earlier parts of this chapter, Labre's example of silent, filthy, unhealthy, unproductive dependence looms as a grim inversion of enlightened economic theory. Against the claim that human morality is based on negotiations toward a harmony of sympathies, he did not offer thanks or minimize the appearance of his suffering. Against the claim that beggars are simply part of the exchange game, he gave away even the few alms he collected and put him-

97. "Un tel spectacle provoqua en moi des sentiments de compassion et je crus voir l'image du Christ Notre-Seigneur au milieu de soldats du Prétoire qui le raillaient, le rudoyaient, l'injuriaient et le frappaient." Richard, *Vagabond de Dieu*, 116-17.

98. ". . . quand je considérai attentivement ce grand serviteur de Dieu, si pauvre, si exténué et tout à la fois si joyeux, mais d'une joie tout céleste . . . il me parut reconnaître en lui, proportion gardée, le portrait le plus parfait du Crucifié, provenant du fait qu'il avait constamment dans son esprit ce divin exemplaire dont le Père éternel a daigné nous inculqué l'imitation." Richard, *Vagabond de Dieu*, 74.

self to the arduous and financially unproductive work of pilgrimage. Against the claim that morality aims at overcoming the body's sloth through hard work and self-control, he welcomed hunger and filth, imitating Christ's suffering and his useless crucified body. Against the claim that those who fail must, regrettably, be left to their fate, he identified himself with the masses of unemployed wandering "surplus labor." Against the claim that charity must leave terror intact for the common good, he rejoiced in his poverty. Against the characterization of the good life, the life of human dignity, as strong, productive, and independent, he remained weak, poor, useless, and reliant on gifts from others.

The contrast could not be sharper, and it was noted by a speaker in the French Senat the year of Labre's canonization, 1881.

> This was a man covered with vermin who all his life lived at the expense of others, on the work of others — very moderately, I admit — prostrated at the foot of altars. This is the most heroic type of self-denial. . . . Such are the lessons that the Church gives to modern society, to this society which works, which takes things on, which has a passion for all great things. . . . Now, if you want to know what the difference between modern society and Catholic society is, take the list of the saints, taking care to add to it especially the last, saint Labre. Then go before the Palace of Industry. Make a tour of it and you will see *our* saints.[99] [. . .] You'll see there the names of three or four thousand mathematicians, artists, builders, inventors, workers of all sorts; you will not see there even one man included for his piety, but only for his work. You will not find people who have cared for their other-worldly salvation, but who have sought to give service to humanity in this world. Here are the two sides of the contradiction. On the one side, humanity detaches itself from the things of the world, thinks only of heaven, and allows itself to be led to heaven by the hand of the Church.

99. "C'était un homme couvert de vermine et qui toute sa vie vivant aux dépens d'autrui, du travail des autres — très médiocrement, je l'avoue — se prosternait sur la dalle des autels. C'est le type le plus héroïque de l'abandon de soi-même. . . . Telles sont les leçons que donne l'Eglise à la société moderne, à cette société qui travaille, qui entreprend, qui se passionne pour toutes les grandes choses. . . . Maintenant, si vous voulez savoir quelle est la différence entre la société moderne et la société catholique, vous prendrez la liste des saints, en ayant soin surtout d'y ajouter le dernier, saint Labre. Puis, vous irez devant le Palais de l'Industrie. Vous en ferez le tour et vous verrez nos saints à nous." From *L'Officiel,* 3 juin 1881. Cited in Richard, *Vagabond de Dieu,* 257 n. 1.

The other side of the contradiction is that humanity thinks no longer of eternal happiness, but cares for the interests of this world and tries to take possession of the earth by science and work. There are the two sides of the contradiction. The Revolution has suppressed the first and left the other standing and glorious. Behold the Truth.[100]

While Corbon's insinuation that mathematicians, artists, builders, and so forth are alien to Christian sanctity is erroneous (Pascal's associations with Jansenism should be enough to indicate that even that branch need not be hostile to sophisticated intellectual work), this little speech indicates the significance of Labre's witness, staking out the territory of Catholic opposition to nineteenth-century ideals. Labre's life revolved around sacred places, the contingencies of Christian history rather than the logical efficiency of system. His vocation was physical and material: not in the sense of engineering and medicine, but the hunger and cold of a pilgrim's life, the blisters, the itch of lice, the smells of a beggar's companions. His calling was also social, though not in the orderly sense of the centralized state or an economic system. He simply could not afford the luxury of privacy because a beggar cannot survive alone. Though he was quiet, even taciturn, he lived continually exposed to public gaze and dependent on strangers, do-gooders, police, neighbors. Labre's population was not an abstraction that could be charted, but characters in a narrative he created, a few families in towns on his routes, some police, a confessor, the impoverished who waited with him for a handout or to whom he offered his alms. His need generated a network of personal meetings and

100. "Vous y verrez 3 000 o 4 000 noms de mathématicien, d'artistes, de constructeurs, d'inventeurs, de travailleurs de tout genre; vous n'y verrez pas figurer un seul homme pour sa piété, mais seulement pour son travail. Vous y trouverez des gens qui n'ont pas songé à leur salut dans l'autre monde, mais qui ont cherché à rendre sevice à l'humanité dans ce monde-ci. Voilà les deux termes de la contradiction. L'un des deux termes c'est que l'humanité se détache absolument des choses de ce monde, ne pense qu'au ciel et se laisse conduire au ciel par la main de l'Eglise; l'autre terme de la contradiction, c'est que l'humanité ne pense plus à la béatitude éternelle, mais songe aux intérêts de ce monde, et cherche à prendre possession de la terre par la science et le travail. Voilà les deux termes de la contradiction. La Révolution a supprimé le premier et elle a laissé l'autre debout et glorieux. Voilà la Vérité." Continuation of citation from Richard, cited in Jean-Pierre Ribaut, "La sainteté de Benoît Labre: Un défi à l'esprit scientiste de la fin du XIXe siècle," in *Benoît Labre: Errance et saintete: Histoire d'un culte, 1783-1983*, ed. Yves-Marie Hilaire (Paris: Les Editions du Cerf, 1984), 91.

shared convictions. Although both within the church and without it he was taken as a patron of otherworldliness, in fact Labre offered a timely material, political, economic witness.

Labre is a troubling character, perhaps most so because of his evident joy in his life of destitution. There is something monstrous, something immoral about it. Other contemporaries of Labre's could have, and in the minds of some, should have earned the acclaim of the church in his place. Abbé Leclerc de Montlinot, for example, holder of doctorates in both medicine and theology and the writer of controversial pieces providing theological defense of, among other works, the *Enyclopédie*,[101] won a prize in 1779 from the Agricultural Society of Soissons for an essay advocating an end to *dépôts de mendicité,* the places of confinement for beggars. Instead, unemployed *valides* should be auctioned off to farmers, the lowest bidder winning payment from the local community to take the beggar on as a laborer. In this way, he claimed, they would end that false charity by which the rich kept the poor kenneled until they needed them. The former beggar would have good work, outside, among peers. Rather than being left a passive recipient, she would become a worker who had the dignity of earning a living (assuming the low bid provided a living wage). Montlinot worked energetically to make the *dépôts* healthier places where beggars could be retrained for work and consumption in the new order. He organized the life of the *dépôt* he directed at Soissons so that its residents could earn privileges for themselves and become almsgivers to those in worse shape, the insane. Committed and pragmatic, he recognized the limits of what he could do. He recognized that he was only training beggars more effectively to sell themselves in a new labor market, and that other reforms would need to be instituted to further protect them. Facing the misery of poverty and an elite prone to despise the poor, he took the risk of attempting to respond constructively, and if some of his methods were questionable, his energetic attempt to engage the human crisis of his time was not.[102] Why not acclaim

---

101. I have borrowed the example of Montlinot from Adams, *Bureaucrats and Beggars,* 188-211.

102. Montlinot's humanism is an example of that social control Foucault studied to such effect. Montlinot's emphasis on punishment and reward in the interest of producing desirable future effects is connected to an almost Benthamite (though anticipating Bentham) practice of the workings of power in the *maison de travail.* In his annual report, Montlinot wrote, "Let the inspector never be thought absent!" and ordered authority in the *maison* as "an invisible chain [connected] to a single point, as in a center of force."

Montlinot, whose energetic use of the best knowledge of his day seems so much more compassionate a response to poverty than Labre's?

The answer, evidently, is that something in Christianity favors the immoral. John Milbank argues in "Can Morality Be Christian?" that Christianity can be called immoral because it is not a reactive, heroic morality.[103] As against classical heroism, in which the brave and selfless warrior sacrifices his own life to protect a city's fragile interior or in which a generous soul offers his last bit of food to save a starving child, Christianity is based in the overflowing plenitude of the loaves and fishes, in the confidence of resurrection. Classical virtue thrives in an atmosphere of opposition and tragedy, where courage and selflessness are tested, where bodies throw themselves into the breach to save their friends or see justice done to a tyrant. Having no fragile interior, no tragic weakness, the Christian narrative does not need heroes who sacrifice themselves for the greater good. Christianity is not about lighting a candle in the dark; it is about standing in full day.

The reader can be forgiven for thinking that Labre might make an appropriate hero-type. Labre's virtue, so entwined with poverty and pain, so fascinated with overcoming the flesh and the world, does look at first glance dependent on the evil it combats. In fact, though, Labre's life makes sense only in the context of plenitude. He adopted vulnerability precisely to discover and proclaim he had no fragile interior which must be protected against evil. He did not hold off any misery or indignity. He did not flinch or scratch at his lice. He did not share his alms with others to fight off the pain that they were enduring but to testify to the plenty that supplied him. Montlinot bravely fought the battle of good against evil; Labre did not need to. Consumed in the joy of union with God and confident of providential care for himself and others, he behaved in an excessive way, in a gratuitous and new repetition of the Christ-life.

Labre relied on providence, not as a stopgap when his own efforts failed but aggressively, proactively. But providence did not keep him from being in pain, hungry, and filthy, from ridicule, or from a death hastened if not directly caused by starvation. Labre had no stake in proving himself so non-reactive as to be untouched by pain or by others' failures. He was secure, but he could be hurt. This plenitude, this participation in divine gift-

103. "Can Morality Be Christian?" in *The Word Made Strange: Theology, Language, Culture* (Oxford: Blackwell Publishers, 1997), 219-32.

136

giving did not remove Labre from his time and place. It led him to discover, and uncover, a community of mutual need and mutual care in
which dependence, even that of a beggar, is not the manipulation of pity in
a world of scarcity. It is the vulnerability of confident hope.[104]

Around his canonization in the nineteenth century, Labre was upheld
by ultramontane French Catholics as the champion of "otherworldliness,"
of death to the idolatry of the self before the absoluteness of God. His name
became a rallying cry against humanism, a shorthand for the importance of
the religious life dedicated to prayer, and a witness to the utter primacy of
our salvation in God. He did not become a rallying cry against the incarceration of the poor or in favor of the de-professionalization of the works of
mercy, anymore than he started a mass movement of renunciation.[105] The
otherworldiness ascribed to him existed as a dialectic against a certain type
of this-worldliness, and the "other world" was apparently not one present
in places and times. But in this, his admirers may have underestimated the
political import his witness had for a material, political body still present in
nineteenth-century France: the church.

The previous four chapters have offered a reading of various Christian accounts of property in an attempt to unpack the awkward silence surrounding dependent poverty in economic ethics. Seeing the power of Franciscan

104. In reading Labre this way, I am trying to correct a certain merciless flavor to
Milbank's essay. In his attempt to distinguish the Christian "notes" (gift, Resurrection, plenitude, End of sacrifice, confidence) from the heroic "marks" (Reaction, Sacrifice, Complicity
with Death, Scarcity, Generality), Milbank himself produces a strangely Nietzschean account of Christianity. This immoral Christianity approaches the faith of Zarathustra, who
proclaims himself "too rich to give alms": invulnerable (although through the gift of God),
the Christian does not participate in a world of suffering and lack. Triumphant, the Christian is herself removed from need and thereby, it seems, from compassion. This attempt to
speak of resurrection, plenitude, and confidence risks becoming murderously triumphal:
Rom Coles' work on *caritas* argues that those who cannot receive gifts also cannot give them,
except as domination. Invulnerable generosity becomes genocide because it never adequately encounters the difference of the other. Plenitude and confidence can actually destroy mercy and patience. *Rethinking Generosity: Critical Theory and the Politics of Caritas*
(Ithaca: Cornell University Press, 1997). Milbank himself addressed this problem in "The
Midwinter Sacrifice: A Sequel to 'Can Morality Be Christian?'" *Studies in Christian Ethics*,
October 1997: 13-38.

105. There were some imitators, the most famous and consistent of whom was the
poet Germain Nouveau. See Jacques Gadille, "La dévotion à Saint Benoît Labre dans le
mouvement spirituel du XIXe siècle," in *Errance et saintete*, 74-78.

poverty and its attendant scandals, we can better appreciate the impulse toward spiritualizing poverty and making wealth a prerequisite of moral action, which is to say, the impulse to stewardship. That stewardship rhetoric gained power alongside a critique of the church's wealth that was reducing the power of the church to be materially present in monasteries across the landscape. The proposed solution was to make the church poor and leave the management of property to the wealthy laity. Stewardship, as a theological category, is confused and has at times been conspicuously self-serving. But recognizing its failings only sends us back to the problems that preceded it. Certain kinds of power and possessions are necessary to ministers; honoring the lowly as superior can give rise to hypocrisy and refusal of any authority; disassociating economic virtue from respect for rights weakens the binding claims the poor can make on those who take advantage of them. Classical economists attempt to ensure fairness, maximize welfare, and minimize suffering through models of human exchange, but at the cost of supernatural eschatology and communities of public friendship. Still the Christian beggar's witness refuses to die out. Even after Smith's articulation of the fundamentals of liberal economics and Wesley's preaching on the duties of industry, frugality, and generosity, Benoît-Joseph Labre roamed the highways of France and Italy, looking for, and finding, the church that could receive his witness.

These stories are not reducible to analytic categories. But because the last two chapters of this work will examine some of their present-day descendents, it may be helpful at this point to tease out the major categories in play. First, we are talking about the material practice of *humility*. Humility as we meet it in voluntary beggars is not merely a realistic appraisal of oneself in relation to others, nor even a consciousness of one's subjection to God. It is a positive appropriation of and joy in lowliness, weakness, and dependence.[106] It involves shortage of food and clean, well-made clothes; precarity in shelter; and vulnerability to assault and insult. But this material humility is distinguishable from masochism or suicide because it exists within a narrative that disciplines it. Christian humility must stand in relation to *Christology*, particularly a *eucharistic Christology*

---

106. ST II-II, Q.161, a.2. Humility is informed by intellect, but is properly in the appetite. Thomas' account of humility would not be representative of all mendicants, to be sure. But that Thomas, a moderate on poverty among mendicants, located humility in this way rather than as an intellectual virtue having to do with appropriate self-knowledge, indicates the distance between recent and medieval notions of humility.

in which weakness becomes an active and creative position. The loss of self in humility is not about the desire to destroy the self per se, but about a desire to direct the self single-mindedly toward the love of God. The humble saint is not the young Benoît-Joseph Labre, so tormented by scruples that in spite of his devotion he was unwilling to receive communion, but the mature Labre, conspicuous in a crowd of beggars for his joy. Vulnerability as an element of humility is voluntarily assumed, not imposed by someone else; it functions as an invitation to the church, not as an isolation or subordination.

The joy that characterizes the saintly beggars suggests also that humility must be seen in relation to *eschatology*. The constraints of dependent poverty are self-destructive unless they point to the supernatural freedom of union with God and caution those who would prefer the freedom of wealth. The saint-beggars make no flat-footed assertions that the poverty endured by most people is advantageous in itself or that all possession of wealth is immoral. Francis's and Labre's vocations presently and materially make manifest the joy and plenitude of union with God as other than and superior to the goods of material welfare, and in doing so they call the church to join in that witness through the diversity of its saintly lives. Their joy in poverty is an "already" witness to a freedom and health which are "not yet."

This eschatological quality in no way makes their present witness immaterial or non-political. In its implication that wealth is an inferior good and that ultimately freedom comes of submission to God, Christian dependent poverty makes the question of eschatology immediate and economic. The church as the body of Christ already participates in the End, and therefore this eschatological witness is not 'otherworldly' for them. It is precisely concerned with the deepest truth about itself, its participation as historical community in the self-giving of the Trinity as revealed in the self-giving of Jesus.[107] This giving is blissful perichoresis within the Trinity

---

107. I am taking pains here to ensure that the language of eschatology and supernature will not be read as indicating that the reality of grace is in any way separate from human life in all its contingency. It is not a matter of a "higher" or "deeper" reality, and even less of a forensic change that leaves no marks in history. The End made present in the person of Jesus Christ remains present in the church. That something remains to be fulfilled is, however, undeniable. Sickness, death, and sin have not ended, not in the church or anywhere else. Thus while the church is the community of the End, where forgiveness, hope, and even humility have a home, all things are not yet subject to Christ. Indeed, when they

and crucifixion within the Roman empire. Either way, if the gift is not oriented toward joy, confidence, and charity, it is not Christian virtue.[108]

We are also considering humility in light of its potential conflict with *efficiency,* meaning the achievement of a goal with the least amount of labor and material expended so that resources are used to their maximum effect. Within the ethics of stewardship, efficiency is directed toward maximizing return on investment in missionary and social service work. Waste is conflated in Wesley (et al.) with irresponsible use of the goods entrusted to the steward by God. While a rational appraisal of one's abilities is useful for efficiency (since it indicates when to enlist another's aid) the humility of our beggars impedes efficiency by courting ill health and abjuring the use of helpful tools. Insofar as efficiency has been incorporated into the ethics of benevolence and service, humility has come into conflict with an important conception of moral life. It is by this route that stewardship and humility directly intersect, for the effective service upheld as the center of moral agency in stewardship rhetoric requires the right use of power within a stable and relatively predictable order, while the beggars' practice of humility is predicated on renunciation of what are usually taken to be the constitutive elements of power: wealth, security, health, and access to technology and the frontiers of scholarship, not to mention any pretense of predictable order.[109]

Finally, *ecclesiology.* Removed from an ecclesiological context, a material humility would be nonsense. One cannot be dependent without being dependent upon someone else. As we have seen even in the cases of Alexis and Labre, who tried to remain incognito, ultimately recognition is

---

are, faith and hope will pass away, and only love will remain. The already of the church's participation in the end is particularly visible in the witness of ascetic saints, who are full of joy and triumph in the midst of evident deprivation, and whose triumph is recognized in the church. I am thinking particularly of Saints Blandina and Anthony, for example — her physical weakness before her martyrdom and his fasts both resulted in glowing health, for a time. Nevertheless, both died.

108. A fuller discussion of this will follow in my treatment of John Milbank's thought on gift.

109. For this reason Nietzsche uses beggars as the classic example of *ressentiment.* To make them fit into his account of human power-seeking, he concluded that they must be seizing power through the underhanded route of pity. The history of the mendicant orders, it must be said, hardly disproves his claim. Friedrich Nietzsche, *Thus Spoke Zarathustra: A Book for All and None,* trans. Walter Kaufmann (New York: The Modern Library, 1995), 269; also 11, 89, 199.

essential. The beggar must be seen not only so that someone will offer the alms needed to sustain a penitential life, but so that the beggar's invitation into eucharistic economy and witness to eschatological hope are offered. Beggars require alms for their maintenance and recognition for their vocation. Unlike contemplatives who can live relatively independent and inconspicuous lives by basket-weaving or farming, mendicants are continually bumping up against other members of the church, drawing them into some share in the life of poverty. The church provides material support and the narration that can make sense of what the beggar does. While a beggar may pursue this vocation when the church offers little of either kind of support, and while no calling ensures its own success, nevertheless any sufficient account of material humility must take as its center the hope that the beggars' dependence will meet with the return gifts it seeks. A steward may practice her craft without a church, but the beggar must have one.

The previous four chapters have ransacked history for illuminating insights into poverty and dependence, humility and rights, stewardship and economic rationality. We are now in a position to turn with much richer understanding to twentieth-century attempts to describe the virtues of humility and poverty within economic life.

CHAPTER FIVE

Reaping What Was Sown

After our tour of the exotic worlds of beggars, Elizabethan reformers, and philosopher-economists, we land at last on familiar — perhaps all-too-familiar — territory: Stewardship Sunday. This much-dreaded holiday, with its appeals for pledges of "time, talent, and treasure,"[1] is met sometimes with remarkable generosity and often with skepticism. Its detailed financial statements and speeches on the obligations that come with financial blessings; its marketing gimmicks; and the strange mix of boredom and embarrassment that descends on a congregation faced with the topic carry on the histories unfolded in the last four chapters. The congregation's leader turns into a beggar and/or a marketer (recalling the friars of *Piers Plowman*), the congregation into the uncomfortable, harassed, or sanctimonious target of pleas and flattery. The worship service may be accompanied by a business meeting focused on efficiency and transparency, affording a glimpse into the inner life of the parish as a small business with little internal connection to worship, in spite of frequent references to gratitude and self-giving. The church must simultaneously be humble in its following of Christ and well-supplied with the means necessary for effective work in the world, at once generous and efficient.

Stewardship Sunday has generated a vast body of pastoral literature. It has also been the butt of a significant body of jokes. For many congregations, the importance of donations determined on this day lends a kind of

---

1. This phrase was trademarked by the National Catholic Stewardship Council in 1970.

desperate air to it, a kind of gravity which only makes the ever-new, always-the-same tactics for rousing generosity more distressing. The whole affair rings false. Articles on "preaching stewardship" indicate that this activity is in many respects parallel to an NPR pledge drive, accompanied by the same anxieties. Will the appeal for money undermine the internal goods of the community and drive people away? How can one make people recognize their responsibility without being reduced to nagging? How often should the topic be broached? Should the rhetoric aim to make financial problems more noble or to make people's idea of nobility more earthy?[2] But this is no joking matter, for the sharing of goods among Christians is one of the hallmarks of Christian life. If Christians cannot talk about property and needs among themselves, at least, then we can be sure that something is seriously awry.

The past four chapters have been an attempt to illuminate that awry "something." Drawing on the lessons the past can offer, we are in a position now to consider what is going wrong in recent work on stewardship. Stewardship, in theological circles, is not a particularly serious term, and yet the consequences of the problems associated with it are profound. As Archbishop Theodore McCarrick told diocesan fiscal managers in a 1996 address, "[Your job is to see] that the diocese is run like a business, when you know so clearly that it is not a business. This is a contradiction in the life of the church, and you are the ones who are caught in the middle of it."[3] In fact, anyone who has ever endured a stewardship Sunday — from either side of the pulpit — is caught there with them.

This chapter will start with a study of the U.S. Catholic Conference of Bishops' pastoral letter on stewardship, with the "application" document that followed it to see how the legacy of our beggars and stewards is playing out in the present day. Douglas John Hall, Protestantism's leading theologian of stewardship, will provide a more extreme example of that legacy, with its propensity to spiritualize the church right out of its material existence. Then we'll turn to John Milbank's theological work on gift as an alternative, but one that remains unfortunately hindered by its own theological imagination. Our best work on possession still has a long way to go.

2. See, for example, Al Fasol, "Rendering unto God," *Southwestern Journal of Theology* 37 (Spring 1995); P. C. Eniss, "Preaching Stewardship in an Affluent Congregation," *Journal for Preachers* 18 (Lent 1995); John and Sylvia Ronsvalle, "When Stewardship Is a Dirty Word," *Christian Ministry* 25 (May-June 1994).
3. "Dilemmas and Challenges for Diocesan Fiscal Managers," *Origins* 26:18 (10/17/96).

A Swing and a Miss: The NCCB Pastoral Letter on Stewardship

Catholics were latecomers to the language of stewardship, perhaps because the word itself is peculiar to English. Latin does not have an exact equivalent to the term: although *dispensatio* is the translation of *oikonomia* in the Vulgate, it had not been part of the developments of the English Reformation, Methodism, and U.S. missions fundraising and therefore did not function in the same way the word "stewardship" did. In Latin, *dispensator* refers positively to good household management. A separate word, *villicus,* connotes business practice, as in "foreman." Latin here retains something of the Greek distinction between economics and chrematistics (profit-seeking trade), and it is certainly not surprising that a medieval scholastic working in Latin used *oeconomos* and *dispensator* with a discussion of the virtues, as referring to good household management, while matters of business and finance (where *villicus* would be more appropriate) were considered in a treatise on vices.[4] The term that referred to business people as models of excellent virtue was not readily available in Latin.

The term "stewardship" seems to have first gained an important set of advocates among Catholics through the Catholic National Council for Diocesan Support Programs (NCDSP). This group had emerged out of an informal meeting of diocesan finance directors called by Archbishop Joseph Ritter of St. Louis in 1962. The 1950s had seen a great increase in the use of an annual fundraising drive within dioceses, an innovation in Catholic practice, and Ritter saw a need for Catholics to share ideas and resources to improve such endeavors. In 1964, members of that original meeting formed the NCDSP. For their 1967 meeting, Fr. Emmanuel Ballard of Brownsville, Texas, invited Gilbert Stout, Methodist National Director of Stewardship and Finance, to talk on the Protestant understanding of stewardship as a biblical concept to the hundred participants from more than fifty-two U.S. dioceses. Ballard had already introduced a stewardship program in his area, using the existing base of Cursillo groups, and was impressed at the way it brought together spiritual commitment and financial support for the church. Stout himself made quite an impression on the delegates. It is probably due to his influence that when the NCDSP needed

4. See Odd Langholm on John of LaRochelle, *Economics in the Medieval Schools: Wealth, Exchange, Value, Money, and Usury according to the Paris Theological Tradition, 1200-1350* (Leiden: Brill, 1992), 122.

to change its name a year later (so that parish support programs could be included), it opted to become the National Catholic Stewardship Council (NCSC). Within this body, stewardship signaled the attempt to see parish and diocesan fundraising as an integral part of the life of Christians, rather than merely as the paying of dues. The ecumenical flavor of the term may have been an added attraction, although the NCSC was always eager to demonstrate its doctrinal faithfulness to Catholicism and its loyalty to the hierarchy.

Although the NCSC membership was composed of finance and development directors rather than theologians, a number of voices within the group kept the concern for theological and spiritual content alive and well. In 1967 the chair of the NCDSP wrote to Cardinal Dearden, explaining that the group's efforts were "directed to the commitment of the laity and include the sharing of their time, talent, and material blessings for the good of the whole Church."[5] A famous friend of the NCSC better known for his work with the National Catholic Rural Life Council, Luigi Ligutti, managed to have the Decree on the Laity of Vatican II include the statement that "It is for Christians a duty and an honor to give God back a portion of the goods they have received from him."[6] Ligutti's involvement not only with the NCRLC but also the Pontifical Committee for Justice and Peace gave him a broad view of stewardship as a matter of personal, profound engagement in Christ's work. Ligutti was particularly influential in organizing in 1973 the first International Seminar on Stewardship in Rome, which attracted many representatives from Africa and Asia. There, Ligutti took a stand against the idea that stewardship refers to contributions by the rich. "The dimes and nickels of the Irish servant girls paid for St. Patrick's in New York in Manhattan. . . . We don't need the rich to support our Christian institutions — we need loving people who share their poverty with a Church of the poor."[7] Fr. Francis Novak, chosen in 1973 to be the first full-time national director of the NCSC, approached stewardship as a matter of worship. The first annual conference after his appointment had as its theme, "The Spirituality of Stewardship — The Logic of Commitment."

5. Cited in Sr. Mary Roger Madden, S.P., *Gladly Will I Spend and Be Spent: A Brief History of the National Catholic Stewardship Council, Inc., 1962-1997* (Washington, D.C.: National Catholic Stewardship Council, 1997), 20.

6. Decree on the Laity, Ch. 10, #3. Madden, *Gladly Will I Spend*, 27.

7. Madden, *Gladly Will I Spend*, 39.

But in 1979, the board of the NCSC, composed mostly of diocesan development directors and fiscal officers trained in professional fundraising, ousted Novak. The NCSC's own history of the event records that,

> In light of the makeup of the board of directors, it is not surprising that a lack of agreement developed between the National Director, with his deeply felt commitment to a theology of total stewardship and the more pragmatic view of persons whose education and background were that of professional fund-raisers. . . . The perception had developed on both sides that the differences between the Director and the Board were at the level of philosophy and were irreconcilable.[8]

Novak was replaced with a cleric who had been a director of development for fourteen years, evidently in the hopes of honoring the spiritual without giving ground on the practical. In theory, the NCSC remains committed both to promoting stewardship as a way of describing one's total commitment to Christianity and to fostering more effective fundraising techniques. But the conflict that brought about the break with Novak, which some describe as a clash of theology and practice, continues in Catholic thought on stewardship to the present day, as only too evident in the tale of the 1992 pastoral letter on stewardship.

The NCSC had worried for years about how to gain more attention and support from bishops, and they were delighted to be of assistance when the United States Catholic Conference decided to conduct a study of stewardship in 1988. Within the first day that the USCCB's Ad Hoc Committee on Stewardship met, the idea of a pastoral letter had been floated, as members agreed that the problem of stewardship was a spiritual one and not simply a matter of mechanics. For the NCSC the decision to produce a pastoral letter on stewardship was a vindication of more than twenty years of work. For all those concerned with improving the effectiveness and theological richness of stewardship among Catholics, hopes for this letter ran high. Archbishop Thomas Murphy chaired the committee and oversaw the writing of the letter.

To the authors' credit, they seized immediately on the most obvious danger of the term, its use as a pious code name for fundraising and management. They threw great energy into writing about stewardship as a

8. Madden, *Gladly Will I Spend,* 46.

thoroughgoing approach that makes all of life into an offering to God. The idea of stewardship can, of course, function without reference to the gospel, as in its use in environmental movements and business. But the committee clearly intended the term to carry Christian content. From the beginning, they treat stewardship as a subcategory of discipleship. In case anyone missed this in the document's title — "Stewardship: A Disciple's Response" — they make their claim explicit in the first paragraph: "Stewardship is an expression of discipleship" (1). They emphasize that in stewardship Christians "follow Christ and try to live his life as our own" (12). Stewardship is about recognizing all things as gifts from God, "collaborating with God in the work of creation,"[9] and "cooperating with God in the work of redemption" (7). The authors attempt both to limit stewardship under the rubric of discipleship and to broaden it out from its use as code for fundraising throughout the letter. Notably, they claim faithfulness to one's calling to be an act of stewardship, making wise use of the gift of vocation. They associate stewardship with detachment from worldly goods as obstacles to the spiritual life. They tie stewardship into evangelism, which is wise management of the Good News. Most conspicuously, they touch on fundraising only very generally and not at great length.

The "stewardship" of the pastoral is, it should be obvious, not entirely at ease with stewardship as most congregations and offices of development or finance know it. Gratitude for God's gifts, responsible use, and return on God's investment are standard elements of stewardship appeals. The pastoral speaks little of gratitude or return with increase, but it does repeatedly urge detachment from material goods. Detachment is a loosing of reliance on and desire for goods, a discipline of giving up even innocent goods for the sake of focusing more clearly on the source of all goods. In commending detachment, the pastoral is using the language of dispossession for the sake of discipleship, emphasizing renunciation rather than efficiency or even responsible use. It calls "dangers" the very things that stewardship usually names "blessings." The tension between these two rhetorics runs through the entire document, and can be seen particularly in an appeal the letter makes to Ignatius of Loyola. The quotation given from his *Exercises* asserts that created things exist to help people to "praise, reverence, and serve God, and by this means to save their souls," and that, therefore, disciples "are to make use of these things in as far as they help

9. They draw this language from *Laborem exercens,* especially #25.

them in the attainment of their end, and they must rid themselves of them in as far as they provide a hindrance to them." The pastoral's commentary on this quotation reads, "The right use of things includes and requires that they be used to serve others" (20-21). The citation is friendly to an Augustinian selective detachment from goods; the commentary, on the other hand, is stewardly, emphasizing effective use. The pastoral nowhere treats this tension.

The letter also claims that the Sermon on the Mount and the Beatitudes (Mt. 5:3–7:27) "prescribe the life-style of a Christian disciple." Jesus is the steward *par excellence* in his governance of the household of God, because he calls and empowers people to "collaborate with him in the work of redemption for themselves and on behalf of others" (19). To this end, he "does not waste time proposing lofty but unrealistic ideals; he tells his followers how they are expected to live. . . . Although it does not suit worldly tastes, 'the wisdom of this world is foolishness in the eyes of God' (1 Cor. 3:19)" (19). Again, these are surprising steps, though the caution about worldly prudence would have been at home in Wesley. Jesus' fidelity to his mission is usually called *obedience* rather than *stewardship,* and the emphasis on his teachings would seem to imply a corollary about the obedience of disciples. But stewardship, with its managerial image, softens the authoritarian sound of obedience and adds a dash of creativity and initiative that the virtue of obedience, at least as heard by Catholics in the U.S., lacks. The content of the commands is also surprising. The teaching the bishops cite here includes proclamation of favor to the lowly and persecuted people, urges daily trust in God rather than solicitude for the future, and demands non-retaliation and indiscriminate charity, down to giving the shirt off one's back rather than engaging in lawsuits. The components most characteristic of stewardship — gratitude, recognition of God's prior right, responsible use, and return with profit — get no attention, while "turn the other cheek" and "give to him who begs from you" are proclaimed as Jesus' no-nonsense instructions on life. The logic of stewardship has no integral connection to the Sermon on the Mount, and the letter offers no evidence that it does.

In fact, the letter has much more to say about spiritual wealth than money or material resources. Rather than beginning with the Genesis account that gives humanity charge of creation or with Matthew 25 (the parable of the talents) or 1 Peter 4 ("good stewards of God's grace"), the chapter "Living as a Steward" sets out by recognizing that God intends humans to be collaborators in creation and co-operators in redemption. The proclamation of the gospel at Pentecost is their example of stewardship. One might argue that in this episode, the disciples are less collaborators than cowards transformed by God's presence into witnesses. The wise use of human resources is less in the foreground than is God's capacity to renew the world. Where the parables of the talents (Mt. 25; Lk. 19) and the steward ready for the master's return (Mt. 24; Lk. 12) depend upon the owner's temporary absence as the circumstance for stewardship, Pentecost presumes the unquestionable activity of the Spirit, sent by Jesus. The case of Pentecost suggests that Christians do participate in God's work, but in ways that suit God's timing and wisdom and rely entirely on God's power. Again, this is hardly a typical turn for a stewardship lesson.

While the authors claim that it would be an error to say, as Douglas Hall does, that stewardship sums up the entire gospel, they themselves connect stewardship with the priesthood of the baptized; all forms of work; prayer, penance, visits to the Blessed Sacrament, and attending daily Mass; patience in suffering; ecological responsibility; solidarity and social justice; work to reduce "structural forms of poverty," military spending, and war-making; and an invitation to solidarity and a "simpler lifestyle." Stewardship, it begins to seem, refers to every aspect of discipleship — except donations to the church.

When the letter does briefly discuss financial support for the church as a component of Christian stewardship, it does so within the chapter called "Stewards of the Church." In one of the most interesting moves of the letter, support of parish and diocese is treated as examples of a person's good management — but of the church, not of the person's own wealth. The church, not my bank account, is the gift of God I must care for and bring to profit. That care involves the edification of the church through the virtues; through offerings of "time, talent, and treasure" (34); through family life, where children are trained in Christian faith and resistance to consumerism and individualism; and in parishes and dioceses, through "sound business practice," described as adhering to strict ethical, legal, and fiscal standards, to openness and accountability (34).

Yet even in this chapter, with its refreshing read of stewardship as care of the church, financial support for institutions does not merit its own sub-heading. The brief treatment of church support happens within a subsection on evangelization. Why is there no distinct section to deal with the problem of the skimpy financial contributions of Catholics to their parishes and dioceses, when research shows that Catholics rank among the lowest contributors to their congregations?[10] It is one matter to write a letter that emphasizes personal and spiritual engagement, with finances as a component of that. It is quite another to avoid the topic of money so carefully that only a detailed reading of the document can find any evidence that it is an issue at all. After all, stewardship does refer in ordinary usage and in its institutional forms to church support. That is the NCSC's very raison d'être. Its membership is composed of fiscal officers and development directors. It was the concern of the Ad Hoc Committee on Stewardship. Stewardship is still, as in the (now) International Catholic Stewardship Council's summer workshop, often paired with development programs. The letter was most eagerly awaited by offices that would previously have been known as Development or Church Support. Enriching the category of stewardship was a laudable goal; burying the critical discussion makes that "enriching" appear nothing more than a disingenuous attempt to avoid the issue.

In making the decision to embed the section on financial support for parish and diocese within the section on evangelization, the writers implicitly rejected the possibility of treating financial stewardship within the section on solidarity and social justice or within the section on the Eucharist, as a discussion of material sharing in the church. In this respect, it is interesting to note that although the section on solidarity asserts from the start that union in Christ transcends human solidarity and bears spiritual fruit, the remainder of the comments on solidarity discuss divisions rooted in personalities, classes, nations, and even among followers of Christ. The "solidarity" in question here includes the union of believers as one example, but that union so quickly moves into outreach that it itself receives no attention. To have considered financial contributions under the rubric of solidarity within the ecclesial community would have required a more substantive treatment of that community in itself, not merely as evangelizer or agent of justice. The document does not offer that

10. Catholics ranked twenty-first in a study of contributions as a percentage of income in twenty-three ecclesial groups (only ahead of Christian Scientists and Unitarian-Universalists). Statistics gathered for 1987-89. Charles Zech, *Why Catholics Don't Give . . . and What You Can Do about It* (Huntington, Ind.: Our Sunday Visitor, 2000), 12. Statistics from 2004 compiled by the Barna group find Catholics still giving less than half as much as Protestants and about one-sixth as much as evangelicals do to their churches. www.barna.org/FlexPage.aspx?Page=BarnaUpdateID=187

kind of treatment of the church. In a letter rich in scriptural allusions, the sharing of goods among Christians attested in Acts 2 and 4 makes no appearance in this text.

The church, in this document, exists for spiritual and material service to the rest of humanity, rather than its own life or calling. "As all this suggests, our individual lives as disciples and stewards must be seen in relation to God's larger purposes" (37). Between our individual lives and those larger purposes, the church is a mediating organization, not an essential component of the larger purpose, much less a necessary condition of discipleship. The Eucharist, as the letter discusses it, should lead to acts of charity and evangelization, but within itself, the Eucharist is an encounter of the individual with Christ in such a way that the bonds of charity among the disciples and with the rest of humanity are strengthened. The Eucharist appears to be incidentally related to the institution of the church, which is distinct from the union of believers with each other and with Christ. Catholic conscience is understandably tender when it comes to connecting financial donations to the Eucharist. But that very tenderness draws attention to one of the most intransigent problems in Catholic stewardship discourse. Implicitly, the question is still one of how an individual or family's possessions are connected to the institution known as the church. The question is *not* how the family of the church — a body composed of all the baptized — can share its possessions, loving one another as Christ did.

So it is that the singular in the title "Stewardship: A *Disciple's* Response," is no accident. The authors are very concerned with the social ramifications of discipleship. They frequently condemn individualism. Still the notion of discipleship itself remains singular, with the church as the structure through which individual disciples work together to achieve larger ends in the public sphere, never the church itself.

This letter was received with "some disappointment, as well as sharp criticism" (1), according to the resource manual entitled "Stewardship and Development in Catholic Dioceses and Parishes," released in 1996 by the Ad Hoc Committee on Stewardship. As the manual tells the story, "Some thought there was a de-emphasis of stewardship as a technique to raise additional funds for financially strapped and needy church institutions. . . . 'What we expected from the bishops,' a fund raiser said, 'is guidance in how to make donations to the church a religious experience motivated by the high ideals of stewardship'" (1-2). The manual then cites the paragraphs discussed above from the section on evangelism as evidence that the letter did indeed address stewardship as donations to the church. Nevertheless, when the pastoral letter was approved, the Ad Hoc Committee on Stewardship agreed also to produce resources to guide the actual processes of stewardship education and formation. Practical application had to follow the statement of principles.

No one should have been surprised at the strained and confused text that this process produced by way of "resource manual." The manual claims that a development program needs first a "spiritually-based plan" (to be drawn from the pastoral), and then a communications program and a "fundraising program based on stewardship and development principles" that sets out how the parish or diocese will "identify prospective donors" (especially those the manual calls "major gift prospects"), "build strong relationships," and "solicit gifts" (9). The manual is adamant that the "spiritually-based plan" comes first, and that prayer and personal commitment to stewardship by the staff are indispensable. Study of the bishops' pastoral is not so much recommended as demanded.

The manual, however, uses language and logic quite alien to the pastoral. The painstaking attempt to discipline stewardship under discipleship evaporates. The manual translates that effort by emphasizing education and formation in stewardship so that stewardship is not merely fundraising but instead a "faith response." The pastoral itself did not characterize stewardship as religiously motivated donation, but as commitment and obedience to God's call to discipleship in every area of life. But once principles are lauded and safely segregated from practicalities, the application manual pulls back the curtain to reveal that the bottom line is still the bottom line. Fundraisers are, for example, urged to "use the best available ethically sound fund-raising practices" (17). Presumably the authors did not mean that having found an effective fundraising technique, people should ask of it whether it honors the blessedness of the lowly and persecuted, whether it is solicitous or trusting in providence, whether it is consistent with storing up treasure in heaven rather than on earth, and so on. "Ethically sound fund-raising" remains a cryptic phrase in relation to the pastoral letter. Games of chance and social functions as fundraisers are mentioned as decreasing in number, but no moral judgment is passed about them. When a kind of categorical refusal is issued, the phrase "minimum giving" is its object (10).

Where the manual does include explicitly moral teaching on stewardship, its reasoning is entirely distinct from the teaching of the pastoral. The manual teaches that "self-giving is good for the spiritual health and vitality of the individual, family, or community" (23). This is a far cry from the pastoral's repeated warnings that attachment to wealth is dangerous. In the manual's formulation, giving is like jogging or eating an apple a day; the pastoral implies it is more like the antidote to poison. Similarly, the manual speaks firmly on "accountability" as an ethical requirement of good stewardship, even as "central to our understanding of stewardship and development" (21), and it defines accountability as giving evidence that those who receive the donation will use it in ways that are effective, stable, and will continue to grow. Like the "deserving poor," they must show themselves "'worthy of investment'" (21). Although the pastoral does call for careful record-keeping and conscientious openness about financial matters in parishes and dioceses, the necessity of demonstrating potential for growth is alien to their document. The manual urges parishes and dioceses to use fundraising techniques "that respect and reinforce stewardship themes of gratitude, accountability, generosity, and returning to the Lord with increase." Of these themes, the pastoral lingers only on generosity. "Returning to the Lord with increase," a phrase open to numerous interpretations, is altogether absent from the bishops' account of collaboration through the work of the Holy Spirit.

In sum, this manual offers quite a confused notion of stewardship. The authors claim on the first page that on the judgment day, "God will have the right to ask, 'What did you do with my world?'" (1). Stewardship is the obligation people have to the true Owner of the world, who has a claim of right against humans for that property. In spite of this dramatic opening, they then urge stewardship staff to avoid using appeals to obligation or guilt in their work (10). At this point in the text, stewardship asks, "How much do you want to give?" (25). Later in the same document, the content changes again to concern for the preferences of those Catholics who "need assistance in estate planning" (14), whose "personal and financial objectives are of primary concern in the decision whether to make a planned gift . . ." (13), and who will be happy to learn about ways to contribute that in addition to awakening them to their stewardship responsibilities, can "provide very practical suggestions on how to increase income, save taxes, and contribute to the Church" (14). Those who will most appreciate this sort of opportunity, "major gift prospects," are to be included in stewardship campaigns early so that they can contribute to the entire process. The implication that they should be courted is not spelled out, but neither is it corrected. Nowhere in the document is the New Testament teaching against favoritism to the rich cited. The terms "stewardship," "sacrificial giving," and "philanthropy" are used almost interchangeably (9, 23, 25). Their easy association with each other in this document makes clear the functional irrelevance of their theological content.

All of this simply tells us that the authors were limited by a lack of preparation to think theologically about financial matters, and in that shortcoming they have a great deal of company. The authors of the pastoral attempted a theologically full-blooded account of stewardship, but that attempt became incoherent because it had no edges and ignored its own key concern. Above all, failing to present the church as more than an association of like-minded disciples holds back not only the pastoral, but this "practical" addendum to it. The authors of the pastoral seem reticent to make the church central to stewardship, in a way that would make contributions to the institution itself as morally serious as other issues they raise. The authors of the resource manual present the church as a worthy and honest competitor for financing in a competitive market, and the pastoral letter did not offer them an account that would have helped them to claim a more central identity, to think of the church as a community of peace in which goods are shared as a work of love within the Body of Christ.

The failure of the pastoral to address financial sharing in the church directly was not cowardice or evasion. The authors believed that emphasizing full discipleship does address the core issue and ultimately will result in a stronger faith and a correspondingly greater willingness to share in the financial burdens of the congregation and diocese.[11] Nevertheless, this approach in the pastoral letter — if we focus on stewardship-as-discipleship, then stewardship-as-fundraising will take care of itself — resulted in the production of a separate application document that filled the gap. Someone had to directly address fundraising for the benefit of those in charge of stewardship and development offices because the theological writers failed

11. See for example the comments of Monsignor Thomas McGread of St. Francis of Assisi parish, in Bob Zyskowski, "True Stewardship: It Takes More Than Money to Keep a Parish Afloat," *U.S. Catholic*, March 2003. Msgr. McGread recently gave a talk for fundraisers about his parish, entitled, "The Story of St. Francis: How Stewardship Became a Way of Life," available online at http://www.catholicsteward.com/Images/MsgrMcGread.pdf.

THE FEAR OF BEGGARS

to do it. The result: the word "stewardship" was reinterpreted in the pastoral, but the structures within which the word functions were unchanged, and therefore the reinterpretation had to be glossed back into line. What the authors of the pastoral gestured toward as practical advice did not match the institutional practices of U.S. Catholicism and therefore was not received.

The pastoral announced that the Sermon on the Mount is practical advice, and meanwhile the pastoral itself was read as containing principles, high spirituality, and not a bit of practical advice for those who have to find funding for congregations and dioceses. Directors of stewardship and development offices can hardly be blamed for this. They are after all embedded in the distinction between an intellectual-spiritual class that knows little of money and a practical-managerial class that does the dirty work. That distinction has deep roots in the origins of stewardship in the English Reformation, when the laity took on the burden of wealth so that the spiritual elite could, for their own good, live in poverty. The fault lies more with the authors of the pastoral, who never acknowledged the real problem: fundraising as we currently know it is foreign to discipleship. The problem was not that the pastoral gave only theory. The problem was that the pastoral spoke as though it belonged to a different kind of application than it did. After all that the pastoral claimed stewardship meant, the International Catholic Stewardship Council's Institute for Stewardship and Development in July 2003 (held, ironically, at the San Damiano Center of Danville, California) did not advertise sessions devoted to justice issues or to the environment. A number of liturgical and devotional events were scheduled, but no discussion or training events had prayer and penance as their topics of reflection, nor did those topics feature prominently in the description of the Institute. Instead it advertised sessions specifically concerned with major gift fundraising and planned giving, as well as a discussion of the pastoral letter in which, no doubt, the point was made that stewardship means more than stewardship means.[12]

Charles Zech's study, entitled *Why Catholics Don't Give . . . and What Can Be Done about It*, like the resource manual a "practical rather than theological" work, exemplifies the tragic outcome of that theology. Throughout the book, Zech, an economics professor at Villanova Univer-

---

12. Registration information for this institute was posted on the ICSC website, www.catholicstewardship.org.

sity, applies the logic of rational choice and utility to analyze the notoriously low amounts given by Catholics to the church. Zech considers characteristics of target groups, what they look for in a church, and what would cause them to give more to the church, and he uncovers some intriguing results. For example, more than half of his sample Catholics, when asked if they would give more to a parish that was more spiritually nourishing, said they would not. More than sixty percent said they would not give more if the preaching were better. Zech explains that people probably are satisfied with the spiritual life and preaching of their churches and therefore don't see an increase in quality making a significant difference in their giving.[13] This rather unlikely explanation aside, Zech's training sets up a model that does not suit the community under consideration. This logic, that a better or better-targeted product can attract a better price, is suited to the church only if we have assumed that the church is a voluntary association of spiritual consumers. Zech gets odd results because the discourse of utility is incommensurable with Catholic ecclesiological habits. Catholics likely will not give more to a more spiritually nourishing parish because many Catholics do not go to a parish to be spiritually nourished. They go because attendance at Mass is an obligation. The efficacy of the sacraments is not commensurable with increased spiritual "satisfaction." Even if better preaching actually would increase contributions, a Catholic might find it insulting to admit it. Awareness that the institutional church is necessary, that it is the body of Christ, makes people willing to give money to keep the furnace running.

Similarly, Zech found the "perplexing" result that Catholics who contributed more were more likely to emphasize the importance of changing unjust social structures or of participating in sacraments than of following the teachings of Jesus,[14] but this finding makes perfect sense if we acknowledge that the first two emphases require a material existence of an institutional church and the second is often thought to require no such institution. In spite of the fact that his research shows a strong correlation between those denominations which hold that their church plays an indispensable role in salvation and the denominations which are most strongly

---

13. Zech, *Why Catholics Don't Give*, 80-82. Having listened to many Catholic homilies and to many Catholics complaining about the quality of their priests' homilies, I find this explanation highly unlikely.

14. Zech, *Why Catholics Don't Give*, 54-55, 60.

financially supported, Zech seems not to notice that those who see some urgency in the existence of the material, political church are the ones willing to pay for it.

In his final comments, Zech pronounces stewardship as a spiritual commitment to be more important than the mere technique of fundraising, but he does so in a way that demonstrates just the opposite.

> In short, these other recommendations [fundraising techniques] should be viewed as *pre-conditions* to successful parish stewardship. Stewardship is *primary,* but without these other factors *in place,* any stewardship program will, at a minimum, be less effective than it could be, and may even be doomed to failure.[15]

The pre-conditions which must already be in place before stewardship can "be effective" (i.e., increase financial contributions) are themselves, by definition, primary, in spite of the author's attempt to insist that that honor goes to stewardship as a lifelong faith.

These discussions are full of confusion and self-deception, and the culprit is the incoherence of stewardship rhetoric itself. At its emergence, stewardship allowed lay people to claim the crucial and (in its redefined sense) humble role of managers of ecclesial wealth, to preserve holiness in the purity of poverty. The habits of that separation linger in the church's life, around that term and around the financial necessities of parishes and dioceses. And now, when those most engaged in thinking about financial welfare are trying to argue that financial welfare must be secondary to discipleship, the problem is woven into the structures of thought and institution that separate financial responsibility from leadership in sanctity.

The focus on the property an individual owns without investigation of whether that property was justly gained; the idea that managing wealth is a humble service in comparison with the purely spiritual (which is to say, useless, and finally impossible) poverty of the church; and the tendency therefore to downplay the church as a body — these are the heritage of the accounts of stewardship we considered in Chapter Three.

The confusion of well-intentioned leadership in this matter also owes some thanks to habits descending from Smith and Malthus. A fully

---

15. Zech, *Why Catholics Don't Give,* 139. Emphasis added.

frank discussion of needs and resources would be necessary so that property could fulfill its social destiny or so that the community of faith could attest to its mutual love because of Christ. That kind of discussion would presuppose a forum in which it could take place, which is not commonly available. It also would presuppose a mutual trust deeply foreign to those who have imagined Malthus's overturning of Nature's table. It would presuppose an understanding of a common good such that admitting one's need is not the pathetic whining of Smith's beggars, or the greatest humiliation of a person schooled in impartiality. It would require the end of patterns of thought that determine the potency of moral characters by how much they can give. Because the stewardship ethic, as we find it to some extent in the NCCB document and much more frankly in the resource manual, presumes that the moral agent is an individual charged with personal responsibility for certain resources, dependence will present for it the same sort of problems it does for Smith: reception of a gift will imply some moral lack in the recipient.

Unresolved traditional issues about rights also haunts current stewardship practice. Stewardship denotes God's right over all goods. In fact, on the surface of it this is the strongest claim implied. But accounts are not yet being settled, and, in the meantime, stewardship denotes the rights and duties of present holders of wealth, without raising questions about the justice of that status quo. It therefore endows the stewards with a *pro temp* right of possession and distribution. Given that the details of their commission to use goods in accord with God's intentions remain rather vague, an individual steward has a fair range of control. Still, stewardship also implies that a claim can be made by those in need, and particularly by the church. The church does not claim a right over the goods of its members, but it can insist that as stewards they have an obligation to God such that they should use those goods for certain pressing needs. Instead of simply asking for what it needs, as a member of a family or a beggar might do, the church walks this fine line, making its claim without appealing to a right of its own.

Plus ça change. . . . Stewardship, earlier in its history, was an appeal made by those who hoped to purify and/or impoverish the church. Now it is used in an attempt to build up that institution. It emerged as part of a justification of a claim against the wealth of the church: lay stewards have an obligation to care for the goods of the earth on behalf of God's work. Now it is turned into a claim the church makes on others: lay stewards have an obligation to use those goods *on behalf of God's work.* Calls for stewardship avoid the authoritarian tones of demands for obedience or loyalty, but they also avoid direct cultivation of fellowship in the Body of Christ. Stewards' obligations are to God, not to those in need. When, then, the church is in need or wants to appeal on behalf of another's need, it talks not about that need within the Body, but about an obligation the individual steward has to God. The appeal can be made without any admission of need, without any sharing in the lack or danger that need creates, without what would usually be called begging. It is also made without any rights of the poor or of the church being invoked, which would imply some conflict between those holding wealth and those invoking the right. The right is re-routed through obligations to the long-absent Owner. Avoiding the conflict of asserting rights, stewardship simultaneously tries to avoid the beggar's admission of need and lack of control, and the humiliation of receiving a gift. Too often, it achieves only confusion and skepticism.

In the stewardship literature just considered, the potential for gift to be humiliating goes unrecognized, as does the possibility that a community of Christians might be able to work together toward a common good in such a way that dependence is no offense to dignity. The NCCB letter fails to consider that the church may be a community within which material sharing happens in a distinctive way.

Even those with generous intentions are finding their efforts inhibited. Fr. Doug Haefner of St. Matthias in Somerset, New Jersey, interviewed as an advocate of a full-blooded approach to stewardship, commented that the word *stewardship* just had all the wrong associations for the rich call to prayer, engagement in the church, and love of the world that he fostered in his parish. "I'm trying to find a linguist who can help us come up with a different word that doesn't have the money aspect to it that the word *stewardship* does," he says. "I think there must be a word in a different culture that would express all it is."[16]

Stewardship is the account of material faithfulness promoted for congregations, and none of the foregoing critique is to deny that sometimes under that name growth in generosity, commitment, and prayer does happen. But the logical contortions barely concealed within the rhetoric all too often only further enmesh us in our economic disorders. We live within histories that shape our thoughts as they shape our institutions

---

16. Interviewed in Zyskowski, "True Stewardship."

and material habits. Stewardship stands at the confluence of histories that undermine a rich sense of eucharistic sharing, and the Catholic church in the U.S., at least, seems to be caught in the currents.

Foul Ball: Douglas John Hall on Stewardship and the Cross

Douglas John Hall, Emeritus Professor of Christian Theology at McGill University in Montreal, trained at Union Theological Seminary under Reinhold Niebuhr and ordained in the United Church of Canada, has authored several works on stewardship as a theologically robust category. Hall's theology shares little with that of the NCCB document, except in one respect: in Hall's work the tendency of stewardship to mean elimination of the church, a tendency crucial to stewardship's history and subtly damaging to the NCCB documents, returns in full force.

According to Hall's thesis, the hellenization and establishment of the church are the chief culprits of Christian history, and it is only among the "disinherited" that the symbol of the *steward* has been recognized and used. Adopting Harnack's familiar narration, Hall asserts that in this hellenization, the church lost its Hebraic "earthiness" and developed a penchant for "anti-material, anti-world spiritualism." Furthermore, the eschatological expectation of the early church made the notion of stewardship as "everyday worldly responsibility" subordinate to the "stewardship of God's grace."[17] The establishment of Christianity as the religion of the Roman Empire reduced the sense of personal responsibility that Christians had for themselves and their churches, since financial and moral support were offered from the larger society. Christians also, he claims, became less able to understand themselves in solidarity with other oppressed people and more likely to seek power for itself by associating with the powerful. "It was quite unlikely that any church bent upon achieving a foothold with the powerful would ever seriously explore the meaning of stewardship — especially its worldly meaning." From Constantine through the Middle Ages the church was too concerned with maintaining political power to permit thought on such humble service as stewardship.

But stewardship "came of age," according to Hall, with the Christianity of North America, where churches were disestablished and had to rely

17. Zyskowski, "True Stewardship," 60.

on the personal commitment of members to pay salaries and maintain buildings and carry out missionary efforts. North American churches assumed disestablishment rather than fighting it, and for that reason they have been given the charism of stewardship as an insight to share with the rest of the world, as Latin Americans were given an understanding of liberation, for the upbuilding of Christians everywhere. In his account, the idea of "stewardship" lay dormant in Scripture until disestablished churches drew it out.

Hall has himself criticized the propensity among Christians to use the term in a superficial way, and his intent in treating the topic is to offer a more theological and challenging image, one which is explicitly critical of capitalism and applicable as a symbol for the entirety of the Christian life. In fact, Hall's work on stewardship grows out of his critique of North American Christianity for its refusal to face up to reality, both about its own weakness and about the persistence of doubt and meaninglessness within contemporary culture. Much of Hall's earlier work charges that a lack of humility in mainstream North American Christianity keeps Christians from conversing frankly with a world suffering from despair. In his 1976 book *The Reality of the Gospel and the Unreality of the Churches*, Hall condemns the façade of security to which mainstream churches cling in a post-Christendom world. That façade causes the churches not to address the "darkness" of the world around them. The churches, he asserts, are afraid that if they cannot control the problems they face, then they are failures; so they hide their heads in the sand and mistake that for success. Meanwhile, the world is turning to Christianity, like Nicodemus in the night, hoping for guidance. Why do the churches not speak truthfully in this time of fear? Hall blames a lingering constantinian desire to appear to be in control. To speak truthfully will involve admitting fear and uncertainty, siding with those who search rather than those who dominate. To speak truthfully would require humility, and this, says Hall, the churches sorely lack.

Against Christian pretensions to power, Hall proposes his own version of the *theologia crucis*. Hall takes the last written words of Martin Luther, "We are beggars, that is certain," as a central notion for the theology of the cross.[18] As opposed to the theology of glory (Luther's terms, though Hall freely adapts them to the twentieth-century context), the theology of

---

18. Douglas John Hall, *Lighten Our Darkness: Toward an Indigenous Theology of the Cross* (Philadelphia: Westminster Press, 1976).

the cross faces human weakness and limitation head-on. Humans are never masters. The triumphalist theology that would claim power and control through proximity to government or wealth is making its last stand, Hall claims, in pretensions to doctrinal certainty. The true triumph of the cross is not about political or even cultural power. Christians, he urges, should "let the Crucified and not the bourgeois culture with which they are identified define his triumph." He continues:

> At the most personal, concrete level, this means the willingness of the people of the cross to give evidence that they are men whose faith lives only in company with unfaith, whose hope is a dialogue with despair, whose sense of the meaning comes out of an ever-renewed confrontation with the sense of meaninglessness and the absurd.[19]

The "logic of the cross" recognizes that salvation is a matter of suffering solidarity rather than resolution; that only viewing the tragedies of human history without escapism makes possible the hope that they are not meaningless; and that grace and faith remain strange to human life, but nevertheless are real.[20] Hall's "theology of the cross" pronounces an unresolved "beggarliness" on all creation, and identifies Christian faith with the recognition of this truth.

> The predisposition of the ethic of the cross is thus to seek the prevenient action of God, the *a priori* of all Christian ethics, in those places especially where the God of glory and power seems absent. In human suffering and degradation, in poverty and hunger, among the two-thirds who starve, in races that are brought low, in the experience of failure, in exposure to the icy winds of the nihil, in the midst of hell — there it looks for the God whose acting is the precondition of Christian obedience.[21]

This conflation of poverty (the two-thirds who starve) and philosophical nausea (the icy winds of the nihil) under the category "cross"

19. Hall, *Lighten.*

20. The importance of Reinhold Niebuhr in Hall's development should be evident, but Hall himself writes of it in "The Cross and Contemporary Culture," in *Reinhold Niebuhr: A Centenary Appraisal,* ed. Gary A. Gaudin and Douglas John Hall (Atlanta: Scholars Press, 1994).

21. Hall, *Lighten,* 151.

lurks all through Hall's work, which he has characterized as a contribution to a liberation theology for North America. He claims that the people who live in darkness, with whom Christians are to identify, are "not only the poor, but those who genuinely 'understand' — the real 'intellectuals.'"[22]

Hall continued to develop this line of thought in his next work, *Has the Church a Future?*[23] Making a hybrid of Rahner's "diaspora church" and H. Richard Niebuhr's "Christ transforming culture" model of church life, Hall claims that while Christians have serious concerns about a loss of distinctiveness in Christian ethics, the greater danger is that the church will become a "Holy Clique,"[24] not of pacifists or counter-cultural sectarians, but of mainstream orthodox Christians as isolated by the security of their own tradition as any Amish community. He urges the churches to live "on the boundary," and not to be afraid of engagement with the world.

> The church of the future will be asked to go a long way — more than the second mile — with persons and groups who live far away from the boundary. It must go. There is no alternative. Even at the risk of losing everything! Even at the risk of not remembering the message! The call of God is never to preserve correct doctrine but to preserve life.[25]

Too often Christians are like the priest in the story of the good Samaritan (Lk. 10:29-37). Valuing ritual purity above compassion, they walk by on the other side of the road while the world bleeds. "Even if the church loses something of its gospel; even if it compromise something of its ultimate loyalty to its Lord, it is bound to remain with the world God loves."[26]

But to be exact, Hall does *not* want the gospel to get lost. He believes that this willingness to lose the gospel *is* the gospel, the *theologia crucis*, Christian humility. True faithfulness will require us to act in ways others might judge unfaithful to doctrine, but it is nevertheless true faithfulness.

22. Hall, *Lighten*, 223.
23. Hall, *Has the Church a Future?* (Philadelphia: Westminster Press, 1980).
24. Hall, *Has the Church a Future?* 73-75.
25. Hall, *Has the Church a Future?* 80.
26. Hall, *Has the Church a Future?* 80.

Mainstream churches (or in his later writings, particularly the more evangelical Protestant communities) think only doctrinal rigidity can be faithfulness. They are unable to do the improvisation that true faithfulness requires, and they cling to the security of a Christian distinctiveness based in bureaucracy or perhaps in the pathetic idea that the state still cares what they say.

Turning from their self-engrossment and toward imitation of Jesus' self-denial, the churches can join forces with other groups campaigning for human welfare. They can find the courage to give up their security, if they will, that Christianity is a story about a person, not a set of doctrines, and that the Person possesses the churches, rather than they him. In this way, churches can adopt a humble openness toward other religions instead of claiming to be the sole possessors of truth. They can witness to faith in the cross, which establishes "the solidarity of the loving God with anguished, searching humanity, in all its many quests for salvation."[27]

Hall refers to this service to the world in passing as "priestly stewardship."[28] He does not at that point draw the contrast, but he is evidently referring to an idea he touches on briefly in his earlier book that *stewardship* is a more humble and appropriate term for Christians to use than *dominion* when speaking of humanity's role in the natural world. Stewardship means responsibility without possession. Christians are at work in a world they do not own, but within which they have a calling to serve God's purpose — not to turn the world into more property and power for the churches, but to encourage human flourishing within all religions, all institutions, all nations, each in their own way. The Christian call is to stewardship, a service of form more than content. Hall's later career as the foremost theologian of stewardship builds this idea into a "gospel in miniature."[29]

Hall, under the influence of Reinhold Niebuhr, insists that anyone who is going to take part in the ambiguous and imperfect work of justice in the world will have to have humility regarding our ability to know truth and do good. But more than that, being humble about our ability to know truth and to do good is constitutive of knowing truth and doing good, much as the basis of scientific knowledge is understanding scientific method, and the basis of Adam Smith's philosophical anthropology, as we

27. Hall, *Has the Church a Future?* 108.
28. Hall, *Has the Church a Future?* 131.
29. Hall, *The Steward*, 49.

shall see, is impartial judgment among strangers. This broad trend associates humility with epistemological modesty, in morals as in science. Humility is the virtue of the modern individual.

At the request of the Commission on Stewardship of the National Council of Churches, Hall produced in 1982 his original work dedicated to the theology of stewardship, *The Steward: A Biblical Symbol Come of Age*. The book went through four printings and spawned two independent study guides for church groups before Hall offered a revised edition in 1990. The revised edition reflects his ongoing work on stewardship in two other books, *The Stewardship of Life in the Kingdom of Death* and *Imaging God: Dominion as Stewardship*.[30] In this literature, the earlier lines of Hall's thought on the churches' lack of humility come into focus in the term "stewardship."

The humble image of the steward speaks directly to the situation of post-Christendom churches, as Hall understands it. Christians now carry on their office as servants, not owners, and in this they come to appreciate their self-sacrificial calling as stewardship. He means that the cross calls Christians not to seek to further the churches as institutions or the gospel as doctrine, but to serve "life" without any aspiration to further power. This is the meaning of post-Constantinianism: to have given up the pretension that Christian institutions or doctrine will ever rule the world and to have turned instead to humble service. We must not be naïve about the possibility of worldly success for steward-Christians. Faithfulness in service to humanity — not success in winning converts or turning the earth into a kingdom of heaven — is the way of the cross. This "service to humanity" is spelled out in Hall's *Stewardship of Life in the Kingdom of Death*,[31] a series of meditations on Christian mission as stewardship. The Christian call is to service of life. Citing Irenaeus's line, "For the glory of God is a living man," and Jesus' "that they might have life, to the full," Hall claims that the essence of Christianity is to work for life in a world of death — specifically, for peace and more socialized economic systems. The details of this "service to life" remain otherwise vague, a fault common in theological work but disappointing from an author adamantly opposed to

---

30. Douglas John Hall, *Imaging God: Dominion as Stewardship* (Grand Rapids: Eerdmans, 1986).

31. Douglas John Hall, *The Stewardship of Life in the Kingdom of Death* (Grand Rapids: Eerdmans, 1985).

spiritualization and in favor of engagement in the nitty-gritty details of human life.[32]

Skipping the details on these questions may be nothing more than the understandable shyness of a theologian faced with the complexity of policy issues in which he is not trained. Then again, it may also be the return of the constantinian aspirations Hall denounced, only in a new form. Stewardship advocates have used the language of humility to bolster property rights; Hall's theology of the cross ends up using the language of humility to place Christians once again in proximity to power. Hall's "service to life," for example, reduces all human problems to similar terms, neglecting significant disputes over what constitutes a good life. The hope to be in service to this universal good — defined, perhaps, by the intellectuals who face the icy nihil? — gives Christian service the potential to be helpful, admirable, and ultimately necessary within every philosophy and system. Irenaeus did say, "For the glory of God is a living man," but Irenaeus went on to explain, "and the life of man consists in beholding God."[33] Hall's omission of this qualification leaves "living man" open to every interpretation, so that Christians working on behalf of life can claim to do so without any further theological baggage. Irenaeus's own formulation means human life, the glory of God shining out in the human person, is not self-sufficient. Pursuing human life will require pursuing the vision of God, which in a circular way leads again to the human, in the light of that vision. This circularity is Christological, for Christ is the one in whom the living human and the glory of God are joined, and so for Irenaeus, the life Christians should honor and pursue is understood, always, through the Incarnation.

Hall's formulation removes those matters of Christian doctrine that might cause awkwardness in mainstream conversations on social welfare. Regarding secular science, he demands that Christians not kid themselves by adopting any stance that "rules out *a priori* the prospect that man may indeed be nothing more than a naked ape."[34] Philosophically, he insists that Christians accept the academic truism of a fundamental epistemo-

---

32. In a question and answer section in *Stewardship of Life,* Hall claims that we should "get a new economic system." The specifics of that system and how "we" should "get" it are unspecified.

33. Irenaeus, AH, IV, 20, 7. Available online at http://www.newadvent.org/fathers/0103420.htm.

34. Hall, *Lighten,* 209.

logical suspicion against Christianity, as against any truth claim. Looking at the history of Christian witness to the state, he reads the Barmen Declaration's refusal to acknowledge any revelation other than that in Jesus Christ to mean, "Be vigilant against tyranny and all pretensions to finality."[35] In each case his position derives from the conviction that Christianity is about humble service and self-sacrifice; and ends with the assertion that Christians should set aside controversies within their own tradition in favor of the dominant view of science, philosophy, and democratic process.

For all his talk of the disestablishment of the churches, Hall's notion of Christianity is deeply amenable to the national governments of the United States and Canada, as well as to the U.N., which are those centers of power most able to engage in effective service to the world, and to justify themselves on that ground. Disestablishment and humility may merely mean granting certainty and power to secular intellectuals and philosophically liberal government leaders and gathering around them as willing servants. As we have seen, theodicy and the attempt to foster virtues were key concerns of Smith and Malthus. The desire to be in service to "life" would hardly be problematic for them. While mainstream economics presently holds to an ostensibly amoral empiricism, many enter the field in an attempt to foster human life, ordering a tragically limited world into the best possible arrangement. In this, Hall's demand of Christian service is not apparently in conflict with any economic system, since all will claim to defend life. Even Malthus only consented to the deaths of the poor on the argument that permitting some to end in misery prevented the same end for many times more. Hall himself, I do not doubt, would find this comparison irritating, as he advocates humane economic reform. But he has argued himself out of theological content with which to make substantial claims about the exact nature of the "life" Christians are committed to. Worse, he has argued the community that could hear those claims out of existence, for a church which insists on its own tradition is implicitly refusing the humility he prizes.

The moral imperative of effective service of "life" requires the continued possession of power so that it can be used to foster health and jus-

35. Douglas John Hall, *Confessing the Faith: Christian Theology in a North American Context* (Minneapolis: Fortress, 1996), 14-15. It is interesting to note that Hall in certain cases claims more for Christian doctrine, as in his appeal to faith that creation is made good and that human mistreatment of it will not have the last word. Hall, *Professing the Faith: Christian Theology in a North American Context* (Minneapolis: Fortress, 1993), 358.

tice. In Hall's work, that moral imperative being the only moral imperative means such possession is a mandate. He rejects pacifism because, unlike the theology of the cross, it refuses to serve life; he must reject the practice of humble poverty on the same grounds. Hall represents the culmination of a history which, faced with unsettling witness of beggars, has refused the possibility of humility-as-lowliness. Institutions can be humbled by renouncing their claims to be a true society, but a personal economic practice of humility is opposed to the preservation and well-being of life, making its practitioners fragile and useless in a time when strong workers, heroes in an endless battle, are most needed.

Strike Three: The Confidence and Despair of Gift-Giving

Hall, the leading theological proponent of stewardship, has reclaimed humility for Christianity by associating selflessness with doctrinal self-immolation, and the Catholic bishops' attempt to read stewardship as discipleship only breeds confusion. Protestants and Catholics seem both to need some alternative ways to think about dependence and generosity. Fortunately, a rich mix of theological and philosophical notions connected to property and exchange has been brewing around the category of gift. Unpredictability, need, and intimacy — categories made alien by the moral importance of independence and efficient use of wealth — have found new advocates in those who hold that human love is indeed always exchange, but an exchange of gifts which is uneven and unpredictable, a function of histories rather than mathematics, secured by trust rather than by doubt. Can a theology of gift free Christian imagination from the traps of stewardship rhetoric?

The problem of gift is initially whether such a thing can exist. Isn't gift-giving really always just another form of self-interested exchange, as the giver seeks a return or at least the satisfaction of having given? Derrida developed a darker version of an insight Adam Smith would have broadly approved: those who aim for altruism are really seeking death, because the only human gift free of self-interest is an empty one offered by a dead person. Theologian John Milbank, whose work on Christianity's immorality was considered briefly in Chapter Four, countered that a gift can be given, because gift-giving is not about altruism. A desire for a return gift and the satisfaction of having given a gift are not the enemies of love because gift-giving is an economy, a dance of exchange. The difference between gift and sale is not that only one is reciprocal, but that only one is predictable, requiring immediate return of an equal good. In gift-giving the return is delayed, unpredictable, and non-identical, not because it is some sort of deficient transfer, but because those who give gifts count cultivating their relationship as the real foundation of the exchange.[36]

Milbank's position holds promise for complicating theories of self-interest that end up reducing humans to monads incapable of real commonality. When he speaks of beggars, for example, Milbank writes that a gift cannot be given to a beggar if that "gift" is premised on the ongoing isolation of the poor from the rich. If the almsgiver is using the existence of the poor as an occasion for demonstrating generosity, then it is this "gift" that is really the failure of generosity. The only gift that can be given to a beggar, he holds, is one that initiates a friendship between the two parties, in which both sides can give and receive with some confidence in each other. Ignoring the human desire to give and receive in return is no virtue; instead, that desire is the occasion for cultivating friendship.

Gift can only really flourish within the confidence of "marital fidelity,"[37] for there the delay and inequality inherent in gift exchange do not become injustice. Each unpredictable, unequal gift earns no guarantee or timetable for equal return, nor in this context does it need them. Confidence permits patience and a willingness to live with inequality. Living with inequality is not easy. It is always possible that gift-giving between those who are not equally able to give is an act of violence, power masquerading in the guise of generosity to justify itself and catch the recipient off guard. Where the giving moves in only one direction, offerings may actually be about domination of the weak under another name.[38] In spite of this danger, marital confidence can maintain its trust because it rests on a deep foundation of mutuality. Only that context of friendship makes pos-

---

36. John Milbank, "Can a Gift Be Given? Prolegomena to a Future Trinitarian Metaphysic," *Modern Theology* 11/1 (January 1995): 119-61.

37. Milbank, "The Midwinter Sacrifice: A Sequel to 'Can Morality Be Christian?'" *Studies in Christian Ethics* 10, no. 2 (October 1997).

38. Coles, *Rethinking Generosity: Critical Theory and the Politics of Caritas* (Ithaca: Cornell University Press, 1997). I do not mean to dismiss Coles's critique here. His study establishes that the rhetoric of gift has indeed acted as a cover for violence. The point is only that these abuses do not destroy the possibility of a gift relationship in which mutuality is based on more than timely return-gift.

sible Christian sacrifice, the gift of grace that receives no adequate or evident return. It is the privilege of intimacy to live with such unevenness. There gifts can be exchanged without the self-protection necessary in an economic order of strangers.

This is also the sense of Milbank's "ontology of peace." Where modern social theory tends, according to Milbank, to see nature red in tooth and claw as the unquestionable foundation for understanding human society, Christianity begins in the wonder and sheer grace of creation, the triumph of cross and resurrection, the outpouring of the Spirit, and the joyful hope of the kingdom. For those steeped in this ontology of peace, the pains and challenges, even the horrors, of modern social life exist within a framework of unswerving confidence. Giving and receiving need not be equal, because redemption for all is surely unfolding.

But even as it commends this "marital trust," "The Midwinter Sacrifice" acknowledges a limit to trust. The effect of the doctrine of original sin is to leave the Christian uncertain that any good can be done in any circumstance. Hall would smile in recognition to hear Milbank admit that Christian confidence in no way means that Christians can claim to act unambiguously.

> On the contrary, the Christian can rather be seen as the person who recognizes that there is no *apparent* good to be found or performed in any given situation. . . . Hence hope, hope that it may be given to me in the next moment to act well, is inseparable from hope that there may be universal acting well, and at last a non-futile mourning; to be ethical therefore is to believe in the resurrection, and somehow to participate in it.[39]

This is a pregnant "somehow." It honors the pervasiveness of sin and the elusive, tactical quality of hope. "We can only receive instances that we judge to constitute such blending and seek, in hope, to perpetuate them: here hope is conjoined to receptive charity." To believe in resurrection and therefore to act in the confidence of resurrection is to be able to act prior to, but logically in confidence after, the wedding banquet of the Lamb. This is not a reckless self-destruction, but it is vulnerability adopted in the hope of, and indeed already in confidence of, a fuller and new return.

39. Milbank, "The Midwinter Sacrifice," 24.

This eschatological ethic strikes at the heart of those who would make "Christian altruism" the sacrifice of self which is most fulfilled in the empty gift of the dead giver. Hall's version of Christian service as self-sacrifice falls prey to Milbank's critique. His claim that Christian humility and service have finally been fully set free to be themselves in the secular world, in which Christians receive no self-satisfaction, no increase in their fellowship, no deepening of their own story, and no confidence of return-gift, is only a more popular version of the claim that a true gift must mean death. Hall's Christian stewardship is the empty ownership of that which is given freely and which has no (acknowledged) content, the gift of kenosis taken to a secular limit. It is, in its emptiness, inviolable. Christianity's victory is destroying itself. Hall's service, not Milbank's confidence, is most unable to receive a return-gift and which is liable in Coles's terms to be murderous domination under another name.

The great weakness of Milbank's position, however, is his inability to say what he is talking about. That is, in spite of his own claim that only receptivity to examples (rather than theory) can draw us into Christian hope, that no account of gift which does not contend with the specificity of the gift and the concrete otherness (rather than generalized alterity) of the receiver can coherently claim to be about gift, he does not offer such specificity. In fact, he is in this respect a victim of his own success. Once he has clearly established that gift depends upon resurrection and a community of trusting non-identical reciprocity, then gift among Christians can only be narrated on the other side of the eschaton. Concrete particular accounts offered now would tend to make the unilateral gift typically required in the midst of sin normative, glorifying a tragic altruism or reducing the horror of martyrdom to simple purchase of glory. Yet, by his account, such narrations are sorely needed so that Christians will be able to recognize and participate in nonidentical gift in hopeful anticipation of resurrection. Nonidentical repetition requires some narrative training in the givers and receivers. Content is pivotal for Milbank, and yet he finds giving it awkward.

In his introduction to *The Word Made Strange*, Milbank presents a tragic, reactive account of the church which is not notably characterized by plentitude and confidence.

> For all the current talk of a theology that would reflect on practice, the truth is that we remain uncertain as to where today to locate true

Christian practice. This would be, as it has always been, a repetition differently, but authentically, of what has always been done. In his or her uncertainty as to where to find this, the theologian feels almost that the entire ecclesial task falls on his own head: in the meager mode of reflective words he must seek to imagine what a true practical repetition would be like. Or at least he must hope that his merely theoretical continuation of the tradition will open up a space for wider transformation.[40]

That is, Milbank does not see the immoral confidence and plenitude enacted in the church, and failing to see it, he takes upon himself the necessity of linguistically recreating it. He not only fails to articulate examples: he does not see them. Such a posture is oddly lacking in that confidence and plenitude which Milbank claims is the sign of true Christianity. Milbank himself adopts the heroic ethic that presupposes danger, not confidence, as one lone voice must light the candle in the darkness.

The eschatological razor's edge Milbank walks in "The Midwinter Sacrifice" leaves not only discussion of but also recognition of virtuous action deeply problematic. Milbank's lack of confidence in even tactical appearances of the good under aspect of hope within the church makes apparent the difficulty of sustaining a narrative which must continually refer to "apparently" unilateral gifts of self as "really" components of a marital relationship of non-identical and indefinitely delayed yet confident gift-exchange. The reality that under original sin, contingent as such a situation is, mourning is futile and charity is not returned, that the feast is as yet abortive and the "gift" abandoned, cannot be avoided. How can one look the history of the church in the face while developing a strong account of resurrection?

While "The Midwinter Sacrifice" goes a long way toward illuminating the "immorality" of Christianity, Milbank's work continues to teeter on the razor's edge, with the risk of charitable violence on one side and despair on the other. That razor's edge is inevitable, given Milbank's argument that Christianity is not reactionary. Confidence in resurrection involves a certain heedlessness of death. "Plenitude" in a world in which as a matter of fact millions starve to death will have to mean, whatever else

---

40. Milbank, *The Word Made Strange: Theology, Language, Culture* (Oxford: Blackwell Publishers, 1997), 1.

Milbank might have in mind, a refusal to narrate the events as tragedy, a refusal to hate God for the horror of human pain, a refusal to destroy oneself in sacrifice. Locating Christianity squarely in the divine *comedy* seems to leave it shockingly short on righteous hatred of evil. The invulnerable community of Christian confidence (which do not include hope and patience) may be left waiting for return-gift, but their confidence is such that they can hardly admit any lack, any uncertainty, any pain. Milbank himself can hardly narrate the Christian community's continuing ambiguity and inability to give other than abortive gifts without despair.

On the other hand, Christianity is not incapable of coping with this eschatological inarticulacy. The Johannine "lifting up" of Jesus which refers simultaneously to the horror of crucifixion and the glory of resurrection strikes the needed chord. Milbank's own claim that the church in continuing to act in the name of Jesus carries on non-identical repetition of his ministry begs for a kind of thick narration of church history in which these abortive, unilateral witnesses are seen in light of eschatological fulfillment. A historical narration can make sense of the claim that humility, patience, and forgiveness are the essential qualities of this immorality of confidence and plenitude.[41] When, on the other hand, we actually turn in Milbank's confidence to the ongoing history of the church, to the institutions and personalities, persecutions and martyrdoms, the endless political maneuvering of church-people, how will we honor his insight into confidence? Gift-giving, says Milbank, is possible, but apparently not in the church as he knows it, or indeed in history at all. Narrating eschatological (im)morality will be no small task.

The answers may come from a theological writer who does not have the luxury of such a tragic view of the church: John Paul II. In his second encyclical letter, *Dives in misericordia,* the pope cuts through this eschatological inarticulacy, repeatedly citing John 14:9, "He who has seen me has seen the Father."[42] The fullness of the eschatological gift-relationship is lacking; revelation and the necessary language for speaking of Christian life on the road are not. In this letter, John Paul II draws on mercy as a term

41. Novelists have perhaps been most successful at this. Graham Greene's *The Power and the Glory,* Evelyn Waugh's *Brideshead Revisited,* and Robert Duval's film *The Apostle* have achieved accounts of tragedy within and re-narrated by divine comedy, without evading horror and grief.

42. All citations are from *The Papal Encyclicals,* ed. Claudia Carlen (Ann Arbor: Pierian Press, 1990), 275-98.

necessary to the Christian account of justice. In Milbank's terms, mercy is inevitably reactive. One only needs and only shows mercy in the face of some sort of failure. John Paul asserts that in Jesus' mercy, we do in fact see the Father's love. Mercy, he says, is love's second name, for it is love working under duress (79).

This encyclical makes mercy do real work toward speaking of the church as a community already shaped by its end even as it is on the road. It claims that the modern fascination with control and system gives rise to a justice which renders mercy an insult. Justice, therefore, tends to become brutality in the interest of upholding dignity. "The word and the concept of 'mercy' seem to cause uneasiness in man, who, thanks to the enormous development of science and technology never before known in history, has become the master of the earth and has subdued and dominated it" (9). In this brief analysis, the pope indicates the source of the problem: scientific and technological development, "understood in a one-sided and superficial way." He does not demand a Luddite revolution among Catholics, but he does want to explain that the control created by technology is illusory and dangerous. Perfect control, which is the inherent desire of technique, is impossible with live human beings. Using justice as rules of control will tend to produce hatred (119), annihilation of the "enemy" (120), or "'peaceful' subjugation of individuals, of environments, or indeed of entire societies and of nations that for one reason or another might prove inconvenient for those who possess the necessary means and are ready to use them without scruple" (111). Justice alone can lead "to the negation and destruction of itself" (121).

We have seen this dynamic before. In economic terms, this is to say that the giving of a gift is an insult. In Smith's stoic ethic a gift suggested a bribe and in Malthus an imprudence, and in both of them an interference in a system or process to which all people are subject. This impersonal, systematic justice, whether a justice of equal competition or of survival of the fittest or of workers controlling their productive power, offers dignity to those who play by its rules and shame to those who interfere. Mercy is just such an interference. The pope himself makes this connection, referring to the "defective machinery . . . at the root of contemporary economics and materialistic civilization" (114).

Neither justice nor mercy, the encyclical teaches, work this way in Christian theology. God's justice unfolds in the history of the Jews, of Jesus, and of the church, and its subordinate role in relation to love "seemed so obvious to the psalmists and prophets that the very term justice ended up by meaning the salvation accomplished by the Lord and his mercy" (36). Biblical justice is God's setting all things right, through mercy, which is love working under duress, "in contact with suffering, injustice, and poverty — in contact with the whole historical 'human condition,' which in various ways manifests man's limitation and frailty, both physical and moral."[43] Mercy restores humans to their true dignity so that the justice of God can be done. In a lengthy discourse on the parable of the prodigal son, the pope insists that the turning point for the son is in recognizing the loss of his dignity: "Father, I am no longer worthy. . . ." Nevertheless, his sonship is not lost, and "love for the son, the love that springs from the very essence of fatherhood, in a way obliges the father to be concerned about his son's dignity" (58). The merry-making of the father celebrates the restoration of that dignity, lost by the son but never surrendered by the father. The offer of mercy is made in respect of, not because of a lack in, human dignity.

More than this, John Paul II insists that this mercy is never one-sided. Mercy participates in a gift-relation of mutuality. Lest it appear that the pope means merely that wealthy Americans who help out in a homeless shelter "get as much out of it" as they put in, a figure of speech which carefully conceals the state of injustice preceding this act of mercy, he claims Jesus' crucifixion as the "disquieting model" of merciful reciprocity (142). The model can be disquieting in two directions, it seems: that our showing (or failure to show) mercy is accepted by Jesus as directed toward himself (as in Matthew 25) and that our model of mercy is suffering a brutal death for those who offer no thanks. The reciprocity, at any rate, does not originate in humans, but in God's display of mercy. Yet, because this display takes place in the finitude of human life, amid weakness, poverty, and suffering, it always already is an appeal for a response. That inherent reciprocity, the pope teaches, is a revelation of the Father. In this way, it is mercy which fights for equality, since mercy is the power which calls for the laying down of one's life for others, for becoming one body. Through Christological reflection, John Paul II aligns present justice with the eschatological achievement of God's charity.

The pope is eager to uphold more conventional accounts of justice as

43. John Paul II had already described mercy as the revelation of God's love in Jesus in *Redemptor hominis*, 9.

useful in limited contexts, and even indicates its sufficiency in economics: justice is "in itself suitable for 'arbitration' between people concerning the reciprocal distribution of objective goods in an equitable manner" (145). But acknowledging the centrality of mercy as both the means and a constituent of the end "shows that, over and above the process of 'compensation' and 'truce' which is specific to justice, love is necessary so that man may affirm himself as man" (158). This apparent permission of justice to govern the "economic" while the personal, spiritual, or perhaps political orders require mercy shifts the tone from the rest of the letter. It is of course theoretically true that when two farmers must agree on an exchange rate between the excess of wheat held by one and the excess of butter held by another, they may be able by calculation of their respective costs to achieve a just price. Scholastic theologians as well as Kenneth Boulding, however, remind us that such just exchange always already includes some order of mutual charity to underpin it.[44] Furthermore, such calculations can be done by different rules: should demand drive the price? What if one farmer has cornered the market? Must the needs of the seller or the gullibility of the buyer be taken into account? "Mere" justice does not exist, and the suggestion in that passage that it is sufficient with regard to "objective goods" is naïve and weakens the pope's position. Nevertheless, his assistance in reclaiming the peculiarities of Christian virtue as open to human speech and to narration within history points toward the possibility of what I will call *viator* economics, economics on the way. After all, only an economics which can include humility will be able to make economic sense of our beggars and save generosity from the inadequacies of stewardship.

This chapter considered in turn three twentieth-century approaches to property and humility, each marked by earlier struggles over begging and stewardship. Douglas John Hall's work reads the humble service of stewardship as necessarily implying that Christians cannot come into conflict with the intellectual leadership of philosophically liberal and left-leaning Western democracies. His commitment to following the person of Christ, not any artificially secure system, fails because he makes the person of Christ only a cipher for self-sacrifice. Here are echoes of the English Reformation,

---

44. See Kenneth Boulding, *Beyond Economics: Essays on Society, Religion, and Ethics* (Ann Arbor: University of Michigan Press, 1968).

in which humble service was not always easy to distinguish from destruction of the church as a force that could stand against the government.

The U.S. Catholic bishops' pastoral letter, on the other hand, made
interesting attempts to teach stewardship as discipleship, and discipleship
as a life that takes seriously the commands of the Sermon on the Mount,
the testimony of the saints, the example of Mary, and the sacramental life
of the church. Stewardship, in this case, is about taking personal responsibility for one's calling as a Christian, accepting God's invitation to become
active and creative within the work that God is doing, to be God's friends.
The letter failed, nevertheless, from two directions. First, its poor
ecclesiology left the work of the steward still external to the church.
Though it condemned individualism, the letter failed to name and challenge patterns of individualism, including that which sees Christian responsibility as a question of individuals or families contributing to a structure outside themselves. This has been a characteristic turn of stewardship
thought from the beginning, as it named the role of people outside the institutional structure, and therefore, in common parlance, people who are
not themselves "the church."

Second, the letter failed to address frankly and fully the financial
problems of congregations and dioceses. The authors did so in hopes that
a call to discipleship would lead to a greater awareness of and commitment
to a common good, and therefore a greater willingness, or even eagerness,
to share with each other out of love. But the Smithean nobility of limiting
of our expression of needs; the Malthusian fear of endless needs; and the
widespread agreement that God's goodness is not inconsistent with grave
inequality and economic estrangement even among fellow Christians —
these are obstacles that will not disappear on their own. In practice *stewardship* means fundraising, drawing on a kind of theological marketing
painfully reminiscent of Franciscan salesmanship in *Piers Plowman*. In
economic and ecclesial habits, gifts remain dangerous, and those who
would ask for them tricksters or villains.

Milbank's work on gift as a concept has the advantage of naming the
crucial issue: there can only be candid sharing within a relationship of
trust. Sacrifice and gift, if they are not to be bribery or insult or domi-
nance, must take place within a relation of mutual exchange, but an exchange not dependent upon equal or scheduled return. Milbank's characterization of this marital trust is so rich that he undercuts his own ability
to speak of the church's life, in which that trust is continually failing, or the

need for it is not even recognized. John Paul II's *Dives in misericordia* offers a limited but useful corrective, in its claim that mercy is the second name of love. The order we see of failure and distrust, so long as it continually meets with mercy, really is already the order of love and trust that Milbank longs for. The challenge is to narrate and build up that order of economic mercy, which is not yet the marital trust of the fullness of time, but in which we nevertheless truly see the Father.

CHAPTER SIX

Why Not Be a Beggar?
Peter Maurin and Viator Economics

The preceding five chapters have taken up a series of approaches to the fear of being poor and dependent. Francis of Assisi, for all the richness of his love of poverty and espousal of vulnerability, produced a way of life that was an occasion of pride and dissension for his followers and a legal conundrum for the church. Christian political economist Adam Smith developed a philosophy of life in which sharing was impossible, and Thomas Malthus foresaw in humanity only a sharing in the fear of misery on the way to an escape from flesh. The advocates of stewardship make the accumulation of wealth an implicit requirement of a morally excellent life or offer a spirituality of service that leaves out the life of the church and therefore fails to touch the structures most in need of its help. In Douglas John Hall's work, the Christian use of power and property involves renunciation of the content of Christian doctrine and universal sharing in the epistemological and moral poverty of sinful, mortal life. In spite of some rich theological work on the primacy of an order of plenty and gift-exchange within Christianity, Christians have little sense of how charity can be economically rational.

We have come to a disheartening pass, and this in itself is a useful accomplishment. Once we understand that Christian praxis concerning poverty and property is in life- and soul-threatening trouble, we may be able to find the nerve to face the deeper challenges lurking within these questions. But for those willing to follow the path, the Christian pilgrimage is not a dead end. Although this work cannot end with "And they all lived happily ever after," it may be able to manage "Maranatha." For in a sidebar to Catholic social thought stands a commentator, widely-read in theology, history, and in economic critiques, who produced a program of action for an ongoing renewal of society and a theologically rich account of a Christian political economy, in which a central role is taken by none other than the beggar.

Peter Maurin, the Unoriginal Beggar

What we give to the poor
for Christ's sake
is what we carry with us
when we die.
We are afraid to pauperize the poor
because we are afraid
to be poor.
Pagan Greeks used to say
that the poor
"are ambassadors
of the gods."
To become poor
is to become an Ambassador of God.[1]

The basis for a Christian economy
is genuine charity and voluntary poverty.[2]

The author of these lines, Peter Maurin, was Dorothy Day's teacher and is commonly called the co-founder of the Catholic Worker movement, although he was not always in agreement with the direction in which Dorothy Day took it. His own vocation was to teaching. Maurin was born in France in 1877, a peasant and the oldest of twenty-two children. He was at times a brother in a religious order of teachers, an unhappy conscript into the military reserves, a Canadian homesteader, a wandering manual laborer, an occasional beggar, a successful French teacher, and a camp caretaker. Though he came from a Catholic family, he said of himself that he did not live, in some years of his life, the way he thought a Christian

---

1. Peter Maurin, "Superfluous Goods," *Easy Essays* (Chicago: Franciscan Herald Press, 1977), 123.
2. Maurin, "A Question and Answer on Catholic Labor Guilds," *Easy Essays*, 30.

should.[3] He spoke little about himself, preferring to speak incessantly about his ideas, so information on his spiritual development is sketchy. By the time Day met him, Maurin was living in voluntary poverty, having given away most of his possessions. Unbathed and unkempt, dressed in old stained clothes, his glasses missing one earpiece and his coat pockets stuffed full of notes and books, he slept in flop-houses on his visits to New York, unless he met someone in greater need than himself, in which case he would give the bed away and stay in the park all night. He showed up at Day's house at the suggestion of a mutual acquaintance from *Commonweal* in December 1932, and she considered him an answer to her prayers. Night after night, he lectured her about Catholicism using sloganistic free verse poems he called "easy essays," a genre he created to suit his oral teaching style.

He did not hesitate to call this teaching "indoctrination" and he liked to be called an "agitator." The essays were designed to challenge assumptions and coax people into a new way of thinking, not to offer information or make subtle arguments. Maurin gathered information and lines of thought from many disciplines, integrating history and theology and economics and art into a coherent diagnosis of and prescription for modern ills. Maurin presented problems and solutions in a simplified way, for he was a teacher and he knew that to change people's views, he had to start by presenting in outline a new way of seeing the world. His essays are not, as he repeatedly insisted, a replacement for a lifetime of reading and inquiry. Some are little more than annotated bibliographies:

> If you want to know
> what industrialism has done to man
> read *Man the Unknown*,
> by Dr. Alexis Carrel.
> If you want to know
> how we got that way
> read *A Guildsman's Interpretation*
> *of History*,
> by Arthur Penty.
> If you want to know

3. Marc Ellis, *Peter Maurin: Prophet in the Twentieth Century* (New York: Paulist Press, 1981), 33.

what it is to be a bourgeois,
read *The Bourgeois Mind,*
by Nicholas Berdyaev.
If you want to know
what religion
has to do with culture,
read *Enquiries Into Religion and Culture,*
by Christopher Dawson.
If you want to know
what to do with freedom,
read *Freedom in the Modern World*
by Jacques Maritain.[4]

The essays do not answer every question because Maurin did not intend them to. Instead they set up a framework for asking new questions and attempting a new kind of answer, or rather an answer "so old it looks like new."[5] Maurin was not original. He was profoundly traditional, and in twentieth-century America, that meant he was radical.

At the center of Maurin's thought is an understanding of the history of Catholic practice of and teaching on economic life, a history that Maurin had assimilated through his own peasant upbringing, his training with the Salesians, his work with French Catholic social movements,[6] his experiments in voluntary poverty, and extensive reading of anarchists, social critics, and utopian thinkers of many stripes. He freely culled useful elements from all of these influences without picking at the details of an argument for flaws. He did not scruple to ignore points with which he disagreed and to commend at the same time authors who disagreed with each other on some points, if he found parts of their work promising. Drawing on family resemblances among a wide array of social critics, especially French and English Catholics, he created what he called a "synthe-

4. "Five Books," *Easy Essays,* 143.
5. "The Purpose of the Catholic Workers' School," *Easy Essays,* 37. This is another of Maurin's signature phrases.
6. Maurin was involved with the Oeuvre des Cercles Catholiques d'Ouvriers and Le Sillon in his youth, although he did not share in the anti-Semitism of the first and ultimately rejected the understanding of Christian democracy in the second. See Ellis, *Peter Maurin,* 23-30 and William J. Collinge, "Peter Maurin's Ideal of Farming Communes," *Dorothy Day and the Catholic Worker Movement: Centenary Essays,* ed. William J. Thorn, Phillip M. Runkel, and Susan Mountin (Milwaukee: Marquette University Press, 2001), 387-88.

sis" based on respect for good work and saintly poverty; a conviction that the good society is one built on and moving toward the love of God, which therefore has the church at its heart; and a reverence for the mystery of the person, who is by God's grace creative, responsible, and at the same time always dependent on and duty-bound to the fellowship of others.

This synthesis centers around what Maurin referred to as the Thomistic doctrine of the common good. This far-reaching notion is stated succinctly in one of the works to which Maurin refers his readers on this matter: "Man in the gospel is part of an organism whose members tend to the same end by different means."[7] All people share ultimately one goal, one purpose, one home, and that is union with the Triune God. Therefore, while roles and means differ, the well-being of each person is tied into the well-being of others because all have their end in friendship with God. Human labor, desire, needs, and abilities are designed to cooperate, so that the individual good is likewise part of the larger good of the entire Body, of which Christ is the head. Christian politics, including economics, is fundamentally peaceable.

Maurin was no collectivist, however, as he established in years of debates with communists on the streets of New York. The doctrine of the common good, as he understood it, does not by any means imply that individual lives should be subordinated to a social purpose. Rather, the social body with its common end is composed of persons, each created by God, creative and profoundly free within his or her own calling. The well-being of the whole body depends upon the personal action of each of these souls as inspired by God, and that personal action can in turn flourish or suffer under the influence of other members. Therefore the shared good of all is not in conflict with the good of each individual, rightly understood as the soul's own union with God through worship and charity, particularly the works of mercy. As each flourishes, the whole will prosper.

Maurin's vivid sense of the common good was practical, not academic. He grew up in a peasant family in the south of France, watching the personal and social life of people tied to the land and to each other over generations. He claimed his family had been there for fifteen hundred years. Farming as he knew it was the great testing ground of personal responsibility and prudence cultivated through tradition and practice. But

7. Alphonse Lugan, *Social Principles of the Gospel*, trans. T. Lawrason Riggs (New York: The MacMillan Company, 1928), 151.

survival, much less a good life, depended heavily on having neighbors who could be counted on. The flourishing of the whole society could only happen when each member played a role, acting to uphold their own and each other's success, as people tended to both their privately owned homes and the commonly-owned pastures and ovens.[8] This functional, practical union of social cooperation, personal responsibility, and charity provided the ground for his critique of modern social disorder.

In Maurin's thought, then, the personal and social, the spiritual and material, and the political and liturgical are not poles in tension with each other, much less mutually exclusive alternatives. The disintegration of this organic whole into confused and competing elements was in his mind particularly connected with the Reformation. The shifts in authority and culture in that period fragmented the social, economic, and moral unity that had been Christendom and paved the way for centuries of further disintegration. Acknowledging the influence of R. H. Tawney and Christopher Dawson, among others, on his understanding of history, Maurin narrated the path by which the secular became severed from the sacred so that people admit no shared ultimate good, unless the individual pursuit of profit could be counted a shared good.

> Modern society believes
> in separation
> of Church and State.
> But the Jews
> did not believe in it,
> the Greeks
> did not believe in it,
> the Medievalists
> did not believe in it,
> the Puritans
> did not believe in it.
> Modern society
> has separated
> the Church from the State,
> but it has not separated
> the State from business.

8. Collinge, "Peter Maurin's Ideal," 391.

Modern society
does not believe
in a Church's State;
it believes
in a business men's State.[9]

Maurin saw modern history as the story of human society gradually being torn apart — the secular from the church and reason from faith, the person from society, art from work, consumption from happiness, and plenty from satisfaction. Maurin's own favorite locus for demonstrating this disintegration into chaos is the legalization of usury, the taking of interest on a loan. Usury is the alienation of wealth from work and community. "Gentlemen are not usurers," he claimed, because real gentlemen do their own work instead of profiting on someone else's labor.

When people used to listen
to the prophets of Israel
and the Fathers of the Church
They could not see anything gentle
in trying to live
on the sweat of somebody else's brow
by lending money at interest.[10]

Maurin pins the permission of usury on Calvin, eliding a long history of debate among scholars about an ever-increasing field of legitimate titles to interest and ignoring Tawney's more nuanced appraisal of Calvin. Maurin's point, at any rate, is that without an understanding of the good to permeate and organize society, business interests begin to follow a limited and destructive logic that separates profit from the real well-being of the community.

. . . money-lending at interest
became the general practice.
And money ceased to be
a means of exchange and began to be
a means to make money.

9. Maurin, "Church and State," *Easy Essays*, 6-7.
10. Maurin, "Is Inflation Inevitable?" *Easy Essays*, 17-18.

THE FEAR OF BEGGARS

So people lent money on time
and started to think of time
in terms of money
and said to each other,
"Time is money."

"Time is money": this claim became a kind of refrain of modern absurdity for Maurin. He heard a kind of mass insanity in this truism, as people commonly accepted the idea that the mere passage of time across a
loan could guarantee profit, without reference to the labor and goods for
which money exists. The idea of a market price for money depends on the
understanding that the lender must be paid for the opportunity cost of the
loan. What has passed between the lender and borrower is not only money,
but the opportunity to use that money for a period of time. Maurin rejected the claim that a lender should be paid interest merely as a function
of the passage of time, while someone else actually did the work that
earned a return.

But his use of "time is money" suggests more than that. His epigram-
matic form leaves the connections to the imagination, but the claim that
"time is money" seems to typify what he saw as the bizarre alienation of
work, personhood, land, community, and faith. Time, a gift from God, is
under no one's control. It is the medium in which lives unfold and in
which salvation works itself out. This constant miracle that God maintains
the existence of the world, which is to say the miracle of time, is the opportunity for work and love, the medium in which lives ebb and flow, nur-
tured by food that is planted, ripened, and harvested on farms; sustained
by goods made painstakingly in workshops through techniques passed
down and improved through generations; warmed and ennobled by famil-
ial love; and sanctified by hours of silent contemplation. Within that unfolding of time, money can play a role as a means of exchange, facilitating
transfers of goods across complex systems. But equating time and money
requires a level of abstraction that appears in Maurin's thought to be not
only fallacious but also malignant. Time cannot be transferred, stored,
amassed, or controlled. Time is sheer gift, given to each and all. It flows
without regard to property rights, and money cannot exchange for it. The
lives that stretch out within time are made of earth and bodies, food and
work and prayer. None of these is the same as money. To leap from money
as means of exchange to money as the portable, mutable form of all else,

including time, is to lose touch with life itself, to move into a rarified and abstracted world in which persons and their work lose their proper dignity. "Time is money" epitomized for Maurin the confusion of a world driven and broken by finance. "Modern society is in a state of chaos."[11]

One of the other voices raised against usury in Maurin's heyday was the personalist movement associated with the French journal *Esprit* and spearheaded by Emmanuel Mounier, another author frequently, if selectively, cited by Maurin.[12] Maurin often called himself a personalist and the efforts of the Catholic Worker a kind of personalist revolution. Personalism insists that persons are not objects within a world, but that persons, as subjects, make the world. The unique and creative power of each human, a power that theological personalists like Maurin understood to be created and sustained by grace, is the crucial element in any account of the world. More fundamental than economic and political systems, more substantial than abstractions of spirit, the person is for these thinkers the real stuff of the world. It is not surprising then that they saw usury as the very antithesis of personalism. As Mounier's *Personalist Manifesto* described it, usury isolates profit from personal work. Linking profit to time rather than persons, usury eliminates the intrinsic connection between a person's work, creativity, responsibility, and income. Time, which should be the gracious backdrop of work, and money, which should be an instrument in the exchange of goods, become an order of their own in which power moves without reference to human labor. Freed from the person, money and time enter into a new disembodied world, independent of history, land, and persons. And, of course, independent of Christian revelation.

Maurin promulgated these criticisms concerning modern society's incoherence as a way of attracting people to his plan of action, which was both radical and pragmatic. He described it as a threefold program: Roundtable discussions for the clarification of thought; houses of hospitality, preferably overseen by the bishop, to be centers of the works of mercy; and agronomic universities, farming communes where workers

---

11. Maurin, "A New Society," *Easy Essays*, 109-10.

12. Maurin commended Mounier's *Personalist Manifesto* to his readers. In fact, on some points Maurin disagreed with positions taken in the manifesto. Notably, the *Manifesto* is deeply skeptical of crafts and back-to-the-land movements; accepts the possible necessity of violence in the cause of creating a new society; and commends voluntary poverty only for the heroic.

could find work as well as study and scholars could broaden themselves through labor. These were, and are, the core practices of the Catholic Worker as Peter Maurin set them out. But Maurin's constructive agenda was both far larger and far more intimate than that list suggests. In the first place, restoring the organic unity of the person, the community, and faith meant restoring the theological center of the community.

> Lincoln Steffens says:
> "The social problem
> is not a political problem;
> it is an economic problem."
> Kropotkin says:
> "The economic problem
> is not an economic problem;
> it is an ethical problem."
> Thorstein Veblen says:
> There are no ethics in modern society."
> R. H. Tawney says:
> "There were high ethics
> in society
> when the Canon Law
> was the law of the land."[13]

To the many critics who claimed Maurin merely had a futile ambition to go back to the medieval period, Maurin, echoing Chesterton, would ask if they thought going forward into a dead-end alley was a better idea than turning around and getting out. Maurin did favor the restoration of a Catholic society, one built on a consensus about the nature of the good life and the good society. Neither authoritarianism nor individual liberty could replace such a consensus, which had to be built from the bottom up, personalist-style. Being a profoundly catholic as well as Catholic thinker, Maurin was well-suited to the work of building such consensus. The ambitious reach of his conversations was notorious. "Peter slept in the back of *The Catholic Worker* office, and he soon brought in an Armenian anarchist poet and a German agnostic to share his quarters with him and to provide sparring partners for round-table discussions."[14] His "Unpopu-

13. Maurin, "Ethics and Economics," *Easy Essays*, 4.
14. Day, "Introduction" to *Easy Essays*, third page of unnumbered section.

lar Front" was built on his belief in a natural alliance among fundamental-
ist Christians who love the Sermon on the Mount and the Ten Commandments; humanists who try to be human; personalist theists who try to be
their brother's keeper; and Catholics who believe in the common good.[15]
He talked enthusiastically with and about Jews, especially in the early for-
ties.[16] He also tried, not very successfully, to foster interracial conversation
in Harlem starting in 1934. He even got himself a gig at the Apollo to try to
win an audience. That particular venture was, not surprisingly, an over-
whelming failure: in his own words, he "got the hook." But he was unde-
terred. The storefront in Harlem closed not after Maurin was beaten nor
after months of finding no way to make a real connection to the community, but only when the owner of the property noticed the Catholic
Worker's pacifism and dropped his support.[17] Maurin never spoke of tol-
erance or pluralism, but he was remarkably inclusive: he would discuss social well-being seriously with absolutely anyone, in the hope that every
person had a unique vocation and would be drawn, as he was, toward the
beauty of truth. "'I will give you a piece of my mind and you will give me
piece of your mind, and then we will both have more in our minds,' he
would say."[18] A peaceful society had to be based in a shared sense of the
good, which is to say a shared theology, and he believed that would be created neither by power over those who are different, nor by allowing others
to go their own, incommensurable, way. He believed the attraction of truth
could unite persons without destroying their uniqueness, because he believed persons were made to love truth. Besides, Truth, when it walked the
earth, loved even its enemies.

In the spirit of Catholic Action, Maurin held that a laity imbued with
the wisdom and spirit of Christianity, led by wise and courageous bishops
and scholars, fired by the example and assistance of religious orders, could
rebuild the secular world from within, restoring order to the chaos of mo-
dernity. His method was not only nonviolent; it was not even about build-

---

15. Maurin, "Unpopular Front," and "Christianity and Democracy," *Easy Essays*, 146,
193.

16. Ellis, *Peter Maurin*, 146-54. In addition to his favorable mentions of Jewish teach-
ing on loans, Maurin wrote several essays specifically defending Jews from anti-Semitism.
The most complete biography of Maurin's life is written, in fact, by a Jewish author, Marc
Ellis.

17. Ellis, *Peter Maurin*, 81-86.

18. Dorothy Day, *Loaves and Fishes* (Maryknoll: Orbis, 1963), 102.

ing a powerful voting block. He aimed to create a well-ordered society by "building the new within the shell of the old" (borrowing in this case from the IWW), particularly among Catholics. Like the Irish missionaries after the barbarian invasions and decay of Roman civilization, Catholics could revive the social order through discussion and education, hospitality, and good farming. "It was on the basis of personal charity/and voluntary poverty/that Irish missionaries/laid the foundations/of the social order."[19] Through the example of "cells of good living," Catholics and their associates in the Unpopular Front would win the world over, persuading one person at a time through appeals to beauty and reason. The church, understood this way, was essential to the personalist revolution Maurin fomented.

In economic life, personalism meant a return to a smaller scale, and especially to farming and crafts. With the English distributivists, Chesterton, Belloc, McNabb and their artist-essayist associate Eric Gill — as well as *Rerum novarum* — Maurin argued for a civilization based on widely-distributed small-scale ownership, where workers personally invested in their labor could do better and more enjoyable work. Within small communities of such workers, mutual accountability and mutual care can and must flourish, for the survival of each depends not on an abstract system beyond anyone's control, but on one's own family, neighbors, and co-workers.

Ideally, a village of farmers and craftspeople would be centered on the parish, so that the material struggle would never be isolated from the Body of Christ, poured out for the sake of "life to the full." Work participates in the sacrifice of love because it is an act of personal creativity and responsible support for oneself and one's family, and beyond that, it is also an act of love for those who will use the product. To enter into labor with love means to spend one's life for others and to risk reliance on the care of others. Although it has to and should expect some return, that exchange can be a real exchange of gifts if it is not simply a mathematical question of balancing rights but a personal commitment to each other.

The moral question about work therefore is not merely whether wages are just, but whether the work is an occasion for charity. Rather than only considering whether workers were paid adequately and their safety protected, he argued that some forms of work — particularly industrial-

19. Maurin, "Reconstructing the Social Order," *Easy Essays,* 17.

ized work — are unworthy of the person, regardless of the remuneration. As work is the personal gift of the worker to her society, production processes that undercut the workers' skills and creativity are intrinsically flawed. The artist Eric Gill, who criticized the industrial organization as failing to produce beautiful and useful goods and by the same token degrading the creative labor of the person, won praise from Maurin for his complaints that the production of cheap plenty through mindless factory work is a blight both for the worker and the consumer. The community of Catholic artists who gathered around Gill at the village of Ditchling in England were for Maurin a great sign of the way liturgy, community, and work belonged together in the Catholic synthesis.[20] This kind of life was summed up by Maurin in two of his favorite slogans — the synthesis of "cult, culture, and cultivation" and the creation of "a society in which it is easier to be good."

Economic personalism also meant that creating the kind of work that could be an act of charity was not a job to foist off on some distant leadership. Direct action was the means, because Maurin's economic personalism saw direct action as constitutive of the good life. Those who want such work will make it for themselves. For example, faced with class conflict, Maurin urged workers to "fire the bosses" and give their work as a gift. In Maurin's view, class warfare was, from either side, a dead end. Owners who exploit workers imperil their souls and create a society in which everyone steps on others to get ahead; workers who negotiate to press for better prices for their labor get treated like commodities because they are acting like commodities. "But the worker would not be exploited/ at the point of production/if the worker did not sell his labor/to the exploiter of his labor."[21] Though Maurin was himself a manual laborer for years and had his own stock of stories about injustice in the workplace, he did not join unions and had no interest in Day's reporting on them. Instead, he offered workers a characteristically radical solution: stop looking to sell yourself to the highest bidder. Reclaim work as an act of personal re-

---

20. The history of Ditchling, like that of many Catholic Worker communities, offers useful, if painfully gained, lessons in the pitfalls of community in which agreements are not clearly articulated in the beginning. Those divisions, however, did not destroy the good example of uniting work and holy life. See Robert Speaight, *The Life of Eric Gill* (New York: P. J. Kenedy & Sons, 1966), 139-49.

21. Maurin, "A Question and Answer on Catholic Labor Guilds," *Easy Essays*, 31.

sponsibility and creativity. Turn work into an act of charity and offer it as a gift, not a commodity.

This claim of Maurin's would certainly have earned him a reputation as a kind of holy fool if his lifestyle had not already done so. Workers whose bosses failed to offer a living wage had little hope that if they stopped contracting for wages they would receive enough to keep them — never mind their families — alive. Without a wage system, how would workers survive? Maurin had an answer, one that he had worked out experimentally. In the 1920s, Maurin, then a French teacher, had announced to his students that he would no longer receive wages but would offer his skill as a teacher as a gift. If his students wanted, they could pay him what they thought it was worth, and he would accept this gladly as a gift. According to Maurin's later articulation of the problem of labor, he became a beggar in preference to being a commodity. Maurin's act was what Gandhi might call an "experiment in truth" conducted by a man of prodigious intellect engaged in years of study and reflection on the problem of Christian life in modern society. The experiment succeeded, although Maurin's somewhat disheartening commentary on the generosity of his students was simply, "They did not let me starve."

Maurin himself was not at all put off by this very modest result, because he did not mistake poverty for failure. Offering his work as a gift presupposed a willingness to become poor, which willingness he thought to be obvious for a Christian. Christians should strive to "keep up with St. Francis," welcoming voluntary poverty as part of their following of Christ. Maurin was not ascetic for asceticism's sake, but neither did he earn all he could in order to give all he could, in the Wesleyan formulation. His poverty was a creative, transformative condition, a way of life to be welcomed and even embraced for the love of God and neighbor.

He meant it, and he lived it. With his peasant background, he knew in his own body about plowing, weeding, harvesting, and digging just as he knew about sleeping out, going hungry, and begging. Work and poverty are hard, but even shoveling manure, if it is part of a life's work that demands skill and serves the common good, can be not only acceptable, but positively good. He respected manual labor so much that he counted it as necessary even, or particularly, for scholars. Making a hybrid of Kropotkin and St. Benedict, Maurin taught that manual labor was necessary not only for the sustenance of the community but also for the welfare of the individuals in it, as refreshment and variation from mental work. Both manual and mental work are necessary for each person, though by training, ability, and temperament people will specialize more in one than the other. Those who become workers need to study both for their inspiration and so that they can continually improve their work. Scholars need to put their bodies to work so that their ideas do not lose hold on present reality and so that they can gain better ideas and insight. Catholic scholarship rooted in the philosophy and practice of the common good would be capable, Maurin was confident, of contesting secular characterizations of economics and guiding Christians into a common life in which "it would be easier to be good."

In this, as in so much else, Maurin taught first by example. He studied and taught in the midst of manual labor, poverty, prayer, and ongoing conversations with everyone who crossed his path, and he both tried out his theories and theorized about events. This practical scholarship bore fruit: Maurin's thought trampled the usual disciplinary boundaries to produce an overarching picture of the good life. "College professors/are specialists/who know more and more/about less and less/and if they keep on specializing/they will end/by knowing everything/about nothing."[22] Overcoming the alienation and disintegration of modern work required the skills of someone with the daring, or naiveté, to be at home in theology, philosophy, economics, history, and social criticism, and more importantly, to be at home among both workers and beggars.

Beggars as Sacraments

Maurin begged for his needs on some occasions, and he urged others not to be ashamed to beg. One of his essays, in fact, is entitled "Why Not Be a Beggar?" He wrote, in a piece urging bishops to lead the way in reclaiming the Catholic tradition of hospitality,

> People who are in need
> And are not afraid to beg
> Give to people not in need
> The occasion to do good
> For goodness' sake.

22. Maurin, "On Specialization," *Easy Essays*, 171.

Modern society calls the beggar
Bum and panhandler
And gives him the bum's rush.
But the Greeks used to say
That people in need
Are the ambassadors of the gods.[23]

Maurin understood beggars to be moral agents in society, carrying the word about the importance of voluntary poverty to the wealthy to invite them to share in it. But Maurin's attention to them is not merely the appeal of a reminder of charity, some positive version of Smith's description of the tug on the cords of sympathy. Maurin's claim that beggars are the ambassadors of God appears to have been influenced, as so much in Maurin is at least indirectly, by the writing of Charles Péguy. In an essay called "The Supplicants and the Supplicated," Péguy argues that in Greek literature the supplicant, not the supplicated, is the dominant character. Having felt the hand of Fate, the one who suffers is closer to the greatest powers and to the truth. Before Priam's supplication, Achilles must bend. All human achievement and power are empty, finally, and it is when one is faced with a beggar that this truth comes home. "Because he has been wax in the divine, superdivine fingers of fate, he has become mysteriously dear to the divine, superdivine heart of fate." It is not a matter of metaphor, but the literal truth.

They are all of them ambassadors. And the ambassadors of a great king. —
     In the face of such an elevation, what do the Greeks make of the meanwhile most important contrast between the just and the unjust, between innocence and crime? . . . What human honor or dishonor — or if this is too modern a term — what human advantage can compare with the advantage of having been chosen to become the plastic material of the gods and of Her who dominates and will model the gods themselves, and govern them in the slumber of death? And that is why the criminal supplicant, or so speak exactly, the former criminal — for, since he is a supplicant he can no longer be a criminal — that is why the supplicant termed criminal is for the Greeks a man infinitely wiser,

---

23. Maurin, "To the Bishops of the U.S.A.: A Plea for Houses of Hospitality," *Easy Essays,* 8.

nearer the gods, more innocent than the wisest and the most innocent of happy men.[24]

Beggars are not just reminders of the need for justice and charity. Beggars have a kind of sacramental role, and the encounter with them calls for reverence. Quite apart from the merit of their deeds or virtue of their lives, those who suffer are close to the heart of God. Against a world of progress and the destruction of human weakness, Péguy ends the essay confessing, "We are as stupid as Saint Augustin [*sic*] and as Saint Paul, as Saint Louis and as Saint Francis and as Joan of Arc. . . ." This ancient sense that those who suffer know the heart of God is a forerunner of the Christian proclamation of Christ crucified. Those who testify to fragility in the face of the healthy and prosperous donors are the ones who stand in the center of the mystery.

Hall understands the beggar as a reminder that all people are equal, because we are all ontologically beggars, mortal. Maurin knew beggars were all about inequality. Some people become keepers of a terrible sacred office, people who live in the cold and heat, who treat dumpsters as pantries and bus stations as bases of operation. Far from advising beggars to accept their sacred function quietly, Maurin urged boldness.

> Although you may be called
> bums and panhandlers
> you are in fact the Ambassadors of God.
> As God's Ambassadors
> you should be given food,
> clothing and shelter
> by those who are able to give it.[25]

What beggars offer is a flash of an economy not based on fear and evasion of each other's needs, an economy that does not rely on rights as weaponry against the weakness of the human condition and against the needs and demands of others. That flash is painful because the transition from the economy where a beggar is a parasite, morally deformed, or a

---

24. Charles Péguy, *Men and Saints: Prose and Poetry*, trans. Anne and Julian Green (New York: Pantheon Books Inc., 1944), 49-51.

25. Maurin, "To the Bishops of the U.S.A.: A Plea for Houses of Hospitality," *Easy Essays*, 8.

metaphor for human mortality to an economy where this beggar could be a friend is shocking. They are a confrontation with the divine that most people can hardly bear to see and that they themselves may never know, if they are not recognized. Beggars — like the Christ-lamb Francis rescued — speak whether they intend it or not of God's own vulnerability in the courts of the unjust. Hall sees in beggars universal human frailty; Maurin saw God's suffering patience. In that theological difference lies the secret heart of the matter.

> True prayer does not consist in asking favors from a king-God, but in giving alms to a beggar-God.
> . . . Strength of spirit and nobility of soul will always have valuable reasons to prefer atheism to faith, especially where God is seen as a king, a judge, a refuge or a consolation, because our ignorance, our egoism and our weakness adapt all too well to that God. But there, where God is seen as exiled purity and perfection begging?[26]

Maurin, like Francis, named the beggar's role as sacramental, because the source and sustainer of all economic life is a beggar. God has poured out and maintains the freedom of the world and now waits for a return gift. The game of freedom then is not how to maximize use of the resources God has entrusted to us to prove ourselves good stewards, but how to give ourselves in love to the One who grasps at nothing.

Stewardship sees God as the Owner who charges his somewhat confused management team to tend his investments. The classic scriptural locus for this image is the parable of the talents in Matthew 25 (and its parallel in Luke 19). Although the word "steward" does not appear in the story in any language — the managers of wealth are called "servants" — the dynamic fits. The owner of all puts riches in the care of his servants and leaves them alone to make use of them. But every investment manager, every franchise owner, every middle management worker knows the secret

---

26. "Le vraie prière ne consiste pas à demander les faveurs a un Dieu monarque, mais à faire l'aumône à un Dieu mendiant. . . . La rigueur de l'esprit et la noblesse de l'âme auront toujours des raisons valuables do préférer l'athéisme à la foi, partout où Dieu se présente come un roi, un juge, un refuge ou un consolation, car notre ignorance, notre égoïse et notre faiblesse s'accomodent trop bien de ce Dieu-là. Mais là où il se présente comme la pureté exilée et la perfection mendiante?" Gustave Thibon, *L'ignorance etoilée* (Fayard, 1974), 187. Cited in *Errance et saintete*, 81.

temptation, the longing to indulge one's own ambition instead of doing the Owner's bidding. The peculiarity of the scriptural story is that the one who disobeys only buries the wealth. His rebellion is strange in content, but familiar in tone. The struggle of stewardship is always how to bring one's independent ambition into line with the governance of the Owner, how to be obedient.

The parable can be read another way, though. A minority of scholars point out that no good ancient ruler would have commended usury in his servants, and the behavior of this sovereign in Luke's version of the tale is more in keeping with brutal tyranny than with Israel's God.[27] The hero of the story, they hold, is the disobedient servant. If money were fruitful, then planting it in the ground would have led to increase. But as in the natural order money does not grow over time, that servant has merely left a sack underground. He uses this prophetic act to confront the unjust ruler, who gathers where he did not scatter and reaps where he did not sow. Defenseless, this truth-telling servant is cast out, into beggary. That servant is Christ, who before the powerful of Jerusalem would tell the truth, suffer for it, and become one of the "least of these" mentioned in the next pericope of Matthew 25.

The reading is unconventional, but it suggests just what the inversion of stewardship thinking finally, theologically, implies. God is not the powerful one who has granted us the freedom of independent but rule-bound use of resources. God is far stranger than that. The source of all, the ever-present sustainer of all, creates a world which is free, and in doing so, is divested of control. God then waits, as a beggar, on the fulfillment of that freedom, which will be the return — gift of love. The freedom granted humanity by the beggar-God does not call for managers to "grow his business" in accord with company policy. The game is not how to make best use of the resources for the purposes of the Owner, but how to give oneself — heart, mind, muscles, home — to the beggar-Lord in love.

This different theological understanding of the freedom of work and the purpose of goods corresponds to a different economic behavior because it shifts the meaning of human work and property. Rather than competing with a rich and absent owner, humanity is called to friendship with one who owns nothing so that goods produced by and associated with the

27. Ched Meyers and Eric DeBode. "Towering Trees and 'Talented Slaves,'" *The Other Side*, May/June 1999: 11-17.

giver can be offered graciously to the receiver, in a fluid exchange of gifts that neither denies a kind of personal property — for how can a gift be given if it never belonged to the giver? — nor entrenches it.

This convergence of these theological and economic issues, the meaning of human liberty before God, the significance of voluntary poverty, and the disorder created by private property run amok, was not unique to Maurin. A series of papal encyclicals commemorating Franciscan anniversaries appeared during Maurin's years of intellectual formation and conversion.[28] These documents drew attention to the need for a renewed proclamation of Francis's love of poverty and peace, and claiming these qualities as relevant to the project of reconstructing the social order. The sense of those encyclicals is captured in Christopher Dawson's comment that ". . . the asceticism of St. Francis no longer involves the rejection of the natural world and the turning away of the mind from the created to the Absolute. The rule of Poverty is a means of liberation, not a movement of negation. It brings man back to the fellowship of God's creation which had been lost or vitiated by self-will."[29] Maurin found these far richer than the better known *Rerum novarum* and *Quadragesimo anno*, which he understood as poor substitutes. "It was as though 'a sad and weary father said to his children who warred continually on one another: you will not follow the ideal so I will present to you another program — organization.'"[30]

This "ideal" of Maurin's was something like the factory in Val des Bois, where the owner, Leon Harmel, established associations of employees and employers to work out together the running of the plant. The factory was committed to offering not only a just wage but also daily mass attended by people involved at all levels of the plant's functioning. Running the plant as a common venture of management and labor in a shared vision of productive work for the community led to the extraordinary result that owners, managers, and workers eventually all became third-order Franciscans. They became a community of charity, relying less on rights

28. Leo XIII, *Auspicato concessum* (September 17, 1882); Benedict XV, *Sacra propediem* (January 6, 1921); and Pius XI, *Rite expiatis* (April 30, 1926). Maurin cites these in "The Third Order of St. Francis." Ellis, *Peter Maurin*, 37.

29. Christopher Dawson, *Progress and Religion: An Historical Enquiry* (Washington, D.C.: Catholic University of America Press, 1929, 2001), 135.

30. Ellis, *Peter Maurin*, 68. Maurin's essay "The Case for Utopia" (*Easy Essays*, 37-40) uses St. Francis to expound Christianity's own kind of both capitalism and communism.

and more on the risk of trust to define their exchange, less on desire to accumulate wealth than on serving the common good to energize their labor. They changed the pattern of work in order to better make an exchange of gifts.[31] In one of his more painful puns, Maurin called on people to become "go-givers" instead of "go-getters." Val des Bois illustrated what he meant.

Actual Franciscans in the U.S., on the other hand, disappointed Maurin. He approached leaders of the first and third order of Franciscans, and in both cases he got an ecclesial run-around.[32] His response, as always, was to speak of them in a way that would encourage them to claim their charism. "Franciscan and Jesuits/believe in the responsibility/of private property/but they believe also/in the practicality of voluntary poverty."[33] The bearers of that tradition should be leaders in rebuilding the social order. Production that embodies the marital trust needed for gift exchange is both possible and useful. Vulnerability to each other and care for each other is practical, while accumulation undercuts both economic and spiritual health.

> To give money to the poor
> is to enable the poor to buy.
> To enable the poor to buy
> is to improve the market.
> To improve the market
> is to help business.
> To help business
> is to reduce unemployment.
> To reduce unemployment
> is to reduce crime.
> To reduce crime
> is to reduce taxation.
> So why not give to the poor
> for business' sake, for humanity's sake,
> for God's sake?[34]

---

31. Ellis, *Peter Maurin*, 26-27.
32. Ellis, *Peter Maurin*, 37.
33. Maurin, "Franciscans and Jesuits," *Easy Essays*, 118.
34. Maurin, "Why Not Be a Beggar?" *Easy Essays*, 78.

When people save money,
they invest that money.
Money invested
increases production.
Increased production
brings a surplus
in production.
A surplus in production
brings unemployment.
Unemployment brings a slump
in business.
A slump in business
brings more unemployment.[35]

Sharing goods and restraining an economy's propensity to produce too much are, Maurin argued, economically sound principles. "The basis for a Christian economy/is genuine charity and voluntary poverty."[36] While beggars have a particular sacramental role, workers who give their labor themselves have some share in it. Both workers who refuse to be a commodity and beggars who are not ashamed to invite people to do good for them are creating an order beyond rights even now, within in a world of rights. Maurin and Francis both saw an economy of rights not ordered to a common good and disassociated from personal duties and affection, and they both understood it to be implicitly contrary to Christian charity. In such an economy, history, personhood, and even work and time get translated into the abstraction of money, and they soon get lost in translation. Maurin's great contribution lay in arguing that such an economy was also counter-productive on its own terms.

And so it is that precisely what makes Maurin so practical is the same thing that causes his example to be so rarely practiced: he advised people to become poor, even in the heart of their productive work. Suddenly beggars generate a new fear, the fear that must have gripped the merchant in Jesus' parable when he first saw the pearl of great price. To give all? Can that be joy? Or can there be any joy in passing this opportunity up, in playing it safe? When the rich young man went away sad, did he ever find again the joy that he could have had?

35. Maurin, "Is Inflation Inevitable?" *Easy Essays*, 19-20.
36. Maurin, "A Question and Answer on Catholic Labor Guilds," *Easy Essays*, 30.

We can only achieve perfect liberty and enjoy fellowship with Jesus when his command, his call to absolute discipleship, is appreciated in its entirety. Only the man who follows the command of Jesus single-mindedly and unresistingly lets his yoke rest upon him, finds his burden easy, and under its gentle pressure receives the power to persevere in the right way. The command of Jesus is hard, unutterably hard, for those who try to resist it. But for those who willingly submit, the yoke is easy, and the burden is light.[37]

Criticisms of Maurin

Maurin enjoyed sparring with intelligent critics, and he has had plenty of them. Perhaps the most serious charge against him came from the one who knew him and honored him most, Dorothy Day. Looking over Maurin's proposed schedule of work and study at his agronomic universities, she remarked on the lack of time for doing housework. Gently, she put a finger on a serious gap in Maurin's thinking: what about families? If poverty is practical, in what sense is it practical for parents and most commonly for women who have charge of children and keeping house? Maurin was not a parent and might well turn the question back on those who raise it, trusting that they would find the answer themselves, as they have begun to, in various ways. Day lamented the ways her work continually dragged her attention away from her daughter, Tamar. She consoled herself with the hope that the Virgin Mary had always been Tamar's real mother, but that consolation did not relieve her of all her grief. But Catholic Worker families have become increasingly common, as some parents, like Padraig O'Neil, insist that bringing their children into their voluntary poverty, shared housing with the poor, and even civil disobedience is simply a way of giving their children the best life they know how to give them. O'Neil has been known to say that he would no more let his child go to the mall to buy designer jeans than he would let her use cocaine. The family that Dumpster-dives together stays together.[38] The question has received

37. Dietrich Bonhoeffer, *The Cost of Discipleship* (New York: Macmillan, 1959), 31.

38. I am paraphrasing from memory comments O'Neil made at a presentation he gave with his oldest daughter, Steve Woolford, Lenore Yarger, and me in Amy Laura Hall's Introduction to Christian Ethics course in early October 2000 at Duke University.

many answers, from O'Neil's confident one to Day's grief, and the conversation continues.[39]

But more frequently, echoing the spiritualization of virtuous poverty so characteristic of the birth of stewardship, readers sometimes dismiss Maurin's emphasis on the works of mercy as lovely and inspiring, but ultimately useless. The real work of systematic change will have to be done by those who are more material and pragmatic. Maurin's program looks to such observers like unrealistic visionary "back to the land" movement paired with holy but ineffective charitable work. Worse yet, it attempts to "go backward," away from industrialism and toward labor organized by guild and local farming communities. Maurin dodged some of these criticisms wittily, quipping that "what is practical is what is practiced" and that when one is standing at a dead end, going backwards is a good idea.[40]

Nevertheless, it is true that his synthesis drew on a large assortment of authors whose greatest common denominator is the extent to which their teachings have not been put into practice, and Maurin's synthesis has to large degree followed their lead. The farms that some of his followers started to be cells of the Green Revolution were called by Dorothy Day herself, "rather less than history." Many of those who took up the challenge of moving from the city back to farming had no training, and as farms, these "agronomic universities" do not have an impressive track record. One disciple, Larry Heaney, died in 1949 at Holy Family Farm in Starkenburg, Missouri, of "work-induced pneumonia while living with eleven people in an unheated farmhouse lacking both electricity and plumbing."[41] Heaney was not the only farmer who died that year, I suspect, but the harshness of rural poverty came as a shock to many who heard in "back to the land" only the hope of a leafy retreat. None other than Monsignor Luigi Ligutti, who organized in 1973 the first International Seminar on Stewardship in Rome, visited the St. Benedict farm near Upton, Massachusetts, and ac-

39. A wonderful resource is the discussion of family and childhood in Rosalie Riegle Troester, ed., *Voices from the Catholic Worker* (Philadelphia: Temple University Press, 1993), 291-332.

40. This second quip he owed to Chesterton, from *The Outline of Sanity* (New York: Dodd, Mead & Company, 1927).

41. Jeffrey D. Marlett, "Down on the Farm, Up to Heaven: Communes and the Spiritual Virtues of Farming," *Dorothy Day and the Catholic Worker Movement: Centenary Essays*, ed. William J. Thorn, Phillip M. Runkel, and Susan Mountin (Milwaukee: Marquette University Press, 2001), 413.

cording to Arthur Sheehan, advised them on how to make more effective use of their property.[42]

Catholic Worker farms continue to work at integrating hospitality, prayer, study, and farming. But whatever must be said of the persistence and creativity of those who live that life, the farms have not become hotbeds of scholar-worker collaboration on reducing unemployment and anomie through a return to land and faith. Nevertheless, people who dismiss Maurin as a visionary have misunderstood his philosophy. The revolution was not about the attainment of those Maurinite villages, much as he believed that they would be a better way to live. Encounter and discussion with people was not the means to the end of a farming commune; the farming communes were themselves just better means to reshape our common life around persons. Maurin carried his utopia around in himself and made it happen everywhere he went, and he expected everyone else to do the same, even if they did not agree with his distributivist ideas. One persistent young man managed to interrupt Maurin one evening in the thirties, to say, "What we've got to do is Christianize the world we're in . . . not try to go back to some world of the past." Maurin responded, "Young man, if that's what *you* think, that's *your* job. . . . You do it!"[43] The revolution was about the wonder of each person, even more than it was about what is often called "Peter Maurin's vision."

Small, persistent successes delighted Maurin, and they have continued in the work of Catholic Worker communities ever since. That these successes were mixed with a good deal of confusion and contention and that they were sometimes short-lived did not change his enthusiasm. Maurin had a profound faith in what one theological influence on and admirer of the Worker called "poor temporal means."

> It is possible that every attempt to transform the social régime along the lines of authentic humanism may fail, at least as far as outward appearances go. In such a case those who love God would exercise an efficacious — though hidden — influence on the temporal by the use of "poor temporal means" not in directly bringing about even a partial

42. Marlett, "Down on the Farm," 410.

43. From correspondence with Arthur Sheehan, quoted in Francis J. Sicius, "Dorothy Day's View of Peter Maurin," *Dorothy Day and the Catholic Worker Movement: Centenary Essays*, ed. William J. Thorn, Phillip M. Runkel, and Susan Mountin (Milwaukee: Marquette University Press, 2001), 422.

reconstruction of the social order, but by fidelity in thought and love
and by the touch of faithful hands on the work of a faithless world.[44]

Dorothy Day wrote that once, when a house of hospitality in Baltimore was being shut down by the city for housing whites and blacks together and for overcrowding, she asked Peter Maurin, "Is this what you
had in mind?" He only responded, "It serves to arouse the conscience at
least."[45] Lament was not his genre. He did not wonder if God was perhaps
secretly at work in the heart of the angry purists, or the alcoholic, or the
apathetic. He knew that God was. The reality all around him was a world
of subjects at the heart of whom is the spirit of God, in all its mystery, begging for their gift. The path to happiness did not lead away from the mess
of human lives around him. Rather, it led into it. There was no other way.

And it is precisely because of this that Maurin's teaching matters.
Maurin is not simply the man who called attention to these other writers,
promoting their critiques and proposals by boiling them down to a couple
of sentences that could be declaimed on a street corner. He made them
practical by modeling not a system, but a path: patient commitment to the
works of mercy at a personal sacrifice in the midst of work and exchange,
rather than only at its edges.

This commitment is the *sine qua non* of his thought, but it only
makes sense if seen in light of the joy of Christian discipleship. To live
rightly in the material and historical world, to create good order here and
now, Maurin taught that one had to have hope in both a better life here
and something beyond this.

> Bourgeois capitalists
> don't want their pie
> in the sky
> when they die.
> They want their pie
> here and now.
> To get their pie
> here and now

44. Jacques Maritain, *Freedom in the Modern World*, trans. Richard O'Sullivan, K.C.
(New York: Charles Scribner's Sons, 1936), 190-91.

45. *The Catholic Worker*, "On Pilgrimage," August 1959, 1, 6, 8. Available online at
www.catholicworker.org, document #754.

bourgeois capitalists
give us
better and bigger
commercial wars
for the sake of markets
and raw materials. . . .

Bolshevist Socialists,
like bourgeois capitalists,
don't want their pie
in the sky
when they die.
They want their pie
here and now.
To get their pie
here and now,
Bolshevist Socialists
give us
better and bigger
class wars
for the sake
of capturing the control
of the means of production
and distribution.[46]

A present life aimed at the happiness of eternal life is more likely to have its own share of happiness than the necessarily violent attempts of capitalists and Bolshevists to create ideal happiness. This is not economic pelagianism; Maurin never claimed to be about building the kingdom of God, but only to aim at creating a world "in which it is easier to be good." Even that aim was chastened: the lice, crowding, the stench of poverty, the long lines of people looking for coffee and left-over bread at the New York Catholic Worker fell sadly short of the kind of gracious hospitality he advocated, which had presupposed many individual Christian homes and parishes welcoming those in need, aided by communities of rural life to employ all who could work. But Peter Maurin could be patient and pragmatic, working against all odds without resort to violence against persons

46. Maurin, *Easy Essays*, 173-74.

or state. When an impassioned group of young intellectuals in 1936 wanted to throw out "the dead wood" (the poor) so the *Catholic Worker* could get on with agitating for its utopian project, Maurin almost shook the dust of the *Worker* from his feet. Day remembered that "he arose from the round table where the discussion was going on and said, 'let us go, let us leave this to them,' like the retiring abbot in the writing in G. P. Fedortov's collection of Russian spirituality."[47] He would not abandon people, even, or especially, the weak. He also would not use force against the purist reformers who were trying to hijack the movement. For a personalist, persons really cannot be the problem, and Maurin saw that such love of persons could only flourish in a spirit of hope. His hope, his "pie in the sky" was practical and political enough to be subject to genuine disappointment, but it was also eternally promised and undefeated, daily renewed in the mass and secretly flourishing in the mystery of many souls. The poor and the drunken, as well as the decadent and foolish were part of that secret flourishing. Maurin neither despaired nor compromised nor turned to violence (legal or illegal) when that secret remained deeply hidden.

In this Maurin exemplifies what I call "*viator* economics." Looking at problems of labor and capital, distribution and production, his aim is to encourage charity and to foster a social order in which charity makes sense. His economic thought is teleological, in the sense that it has a particular social good — the society in which it is easier to be good — and even an ultimate good for all beyond that — union with God. But as he pursues that good without using force to establish it, he has to give attention and patient care to the path toward that good as itself necessary and good, in a limited way. He cannot short-cut around the actual persons who work and do not work, who have and do not have housing. They, and the spirit of God at work among them, are the path to the good end. And so while a society of responsible and interdependent craftspeople and agricultural workers is the economic good at which Maurin aimed, the disgruntled unemployed men among whom he lived were genuinely and necessarily part of that good. Their begging was also a good part of the movement toward it, for by begging they anticipated and urged others to anticipate a society of the common good, a social order in which each was concerned for the needs of each, rather than competing behind a veil of abstractions.

47. Dorothy Day, "The Incompatibility of Love and Violence," *The Catholic Worker*, May 1951, 1, 2. Available online at www.catholicworker.org, document #232.

Maurin's *viator* economics is therefore characterized by two apparently contradictory but in fact mutually necessary qualities: first, a sense of a good economic order rather than merely an adequate one; and second, a pragmatic commitment to the person in the present. These qualities parallel the qualities of pilgrimage. A pilgrim has to have a goal, a specific shrine at which he or she intends to arrive, and at which, barring catastrophe, he or she will arrive. This is the purpose of a pilgrimage and what distinguishes it from meandering. But the pilgrimage, the holy work, does not begin with arrival, but with the road. Because of the end, the road itself becomes good. Peter Maurin called himself utopian, but one can hardly imagine a scholar less given to escapism. The way to his society of gift was each day, each person, each effort by him and by others. That the goal was not yet reached did matter. One has to strive for it and expect to reach it. But no part of the attempt to reach it is a failure or even, properly, an obstacle. As long as we are on the way, the end is already anticipated. He liked to quote from Catherine of Siena, "All the way to heaven is heaven, for Jesus said, I am the way."

As a *viator,* Francis made sense. His critics rightly point out that begging should play no part in an order of grace, that no one should be reduced to that kind of poverty and any romanticization of it or distraction from its horror is immoral. Assisi in Francis's day was no order of grace, and his reaction — renunciation and mendicancy — was critique and witness, a fragment of a gracious order transplanted into a hostile environment. Francis himself did not oppose property, even the holding of significant wealth. He did not urge the poor to become like him anymore than he urged this on the rich. He did not present himself as the answer to the Christian problem with wealth. Rather, he presented himself and his friars as wayfarers following Christ, never at home here, still traveling toward full possession of their inheritance. This is the uneasiness in Franciscan begging — it is not the good at which it aims, but it does participate more fully in that good than more apparently sensible proposals do. To accept it as a static position is to destroy it, but to renounce it in favor of another position may be no better. Christian economics is not a position, but a journey toward a new city, where poverty will no longer be. But the opposite of poverty is not plenty. We know well that plenty and poverty can co-exist in one city, and Maurin teaches us that they can co-exist in more than one way. The opposite of poverty is not plenty, but friendship. Still the journey of that city requires of its pilgrims renunciation — of their fear of poverty of the poor, with all its rationalizations and material defenses, and also of their propensity to despair. The road Maurin will set us on is not an easy one, but knowing where easy answers have gotten us will make it surprisingly appealing. And if it is the right road, the journey is already a comedy.

CONCLUSION

Economic Comedy

Economics has been cast as a science of tragic choices. As described by Malthus, the finite world limits human satisfaction and at times refuses to meet even human need. Economics is the science of facing that finitude, recognizing the limits imposed by nature and human nature, and making the best of it, whatever one judges that "best" to mean. Making and enforcing those judgments is the necessary dirty work of stewards and the intellectual challenge of economists. They look the hardship in the eye, hunger and underfunded schools and small businesses thwarted by interest rates, the balance between unemployment and inflation — and they work to manage it, to overcome it where possible, to make peace with it where there is no other way. They are heroes. Their work is mundane and prosaic, and their commitment to it is all the more heroic for its lack of glamour.

But the beggars of this book are comedians. Their joyfulness, relative to the sober management of our tragic heroes, can seem irresponsible and even immoral in the face of poverty. Labre, Francis, Maurin — the temptation to dismiss these holy fools as "otherworldly" and therefore materially irrelevant to the serious business of dealing with poverty is strong. Worse yet, the cheerful beggar Patience of *Piers Plowman,* though he knows and pities the misery of the poor and denounces the callous greed of the rich, defends holy poverty in the end because, "You need not care about corn or clothes or drink,/Nor dread death or devil, die as God likes/Whether through hunger or heat, at his will it be;/for if you live as he teaches the shorter life the better."[1]

1. C-Version, Passus XV, 257-60.

THE FEAR OF BEGGARS

Can it be holy and wise cheerfully to accept early death? Where is the righteous rage that defends human flourishing?

At its sharpest, the fear of beggars is a fear of war, of being overrun by desperate hordes of hungry people, of the dissolution of the security of property rights, of the breakdown of social agreement into class conflict. Flannery O'Connor's story "A Circle in the Fire" captures the moral horror of being overrun, not by a horde of famine-plagued peasants, but by three little boys. The boys arrive at Mrs. Copes's farm uninvited.[2] One of them, Powell, is the son of Mrs. Copes's former employee, who after leaving Mrs. Copes's employ and consciousness, died. Powell has returned with some friends from his new and apparently unhappy home in Atlanta's developments to show them the wonders of the farm. Mrs. Copes first a little awkwardly greets them as visitors, and then recognizing they are hungry she shifts into the more comfortable reaction of pity. She provides some food, which they hardly eat and for which they offer no thanks. She begins to realize that they intend to stay on the property amusing themselves with her horses and woods. Mrs. Copes fears fire in the woods, and she immediately attempts to control their access, forbidding them to camp on the property anyplace except in the yard near the house. The boys repeatedly break their word to her: they ride the horses they promised to stay away from, and they do not leave in the morning as they say they will. Mrs. Copes cajoles, then chases and admonishes them, but they only become more aggressive, knocking her mailbox down, letting the bull loose, and draining all of the oil out of the tractors. Finally Mrs. Copes's little daughter dresses like an old west sheriff and goes out to get the boys with her toy guns. She finds them in an idyllic setting, washing and playing in the water in a cow trough. She spies on them and hears them scoff at her mother's claim to own the woods: "'Listen,' the big boy said, sitting down quietly in the water with the little one still moored to his shoulders, 'it don't belong to nobody.' 'It's ours,' the little boy said." They toy with their desire to destroy the beauty of the place. "'Do you know what I would do with this place if I had the chance? . . . I'd build a big parking lot on it, or something,' he muttered."[3] As the daughter watches, the boys set the woods on fire, and no

2. Flannery O'Connor, "A Circle in the Fire," in *Flannery O'Connor: Collected Works*, ed. Sally Fitzgerald (New York: Library of America, Literary Classics of the United States, Inc., 1988), 232-51.

3. O'Connor, "A Circle in the Fire," 249.

one except Mrs. Copes is in a hurry to put it out. The story ends with the child's vision of the boys dancing in the midst of the fire, "in a circle the angel had cleared for them."[4]

Throughout the story, Mrs. Copes preaches to others the importance of counting blessings, of being grateful under all circumstances. That her own circumstances are much better than others is no reason for them to be less grateful than she. When invited to speculate on how a woman in an iron lung got pregnant, Mrs. Copes deflects the question, concentrating on the necessity of the woman's gratitude that she was alive at all. How people's situations arose is not her concern. She has a legal claim to the farm and she appreciates that it is a good one, and so she is thankful, or so she says. The boys forthrightly deny her claim from the beginning. They state their intention to sleep on her property, to amuse themselves with playing on it; they eat her food without thanks and in fact with complaints at its quality. They act on her as beggars did on Malthus: she feels she must offer them help, but she also resents their presence, wants to control their incursion into her life, and comes to admit that they are her enemy. Her daughter, less restrained by gentility, fantasizes that she is going to get them "one by one and beat you black and blue. Line up. LINE UP!"[5] They are not just hungry boys, as Mrs. Copes hoped at first; they are weeds taking control of her garden, spreading malicious mischief over the entire farm. Mrs. Copes and the boys are drawn irresistibly into war with each other. Stewards and economists try to negotiate compromises, while our beggars camp in the desert between battle lines, singing songs in the night.

When Francis of Assisi taught his followers "not to make any place their own or contend with anyone for it," to receive thieves and robbers "with kindness,"[6] the note he struck resonated through Christendom. The emerging market economy was already creating an economic world based on individual property rights, rather than on a sense of the common good or of mutual customary obligations. While this could be a moment of opportunity for workers to improve on their situations, it is also a tectonic shift in the grammar of Christian economy, for the question is no longer whether arrangements truly serve the mutual love Christians are to have for one another; now it begins to be possible to conceive of a just society as

---

4. O'Connor, "A Circle in the Fire," 251.
5. O'Connor, "A Circle in the Fire," 248.
6. *Earlier Rule*, Ch. VII. FA: EDI, 69.

merely a matter of equal exchange under contract. Mutual charity can disappear from the scene.

This was the genius of Francis's practice of renouncing property: to defend a right to his property would involve him in an assertion of his own rights against another person's, and he knew, as Mrs. Copes tried to avoid knowing, where that road leads. His poverty was a form of economic unilateral disarmament.

But Francis did not strip himself alone. Because he permitted, and even encouraged, his friars to beg when they needed to, he pulled others along with him into poverty. Opponents complained that the Franciscan movement's exponential growth was a threat to the prosperity of poor families whose devotion led them to give alms to the growing numbers of friars begging for the love of God. Voluntary poverty is one thing; begging in the expectation that others will and should share to some extent in that poverty is another, and starting a movement which permits thousands of religious (and their imitators) to beg is quite something else. The specter of hordes of "virtuous" beggars demanding alms and impoverishing all of Christendom haunted the nightmares of Europe under Franciscan sway. Francis's radical alternative to a rights-based economy of market exchange could be narrated as both an irenic witness to the reign of God and an economic anarchy open to, or even an occasion of, scandalous abuses.

The early theorists of political economy likewise saw the bitter conflict beneath the market. For Smith, this is inevitable, as isolated beings negotiate their psychological and material welfare against each other. Mrs. Copes naturally feels concern for the boys and desires to behave generously, but the moral blindness of the boys makes a harmonious ending impossible. The "truck, barter, and exchange" of human life is constructive social conflict. For Malthus the misery of the victims was more intransigent and the conflict more explicitly horrifying, because he would claim that the boys are only the misbegotten children of Mrs. Copes's wayward impulse to benevolence. Nevertheless, they must be suppressed, victims in a necessary war even God cannot pacify. It was Marx, of course, who most sharply drew the conclusion that market economics *is* war and that the way out of it is to tear away the illusion of the market and reveal the war beneath, so that it could be fought and inevitably won by the workers. But the battle lines had been drawn well before Marx began to marshal his forces.

Within the church, Smith's celebration of economics as unbloody war was as unsuitable as the anarchy of Franciscanism had been counter-productive. The language of stewardship came to bear the burden of articulating a sort of just-war theory of economics. The emergence of the metaphorical sense of "steward" in the same era in which the crown was redistributing ecclesial and monastic goods suggests an attempt to articulate the just management of the church's right to property as a sort of humble service before God, although an immensely powerful one in the world. The language, because applied to secular control of property, was particularly appropriate for describing a necessary moral function of wealth-management to ensure the survival of an increasingly "spiritual" and abstract community known as the church. Attempts at developing this ethic dated back at least to the anti-fraternal debates and to Marsilius; flourished in the work of early Methodists with their aspiration to have a poor clergy supported voluntarily; and became a dominant pre-occupation of Protestantism in the United States, with its survival dependent upon the donations of voluntary members. Mrs. Copes is not the only good Christian whose repeated protestations of gratitude only announced more and more definitively her unwillingness to be accountable to others.

In an agonistic marketplace, where rights are necessary for self-defense and potent as weapons, neither Franciscan attempts to follow the crucified Jesus as the meek and defenseless; nor heroic ethics of the necessary battle for the good of all in classical economics; nor the attempt to grant a limited sphere of participation in that war to those charged with stewardship have provided for Christians a fully satisfactory account of moral economic life. And this should not surprise us. Love among us is mercy, not because love requires a dark background against which to stand nor because love is self-destruction, but because we are in *status viatoris*. The attempt to create a system which will work for all people, in all places, to fight off suffering and offer "full life" is simply in contradiction to that condition. It can only be instituted by force, and more successfully by more brutal or insidious force. The challenge, therefore, to those who would work for a "Christian economics" must be to cultivate hope, mercy, and humility, habits of the *viator* ordered toward an end in which they themselves will finally give way to an all-encompassing charity.

Contrary to common sense, Maurin and his companions demonstrated that hospitality requires poverty more than Mrs. Copes–style property. The beggar-boys who burn the woods know that modern individual property is not a neutral substance that can be used for good or ill, because by definition it excludes them. It is not a question of how one uses property; modern private property rights are founded on a narrative of strangerliness, which is to say managed enmity, and for those on the losing side, the only thing to do with such property is torch it.

But that is not Peter Maurin's way. We can imagine him wandering up to Mrs. Copes's porch, leaning toward her as he warmed up, gesturing eagerly as he spoke, perhaps to encourage her to hold a round-table discussion with the field hands and local politicians about racism, to urge her to be truly genteel by doing her own labor and respecting that of others, to tell her of the beauty of the witness of saints who welcomed even their enemies, and incidentally, why not turn the farm into an agronomic university?

The boys' presence is simply not the same for him as it is for her. As Mrs. Copes would no doubt notice, the company of unruly and enraged beggars was nothing unusual for him, and he had been mistaken for one at least once himself.[7] His propensity to "agitate" and "indoctrinate" at the drop of a hat may have driven some boisterous beggars to look for less exhausting targets. He believed in everyone, and no one got away from an encounter with Maurin unchanged. Day wrote of him that he "aroused in you a sense of your own capacities for work, for accomplishment. He made you feel that you and all men had great and generous hearts with which to love God. If you once recognized this fact in yourself you would expect and find it in others. 'The art of human contacts,' Peter called it happily."[8]

Even with Maurin's talent for drawing out the best in people, he could not advise Mrs. Copes without recognizing the possibility that the boys would damage the farm. Day's comments on the "art of human contacts" continue, recognizing that even Peter Maurin did not bring out the responsible and loving participant in every person. "But it was seeing Christ in others, loving the Christ you saw in others. Greater than this, it was having faith in the Christ in other without being able to see Him. Blessed is he that believes without seeing."[9] Maurin assumed trust and reverence for each person, and if the encounter took an ugly turn and he could not avoid moving quickly into the work of turning the other cheek,

7. Ellis, *Peter Maurin*, 32.

8. Dorothy Day, *The Long Loneliness* (San Francisco: Harper and Row, Publishers, 1981), 171.

9. Day, *The Long Loneliness*, 171.

then that is what he did. He held with a terrible simplicity to the claim that the poor are one's brothers and sisters. Suffering out of love for them is not the problem to be avoided, and given the power of God to use one person's love to do great things, insults and blows endured patiently in the cause of mercy might themselves become part of the creative work of restoration.

Great mountains of literature have been written by Christians, for Christians, about how to avoid becoming poor while still following Jesus' commands. Much of it, in the wake of anti-fraternal debates, favors effective service and humble practicality, or influenced by modern thought on political economy, posits an inevitable individual responsibility which it is psychologically, economically, and spiritually perilous to cross. In all of it, beggars violate boundaries and puncture rationalizations about peaceful individualism.[10] If we cannot be neighbors, they seem to say, it is highly questionable that we can be anything but enemies. Peter Maurin thought that in this they were right, and he set to work describing what an economy of neighborliness would look like and living his part of it as best he could.

After his first visit to the Catholic Worker office where Maurin was staying in 1934, Stanley Vishnewski described it as a small and dark three-room apartment, the front room of which was packed with rickety furniture used in writing and laying out the paper, as well as a clothing donation box available to anyone who came in; the second room was filled with bookcases, suitcases left by homeless people for storage, and Maurin's cot; and the small kitchen in back held a large round table. This place, Maurin's lodging and work, was his version of Mrs. Copes's farm. It was the blessing given to him by God, a place where he could flourish in the company of other people using their talents for the love of Christ, and what made it work was the shared willingness to share poverty. It was a different kind of property, one suitable for life on the road to holiness.

The wandering beggar-poet Peter Maurin sometimes seems like a character from *Piers Plowman* even down to his silly alliteration and puns.

---

10. I am reminded of a beggar who asked me for money one day when I was out of cash because I had been Christmas shopping. When I muttered that I was sorry, he blasted out, "You aren't sorry. They all say that, but you aren't sorry at all." I judged that telling him I was writing a book about beggars probably wouldn't help matters. I ran into him again an hour later and before I even spoke, he apologized for yelling at me. I used a credit card to buy us a pizza. Class barriers did not come crashing down, but there was a little more truth in that moment than in most of my encounters with beggars, and I have him to thank for it.

Maurin's career as a comedian at the Apollo in Harlem was short-lived, but comedy is unmistakably his genre. When, during the master's dinner with Patience, Piers Plowman makes his cameo appearance calling for love of enemy, he ends with, "And lay on him thus with love till he laugh with you/ And if he not bow down for this beating, may he go blind!" (XV, 147-48). Christian love of enemy is participation in the absurd excess of God's generosity. If our enemies cannot be brought to laugh with us at God's goodness, then they will be blind, as they bring on themselves the loss of the beatific vision. As they do with Peter Maurin, laughter and jokes play a small but important role in marking the territory of grace in *Piers Plowman*. The master dismisses Patience's claims to power as "a dysores [popular entertainer's] tale" (XV, 171); Jesus' prosecutor accuses him of making jokes about the Temple (XX, 40); and in the climactic harrowing of hell, Jesus makes a joke that destroys the power of Lucifer, claiming "an eye for an eye" as warrant to use his disguise to steal humanity back from their tempter, who used disguise to take them in the first place. *"Ars ut artem falleret"* [It takes a trick to undo a trick] (XX, 392).

Much of Langland's craft is a lesson in the power of righteous laughter.[11] The stern refrain, *"Redde quod debes"* (Pay what you owe), governs an early section of the work on the obligation of workers to be industrious. The merry-making of truant workers, like the merry-making of the callous rich and of hypocritical friars, is a failure to *redde quod debes,* to do justice. But midway through the work a different refrain takes over: *"Patientes vincunt"* (The patient overcome). In God's good time, grace triumphs, and with it, those who have hoped patiently. Even now, as in the contrast of the gluttonous master and Patience or Peter Maurin's "pie in the sky" economy, a sort of triumph already belongs to the patient.

11. Laughter is found in the pub as well, but there Langland sees joy distorted by gluttony, sloth, and lust, perversions of the good of conviviality. Significantly, the friars are also judged guilty of a wrongful sense of humor. In Langland's terms, the Franciscan malaise can be characterized as a loss of right laughter.

> 3e lordes and ladies and legates of holy churche
> That feden feol sages, flateres and lyares,
> And han lykyng to lythen hem in hope to do 3ow lawhe —
> *Ve vobis qui ridetis —*
> And 3eueth such mede and mete and pore men refuse,
> In 3oure deth-deynge y drede me sore
> Last tho manere men to muche sorwe 3ow brynge. (VII, 82-87)

The humorless business of achievement and fairness, held together by the fear of starvation, is reshaped by this eschatological turn. *"Redde quod debes"* remains a demanding claim on sinners throughout the poem, but it loses some of its resentful shakedown character after the appearance of the triumph of the patient. When justice and charity do work together, laughter becomes an element of salvation. Tellingly, when Piers advocates his ludicrous approach to one's enemies, Reason goes chasing after him. The triumph of the patient both surpasses and attracts reason. It claims a playful generosity to the gospel, which is met in the simple-minded poor, the "lunatic lollers and wandering tramps," who are healthy but witless "merry-mouthed men, minstrels of heaven,/And God's boys [rascals] and jesters, as the book tells" (IX, 126-27). Francis, Maurin, Labre, and even the boy Powell in O'Connor's story are God's own pranksters.

For the *viator* community, gifts are provision for the journey necessary from each and for all. The duty to make use of one's calling and talent has correlative rights, held for the sake of fulfilling the duty, and such obligations, fulfilled in an orderly way, are necessary for the community of peace. Even St. Francis in the RNB allowed his brothers to keep the tools of their trade, assuming, certainly, that the trade in question would be lowly. But where rights serve not as a support to duty for the sake of love, but as a hedge against the war of the market or demands of the state, this comic material humility does disturb their moral mandate. It does not do so, however, by suggesting simply that all people should relinquish the demand for their necessities and suffer in silence. From the Canon of Poverty's leading the poor in protest against the cleric who hoarded grain to Peter Maurin's call to "fire the bosses," the adoption of humility constitutes an appeal to a more fundamental order, in which mutual charity makes demands beyond the mere restraint of war. Claims of right are not always harmful. It is a matter of the center of gravity: rights will help adjudicate and protect, within an order that already knows mere rights are never enough. As the true economic order is constituted by charity, so rights neither solve every problem nor encompass every good. God's comics refuse to play by those rules, up-ending a world founded upon the determination of certain rights. Rights can be a tactic of charity, but charity is no sidekick to rights.

These comics do not claim that all people should imitate them. In various ways, beggars held that their vocation was holy and a privilege, even as they also honored many others vocations. But to say then that "some are called to this poverty, and others are not" is to turn away the riches they are offering. Their calling is a center of gravity for practice of property and exchange, so that even property and exchange no longer fear poverty, but embrace it as the occasion of neighborliness and the site of God's patient triumph. Joy is not in material security, if such a thing as material security could exist. The answer to the fear of the poor is not avoidance, but love itself, acting in a world of suffering under the guise of joyful mercy.

And what, in the end, of beggars? Beggars disrupt economics as system and demand personal responsibility by creating the most localized of economies, one on one. As each beggar and almsgiver are different, no one answer can address the complexities of need, shame, desire, power struggles, race relations, fear, greed, sickness, and despair that may be part of such an encounter. Any disciple of Peter Maurin and Dorothy Day knows that there is no single right answer for all cases. But knowing there is no single answer is at least a step in the right direction; practicing the art of human contacts is another; and becoming poor a giant leap. There is no system for dealing with beggars; there are instead people, bound to each other by a piece of sidewalk, strangers in a world not given to marital trust and gift-exchange. Building the new within the shell of the old, in this case, will require hard practice and honest speech about the gospel. It will require openness to strangers, for a gift can only be given to a beggar if the gift invites the beggar into friendship.[12] Friendship, including the power to accuse and argue frankly and to know ourselves accountable to each other and to relax in each other's homes, is an achievement under the best of circumstances and a marvel in an encounter of almsgiver and beggar. But a wandering preacher, betrayed and crucified, rose with healing in his hands. We have reason to wait in joyful hope.

Strangerliness is a habit that has been learned slowly. We will unlearn it with difficulty, and we will not do so without making changes, in our finances, our locations, our ways of doing business, and our encounters with strangers. This pilgrimage is not safe; staying where we are is worse. "I am at your mercy" is not only a plea for help, but also an invitation to reflect on John Paul II's teaching: "No peace without justice; no justice without mercy." Where else will we find the peace of Christ, but in the deter-

---

12. John Milbank, "Can Morality Be Christian?" in *The Word Made Strange: Theology, Language, Culture* (Oxford: Blackwell Publishers, 1997), 226.

mined and absurd practice of mercy, laying on with love until even our enemies laugh with us?

In a world of fragility and sin, Christianity must cultivate that economic comedy which turns the tables on good and faithful stewardship. Laughter, like perfect love, drives out fear. Getting the joke may be the most important economic virtue of all.

Bibliography

Adams, Thomas McStay. *Bureaucrats and Beggars: French Social Policy in the Age of the Enlightenment.* New York: Oxford University Press, 1990.

Aers, David. *Community, Gender, Individual Identity: English Writing, 1360-1430.* London: Routledge, 1988.

————. Piers Plowman *and Christian Allegory.* London: Edward Arnold, 1975.

Aers, David, and Lynn Staley. *The Powers of the Holy: Religion, Politics, and Gender in Late Medieval English Culture.* University Park, Pa.: The Pennsylvania State University Press, 1996.

Amiand, Arthur. *La legende Syriaque de S. Alexis, l'homme de Dieu.* Paris: Vieweg, 1889.

Anderson, Gary M. "Mr. Smith and the Preachers: The Economics of Religion in the *Wealth of Nations.*" *Journal of Political Economy* 96, no. 5 (October 1988): 1066-88.

Armstrong, Regis J.; J. A. Wayne Hellman; and William J. Short, eds. *Francis of Assisi: Early Documents.* Vol. I: *The Saint.* New York: New City Press, 1999.

————. *Francis of Assisi: Early Documents.* Vol. II: *The Founder.* New York: New City Press, 2000.

Arrow, Kenneth. "Gifts and Exchanges." *Philosophy and Public Affairs* 1/4 (Summer 1972).

Asad, Talal. "On Discipline and Humility in Medieval Christian Monasticism." In *Genealogies of Religion: Discipline and Reasons of Power in Christianity and Islam.* Baltimore: Johns Hopkins University Press, 1993.

Baier, Annette. *Moral Prejudices: Essays on Ethics.* Cambridge, Mass.: Harvard University Press, 1994.

Baron, Hans. "Franciscan Poverty and Civic Wealth as Factors in the Rise of Humanistic Thought." *Speculum* XIII, no. 1 (January 1938).

Bibliography

Bateman, Bradley. "The Force of the River Itself: The Social Gospel and the American Economics." *The National Humanities Center Ideas* 7, no. 2.

Berdyaev, Nicholas. *The Bourgeois Mind and Other Essays.* Freeport, N.Y.: Books for Libraries Press, Inc., 1934, 1966.

Bonaventure. *The Defense of the Mendicants. The Works of Bonaventure,* vol. IV. Translated by José de Vinck. Paterson, N.J.: St. Anthony Guild Press, 1966.

Boulding, Kenneth. *Beyond Economics: Essays on Society, Religion, and Ethics.* Ann Arbor: University of Michigan Press, 1968.

Bruni, Luigino. "Genovesi vs. Adam Smith: Economic Alternatives for Business People." *Houston Catholic Worker* XXI, no. 5 (Sept.-Oct. 2001).

Cavillac, Michel. *Gueux et marchands dans le* Guzmán de Alfarache *(1599-1604): Roman picaresque et mentalité bourgeoise dans l'Espagne du Siècle d'Or.* Bordeaux: Institut d'études Ibériques et Ibéro-Américaines de l'Université de Bordeaux, 1983.

Chesterton, G. K. *The Outline of Sanity.* New York: Dodd, Mead & Company, 1927.

Church, Pharcellus. *The Philosophy of Benevolence.* New York: Leavitt, Lord & Co., 1836.

Clopper, Lawrence M. *"Songes of Rechelesnesse": Langland and the Franciscans.* Ann Arbor: University of Michigan Press, 1997.

Coles, Romand. *Rethinking Generosity: Critical Theory and the Politics of Caritas.* Ithaca: Cornell University Press, 1997.

Coletti, Theresa. *"Paupertas est donum Dei:* Hagiography, Lay Religion, and the Economics of Salvation in the Digby *Mary Magdalene." Speculum* 76 (April 2001).

Constable, Giles. "The Ideal of the Imitation of Christ." In *Three Studies in Medieval Religious and Social Thought.* Cambridge: Cambridge University Press, 1995.

Couvreur, Giles. *Les pauvres ont-ils des droits? Recherches sur le vol in cas d'extrême nécessité depuis la Concordia de Gratien (1140) jusqu'à Guillaume d'Auxerre (+ 1231).* Roma: Libreria Editrice dell'Università Gregoriana, 1961.

Dabney, Robert L. *Lectures in Systematic Theology.* Grand Rapids: Zondervan Publishing House, 1972.

Davis, Natalie Zemon. *Society and Culture in Early Modern France.* Stanford: Stanford University Press, 1975.

Dawson, Christopher. *The Formation of Christendom.* New York: Sheed and Ward, 1967.

————. *Progress and Religion: An Historical Enquiry.* Washington, D.C.: Catholic University of America Press, 1929, 2001.

Day, Dorothy. *The Long Loneliness.* San Francisco: Harper and Row, 1981.

De Certeau, Michel. *The Practice of Everyday Life.* Translated by Steven Rendall. Berkeley: University of California Press, 1988.

De la Gorce, Agnes. *Saint Benedict Joseph Labre.* Translated by Rosemary Sheed. New York: Sheed & Ward, 1952.

Derrida, Jacques. *Given Time: 1. Counterfeit Money.* Translated by Peggy Kamuf. Chicago: University of Chicago Press, 1992.

Duby, Georges. *Rural Economy and Country Life in the Medieval West.* Translated by Cynthia Postan. Columbia, S.C.: University of South Carolina Press, 1968.

Duffy, Eamon. *The Stripping of the Altars: Traditional Religion in England, 1400-1580.* New Haven: Yale University Press, 1992.

Ellis, Marc H. "The Legacy of Peter Maurin." *Cross Currents* XXXIV, no. 3 (Fall 1984).

————. *Peter Maurin: Prophet in the Twentieth Century.* New York: Paulist Press, 1981.

Evensky, Jerry. "Adam Smith's Moral Philosophy: The Role of Religion and Its Relationship to Philosophy and Ethics in the Evolution of Society." *History of Political Economy* 30:1 (1998).

Fish, Simon. *A Supplication for the Beggars.* The English Scholar's Library of Old and Modern Works, vol. 1. New York: AMS Press, 1967.

Fitzhugh, George. *Cannibals All! Or Slaves without Masters.* Edited by C. Vann Woodward. Cambridge, Mass.: The Belknap Press of Harvard University Press, 1960.

Flood, David, ed. *Poverty in the Middle Ages.* Werl: Dietrich-Coelde-Verlag, 1975.

Flood, David, and Thadée Matura. *The Birth of a Movement: A Study of the First Rule of St. Francis.* Translated by Paul Schwartz and Paul Lachance. Chicago: Franciscan Herald Press, 1975.

Foucault, Michel. *The Order of Things: An Archaeology of the Human Sciences.* New York: Random House, Inc., 1970.

Genovese, Eugene. *A Consuming Fire: The Fall of the Confederacy in the Mind of the White Christian South.* Athens: The University of Georgia Press, 1998.

Gerard of Abbeville. "Contra adversarium." Edited by P. Sophronius Clasen. *Archivum Franciscanum Historicum* 32 (1939): 100-117.

Geremek, Bronislaw. *Poverty: A History.* Translated by Agnieszka Kolakowska. Oxford: Blackwell, 1994.

Gill, Eric. *Beauty Looks after Herself: Essays by Eric Gill.* London: Sheed & Ward, 1933.

————. *Work and Property.* London: J. M. Dent, 1937.

González, Justo L. *Faith and Wealth: A History of Early Christian Ideas on the Origin, Significance, and Use of Money.* San Francisco: Harper and Row, 1990.

Grace, Frank. *The Concept of Property in Modern Christian Thought.* Illinois Studies in the Social Sciences: Volume XXXIV, nos. 1-2. Urbana: The University of Illinois Press, 1953.

Groethuysen, Bernard. *The Bourgeois: Catholicism vs. Capitalism in Eighteenth-*

Century France. Translated by Mary Ilford. New York: Holt, Rinehart and Winston, 1968.

Grundmann, Herbert. *Religious Movements in the Middle Ages.* Translated by Steven Rowan. Notre Dame: University of Notre Dame Press, 1995.

Guevarra, P. *Ways and Means for Suppressing Beggary and Relieving the Poor by Erecting General Hospitals and Charitable Corporations.* Translated with an introduction by Abraham Castres. London: James Roberts, 1726.

Gutton, Jean-Pierre. *La société et les pauvres en Europe (XVIᵉ-XVIIIᵉ siècles).* Presses Universitaires de France, 1974.

Haan, Roelf L. "Man and Methodology in Economic Science: About Abstraction and Obedience." In *Social Science in Christian Perspective.* Edited by Paul A. Marshall and Robert E. Vandervennen. Lanham, Md.: University Press of America, 1988.

Hall, Douglas John. *Confessing the Faith: Christian Theology in a North American Context.* Minneapolis: Fortress Press, 1996.

———. "The Cross and Contemporary Culture." In *Reinhold Niebuhr: A Centenary Appraisal.* Edited by Gary A. Gaudin and Douglas John Hall. Atlanta: Scholars Press, 1994.

———. *Has the Church a Future?* Philadelphia: Westminster Press, 1980.

———. *Imaging God: Dominion as Stewardship.* Grand Rapids: William B. Eerdmans Publishing Co., 1986.

———. *Lighten Our Darkness: Toward an Indigenous Theology of the Cross.* Philadelphia: The Westminster Press, 1976.

———. *Professing the Faith: Christian Theology in a North American Context.* Minneapolis: Fortress Press, 1993.

———. *Remembered Voices: Reclaiming the Legacy of "Neo-Orthodoxy."* Louisville: Westminster John Knox Press, 1998.

———. *The Steward: A Biblical Symbol Come of Age.* Revised Edition. Grand Rapids, Michigan: William B. Eerdmans Publishing Company, 1990.

———. *The Stewardship of Life in the Kingdom of Death.* Grand Rapids: William B. Eerdmans Publishing Company, 1985.

———. *Thinking the Faith: Christian Theology in a North American Context.* Minneapolis: Augsburg, 1989.

Hall, Douglas John, and Rosemary Radford Ruether. *God and the Nations.* Minneapolis: Fortress Press, 1995.

Halteman, James. *The Clashing Worlds of Economics and Faith.* Scottdale, Pa.: Herald Press, 1995.

Hausman, Daniel M., and Michael S. McPherson. *Economic Analysis and Moral Philosophy.* Cambridge: Cambridge University Press, 1996.

Hemming, T. D., ed. *La Vie de Saint Alexis.* Exeter: University of Exeter Press, 1994.

Hilaire, Yves-Marie, ed. *Benoît Labre: Errance et saintete: Histoire d'un culte, 1783-1983*. Paris: Les Editions du Cerf, 1984.

Hill, Christopher. *The English Bible and the Seventeenth-Century Revolution*. London: Allen Lane, 1993.

————. *Puritanism and Revolution: Studies in Interpretation of the English Revolution of the Seventeenth Century*. New York: St. Martin's Press, 1997.

Hufton, Olwen H. *The Poor of Eighteenth-Century France, 1750-1789*. Oxford: Clarendon Press, 1974.

Iannaccone, Laurence R. "Introduction to the Economics of Religion." *Journal of Economic Literature* XXXVI (September 1998).

Ignatieff, Michael. *The Needs of Strangers: An Essay on Privacy, Solidarity, and the Politics of Being Human*. New York: Viking Penguin, 1984.

Johnson, Matthew. *An Archaeology of Capitalism*. Oxford: Blackwell Publishers, 1996.

Kantonen, T. A. *A Theology for Christian Stewardship*. Philadelphia: Muhlenberg Press, 1956.

Kaye, Joel. *Economy and Nature in the Fourteenth Century: Money, Market Exchange, and the Emergence of Scientific Thought*. Cambridge: Cambridge University Press, 1998.

Kemp, Margery. *The Book of Margery Kempe*. Edited by S. B. Meech. Early English Text Society #212. London: Humphrey Milford, Oxford University Press, 1940.

Kropotkin, Peter. *Fields, Factories, and Workshops or Industry Combined with Agriculture and Brain Work with Manual Work*. Edited by George Woodcock. Montréal: Black Rose Books, 1994.

————. *Mutual Aid: A Factor of Evolution*. Boston: Extending Horizons Books, 1955.

Kumarappa, J. M., ed. *Our Beggar Problem: How to Tackle It*. Bombay: Padma Publications Ltd., 1945.

Lambert, M. D. *Franciscan Poverty: The Doctrine of the Absolute Poverty of Christ and the Apostles in the Franciscan Order, 1210-1323*. London: S.P.C.K., 1961.

Langholm, Odd. *Economics in the Medieval Schools: Wealth, Exchange, Value, Money, and Usury according to the Paris Theological Tradition, 1200-1350*. Leiden: E. J. Brill, 1992.

————. *The Legacy of Scholasticism in Economic Thought: Antecedents of Choice and Power*. Cambridge: Cambridge University Press, 1998.

————. *The Merchant in the Confessional: Trade and Price in the Pre-Reformation Penitential Handbooks*. Leiden: Brill, 2003.

Langland, William. *Piers Plowman*. An alliterative verse translation by E. Talbot Donaldson. New York: W. W. Norton & Co., 1990.

————. *Piers Plowman*. An edition of the C-text by Derek Pearsall. Berkeley: University of California Press, 1978.

Bibliography

————. *The Vision of Piers the Plowman.* A complete edition of the B-text, edited by A. V. C. Schmidt. London: Everyman's Library, 1978.

————. *William Langland's* Piers Plowman: *The C Version: A Verse Translation.* Translated by George Economou. Philadelphia: University of Pennsylvania Press, 1996.

Lapsanski, Duane V. *Evangelical Perfection: An Historical Examination of the Concept in Early Franciscan Sources.* St. Bonaventure, N.Y.: The Franciscan Institute, 1977.

Lawrence, C. H. *The Friars: The Impact of the Early Mendicant Movement on Western Society.* London: Longman, 1994.

LeJeune, R. P. *Le Missionaire de l'Oratoire: Sermons du R. P. LeJeune, Prêtre de l'oratoire de Jésus.* Nouvelle edition. Paris: Louis Vivès, 1873.

Lis, Catharina, and Hugo Soly. *Poverty and Capitalism in Pre-Industrial Europe.* Hassocks, Sussex: The Harvester Press Limited, 1979.

Little, A. G. *Studies in English Franciscan History.* Manchester: University of Manchester Press, 1917.

Little, Lester K. "Evangelical Poverty, the New Money Economy, and Violence." In *Poverty in the Middle Ages,* edited by David Flood. Werl: Dietrich-Coelde-Verlag, 1975.

————. *Religious Poverty and the Profit Economy in Medieval Europe.* Ithaca: Cornell University Press, 1978.

Llull, Ramon. *Blanquerna: A Thirteenth Century Romance.* Translated from the Catalan by E. Allison Peers. London: Dedalus/Hippocrene Books, 1987.

Lugan, Alphonse. *Social Principles of the Gospel.* Translated by T. Lawrason Riggs. New York: The Macmillan Company, 1928.

MacIntyre, Alasdair. *After Virtue: A Study in Moral Theory.* Second Edition. Notre Dame: University of Notre Dame Press, 1984.

————. *Whose Justice? Which Rationality?* Notre Dame: University of Notre Dame Press, 1988.

Madden, Sr. Mary Roger, S.P. *Gladly Will I Spend and Be Spent: A Brief History of the National Catholic Stewardship Council, Inc., 1962-1997.* Washington, D.C.: National Catholic Stewardship Council, 1997.

Maitland, Sara. "Passionate Prayer: Masochistic Images in Women's Experience." In *Sex and God: Some Varieties of Women's Religious Experience,* edited by Linda Hurcombe. New York: Routledge & Kegan Paul, 1987.

Mäkinen, Virpi. *Property Rights in the Late Medieval Discussion on Franciscan Poverty.* Leuven: Peeters, 2001.

Malthus, Thomas. *An Essay on the Principle of Population.* Selected and introduced by Donald Winch. Cambridge: Cambridge University Press, 1992.

————. *The Works of Thomas Robert Malthus.* 8 Volumes. Edited by E. A. Wrigley and David Sonden. London: Pickering & Chatto, 1986.

Marcett, M. E. *Uhtred de Boldon, Friar William Jordan, and "Piers Plowman."* New York, 1938.

Maritain, Jacques. *Freedom in the Modern World.* Translated by Richard O'Sullivan, K.C. New York: Charles Scribner's Sons, 1936.

Marlett, Jeffrey D. "Down on the Farm, Up to Heaven: Communes and the Spiritual Virtues of Farming." In *Dorothy Day and the Catholic Worker Movement: Centenary Essays,* edited by William J. Thorn, Phillip M. Runkel, and Susan Mountin. Milwaukee: Marquette University Press, 2001.

Marshall, Gordon. *In Search of the Spirit of Capitalism.* New York: Columbia University Press, 1982.

Maurin, Peter. *Easy Essays.* Chicago: Franciscan Herald Press, 1984.

Mauss, Marcel. *The Gift: Forms and Functions of Exchange in Archaic Societies.* Translated by Ian Cunnison. New York: W. W. Norton & Company, 1967.

McCarraher, Eugene. *Christian Critics: Religion and the Impasse in Modern American Social Thought.* Ithaca: Cornell University Press, 2000.

McCloskey, Donald N. *The Rhetoric of Economics.* Madison: University of Wisconsin Press, 1985.

McGreevy, John. *Catholicism and American Freedom: A History.* New York: W. W. Norton & Company, 2003.

McManners, John. *Church and Society in Eighteenth-Century France.* Oxford: Clarendon Press, 1998.

McManus, William E. "Stewardship and Almsgiving in the Roman Catholic Tradition." In *Faith and Philanthropy in America: Exploring the Role of Religion in America's Voluntary Sector,* edited by Robert Wuthnow and Virginia A. Hodgkinson. San Francisco: Jossey-Bass, 1990.

McNabb, Vincent. *Old Principles and the New Order.* New York: Sheed and Ward, 1942.

Meyers, Ched, and Eric DeBode. "Towering Trees and 'Talented Slaves'." *The Other Side* 35, no. 3 (May/June 1999).

Middleton, Anne. "Acts of Vagrancy: The C Version 'Autobiography' and the Statute of 1388." In *Written Work: Langland, Labor, and Authorship,* edited by Steven Justice and Kathryn Kerby-Fulton. Philadelphia: University of Pennsylvania Press, 1997.

Milbank, John. "Can a Gift Be Given?: Prolegomena to a Future Trinitarian Metaphysic." *Modern Theology* 11/1 (January 1995).

———. "Can Morality Be Christian?" In *The Word Made Strange: Theology, Language, Culture.* Oxford: Blackwell Publishers, 1997.

———. "The Midwinter Sacrifice: A Sequel to 'Can Morality Be Christian?'" *Studies in Christian Ethics* 10, no. 2 (October 1997).

———. "The Soul of Reciprocity (Part One): Reciprocity Refused." *Modern Theology* 17:3 (July 2001).

Bibliography

―――. *Theology and Social Theory: Beyond Secular Reason.* Oxford: Blackwell, 1993.

Minowitz, Peter. *Profits, Priests, and Princes: Adam Smith's Emancipation of Economics from Politics and Religion.* Stanford: Stanford University Press, 1993.

Mollat, Michel. "Pauvres et pauvreté a la fin du XIIe siecle." *Revue d'ascetique et de mystique,* Tome XLI, 3:163 (1965).

―――. *The Poor in the Middle Ages: An Essay in Social History.* Translated by Arthur Goldhammer. New Haven: Yale University Press, 1986.

Mounier, Emmanuel. *Personalism.* Translated by Philip Mairet. London: Routledge & Kegan Paul, 1952.

National Conference of Catholic Bishops. *Stewardship: A Disciple's Response. A Pastoral Letter on Stewardship.* Bilingual Edition. Washington, D.C.: United States Catholic Conference, 1993.

―――. *Stewardship: A Disciple's Response. A Pastoral Letter on Stewardship.* Tenth Anniversary Edition. Washington, D.C.: United States Catholic Conference, 2002.

―――. *Stewardship and Development in Catholic Dioceses and Parishes: Resource Manual.* Washington, D.C.: United States Catholic Conference, 1996.

Nicholls, David. "Population and Process: Parson Malthus." *Anglican Theological Review* LXXVII:3 (Summer 1995).

Nietszche, Friedrich. *Thus Spake Zarathustra.* Translated with a preface by Walter Kaufmann. New York: The Modern Library, 1995.

Nisbet, Robert A. *The Sociological Tradition.* New York: Basic Books, 1966.

Noonan, John T. *The Scholastic Analysis of Usury.* Cambridge, Mass.: Harvard University Press, 1957.

Novak, Michael. *The Catholic Ethic and the Spirit of Capitalism.* New York: The Free Press, 1993.

O'Boyle, Edward J. *Personalist Economics: Moral Convictions, Economic Realities, and Social Action.* Boston: Kluwer Academic Publishers, 1998.

O'Donovan, Joan Lockwood. *Theology of Law and Authority in the English Reformation.* Atlanta: Scholars Press, 1991.

O'Toole, Patricia. *Money and Morals in America: A History.* New York: Clarkson Potter Publishers, 1998.

The Papal Encyclicals. Edited by Claudia Carlen. Ann Arbor: Pierian Press, 1990.

Payne, Harry C. "*Pauvreté, misère,* and the Aims of Enlightened Economics." *Studies on Voltaire in the Eighteenth Century* 154 (1976).

Péguy, Charles. *Men and Saints: Prose and Poetry.* Translated by Anne and Julian Green. New York: Pantheon, 1944.

Penty, Arthur. *The Restoration of the Guild System.* London: Swan Sonnenschein and Co., Ltd., 1906.

Perugi, Maurizio, ed. *La Vie de Saint Alexis: Edition Critique.* Genève: Librarie Droz S.A., 2000.

Pfau, Thomas. *Wordsworth's Profession: Form, Class, and Logic of Early Romantic Cultural Production.* Stanford: Stanford University Press, 1997.

Philips, Dietrich. "The Church of God." In *Library of Christian Classics,* XXV, *Spiritual and Anabaptist Writers,* edited by George Huntston Williams. Philadelphia: Westminster Press, n.d.

Pickstock, Catherine. *After Writing: On the Liturgical Consummation of Philosophy.* Oxford: Blackwell, 1998.

————. "Liturgy Not a Museum Piece, but a Life's Work." *Houston Catholic Worker* XXXI, no. 6 (November 2001).

Pieper, Josef. *On Hope.* Translated by Sister Mary Frances McCarthy, S.N.D. San Francisco: Ignatius Press, 1986.

Powell, Luther P. *Money and the Church.* New York: Association Press, 1962.

————. "Stewardship in the History of the Christian Church." In *Stewardship in Contemporary Theology,* edited by T. K. Thompson. New York: Association Press, 1960.

Reid, W. Stanford. "John Calvin, Early Critic of Capitalism." *The Reformed Theological Review* XLIII: 74-81 and XLIV: 9-12.

Reumann, John. *Stewardship and the Economy of God.* Grand Rapids: William B. Eerdmans Publishing Company, 1992.

Richard, Joseph. *Le vagabond de Dieu: Saint Benoît Labre.* Paris: Editions SOS, 1976.

Richards, Norvin. *Humility.* Philadelphia: Temple University Press, 1992.

Ross, Ian Simpson. *The Life of Adam Smith.* Oxford: Clarendon Press, 1995.

Rourke, Thomas R. "Contemporary Globalization: An Ethical and Anthropological Evaluation." *Communio* 27 (Fall 2000).

Salimbene degli Adami. "His Two Journeys through France, Selections." In *XIIIth Century Chronicles,* translated by Placid Hermann. Chicago: Franciscan Herald Press, 1961.

Salstrand, George. *The Story of Stewardship in the United States of America.* Grand Rapids: Baker Book House, 1956.

Sandys, Edwin. *The Sermons of Edwin Sandys, DD.* Edited by Rev. John Ayre. Cambridge: The University Press, 1862.

Scase, Wendy. Piers Plowman *and the New Anti-Clericalism.* Cambridge Studies in Medieval Literature #4. Cambridge: Cambridge University Press, 1989.

Schaller, Lyle. *44 Ways to Increase Your Church's Financial Base.* Nashville: Abingdon Press, 1989.

Schumpeter, Joseph A. *History of Economic Analysis.* Edited by Elizabeth Boody Schumpeter. New York: Oxford University Press, 1954.

Schwartz, Robert M. *Policing the Poor in Eighteenth-Century France.* Chapel Hill: University of Chapel Hill Press, 1988.

Sheehan, Arthur. *Peter Maurin: Gay Believer.* Garden City: Hanover House, 1959.

Bibliography

Shepherd, Geoffrey. "Poverty in *Piers Plowman*." In *Social Relations and Ideas: Essays in Honour of R. H. Hilton*, edited by T. H. Aston et al. Cambridge: Cambridge University Press, 1983.

Sicius, Francis J. "Dorothy Day's View of Peter Maurin." In *Dorothy Day and the Catholic Worker Movement: Centenary Essays*, edited by William J. Thorn, Phillip M. Runkel, and Susan Mountin. Milwaukee: Marquette University Press, 2001.

Skillen, Tony. "Questions of Begging." In *Philosophy and Public Affairs*, Royal Philosophy Supplements 45, edited by John Haldane. Cambridge: Cambridge University Press, 2000.

Smith, Adam. *An Inquiry into the Nature and Causes of the Wealth of Nations.* Edited by R. H. Campbell and A. S. Skinner. Indianapolis: Liberty Classics, 1981.

————. *The Theory of Moral Sentiments.* Edited by D. D. Raphael and A. L. Macfie. Oxford: Clarendon Press, 1976.

Smith, Ben H. *Traditional Imagery of Charity in "Piers Plowman."* The Hague: Mouton & Co., 1966.

Smith, Joseph. "The Faithful Stewardship. A Sermon preach'd before the sons of the clergy, at their anniversary meeting in the Cathedral-Church of St. Paul, December 10, 1719." London, 1720.

Society for the Suppression of Mendicity. *Twenty-Third Report.* London: H. Gosbell, 1841.

Soskice, Janet. *Metaphor and Religious Language.* Oxford: Clarendon Press, 1985.

Speaight, Robert. *The Life of Eric Gill.* New York: P. J. Kenedy & Sons, 1966.

Spiegel, Henry William. *The Growth of Economic Thought.* Third Edition. Durham: Duke University Press, 1991.

Spinka, Matthew, ed. *Advocates of Reform: From Wyclif to Erasmus.* Library of Christian Classics, Volume XIV. Philadelphia: The Westminster Press, 1953.

Stark, Oded. *Altruism and Beyond: An Economic Analysis of Exchanges within Families and Groups.* Cambridge: Cambridge University Press, 1995.

Systematic Beneficence: Three Prize Essays. New York: Carlton & Phillips, 1856.

Szittya, Penn R. *The Antifraternal Tradition in Medieval Literature.* Princeton, N.J.: Princeton University Press, 1986.

Tawney, R. H. *Religion and the Rise of Capitalism: A Historical Study.* New York: Mentor Books, 1954.

Taylor, Charles. *Sources of the Self: The Making of the Modern Identity.* Cambridge: Harvard University Press, 1989.

Thibon, Gustave. *L'ignorance etoilée.* Paris: Fayard, 1974.

Thomas Aquinas. *Summa Theologica: Complete English Edition in Five Volumes.* Translated by Fathers of the English Dominican Province. Westminster, Md.: Christian Classics, 1948.

Tierney, Brian. *Medieval Poor Law: A Sketch of Canonical Theory and Its Application in England.* Berkeley: University of California Press, 1959.

Tise, Larry E. *Proslavery: A History of the Defense of Slavery in America, 1701-1840.* Athens: The University of Georgia Press, 1987.

Titmuss, Richard M. *The Gift Relationship: From Human Blood to Social Policy.* New York: Vintage Books, 1971.

Troester, Rosalie Riegle, ed. *Voices from the Catholic Worker.* Philadelphia: Temple University Press, 1993.

Vogt, Virgil. *Treasure in Heaven.* Ann Arbor: Servant Books, 1982.

von Balthasar, Hans Urs. *A Theology of History.* San Francisco: Ignatius Press, 1994.

Walsh, Michael, and Brian Davies, eds. *Proclaiming Justice and Peace: Papal Documents from "Rerum Novarum" through "Centesimus Annus."* Expanded North American edition. Mystic, Conn.: Twenty-Third Publications, 1991.

Waterman, A. M. C. "The Ideological Alliance of Political Economy and Christian Theology, 1798-1833." *Journal of Ecclesiastical History* 34, no. 2 (April 1983).

The Way of a Pilgrim. Translated by R. M. French. New York: Harper & Brothers, 1952.

Weber, Max. *The Protestant Ethic and the Spirit of Capitalism.* Translated by Talcott Parsons. New York: Charles Scribner's Sons, 1958.

Winthrop, John. "A Modell of Christian Charity." In *The Puritans,* edited by Perry Miller and Thomas H. Johnson. New York: Harper & Row, 1963.

Wolf, Kenneth Baxter. *The Poverty of Riches: St. Francis of Assisi Reconsidered.* Oxford: Oxford University Press, 2003.

Wyclif, John. *An Apology for Lollard Doctrines, Attributed to Wicliffe.* With an Introduction and Notes by James Henthorn Todd. The Camden Society, 1842; repr. New York: AMS Press, 1968.

———. *The English Works of Wyclif, Hitherto Unprinted.* Edited by F. D. Matthew. Second revised edition. Early English Text Society, Original Series, 74. Millwood, NY: Kraus Reprint Co., 1973.

———. *On Simony.* Translated by Terrence McVeigh. New York: Fordham University Press, 1992.

———. *Wyclif: Select English Writings.* Edited by Herbert E. Winn. London: Oxford University Press, 1929.

Zech, Charles E. *Why Catholics Don't Give . . . and What Can Be Done about It.* Huntington, Ind.: Our Sunday Visitor, 2000.

Zyskowski, Bob. "True Stewardship: It Takes More Than Money to Keep a Parish Afloat." *U.S. Catholic* 68, no. 3 (March 2003).

Index